The City Connection

The City Connection

Migration and
Family Interdependence
in the Philippines

Lillian Trager

Foreword by T. G. McGee

Ann Arbor
The University of Michigan Press

1991   1990   1989   1988   4   3   2   1

Library of Congress Cataloging-in-Publication Data

Trager, Lillian, 1947–
    The city connection : migration and family interdependence in the
Philippines / Lillian Trager ; foreword by T.G. McGee.
        p.   cm.
    Bibliography: p.
    Includes index.
    ISBN 0-472-09390-8 (alk. paper) ISBN 0-472-06390-1
(pbk. : alk. paper)
    1. Rural-urban migration—Philippines—Dagupan City.   2. Dagupan
City (Philippines)—Social conditions.   3. Dagupan City
(Philippines)—Economic conditions.   I. Title.
HB2110.D34T73 1988
304.8'09599'1—dc 19   88-22342
                                                                 CIP

Foreword

Studies of the migration process have formed an important component of the literature of the social sciences. Among these studies, the investigation of rural–urban migration has been a major focus. This is hardly surprising, since one of the major spatial transformations of the nineteenth and twentieth centuries has been the shift of populations from rural to urban locations. On a global scale, the numerical dimensions of this shift have far exceeded either international migration or frontier colonization. Studies of rural–urban migration have tended to concentrate upon the demographic and economic aspects of migration, often to the neglect of the wide human dimensions of the process. It is only perhaps the historians such as Oscar Handlin who have given us the feelings of the migrants of the great uprooting from Europe to the cities of North America, through the use of letters and recollections of the migrants. This work shows how migrants create two environments: the place of migration and the homeland, both of which are a part of the totality of their lives.

The City Connection follows this tradition, utilizing microstudies of households to show how migration can be viewed as a process that involves all members of households, despite geographical dispersion. This approach reveals how important urban migration is as an income-maximizing strategy for the household. In the Philippines this often involves making minimal incomes slightly less minimal. It involves many different types of migration: international, metropolitan, and local, reflecting the abilities of households to use their resources, their connections and their information to encourage participation of their members in income-earning activities. In the context of the Philippines of the 1970s and 1980s, these strategies are carried out within a structural setting of considerable political and economic instability, aggravated by world recession, corruption, and bureaucratic inefficiency.

The virtue of Trager's study is that it sets the migration process within the "chaos" (not too strong a word) of the Philippines at the level of the individuals interacting with their households and the workplace. The carefully observed ethnography of the migrants and their milieu is far more insightful than the cold demographic statistics of the census, based upon boundary drawing that makes mockery of the human condition.

Trager's study is an important addition to migration and household studies. It is, in a sense, a cautionary tale; a warning to the planners who use macrostatistics (the fuel of national planning) that they need to put flesh on this data by studies such as this of Trager's. It will certainly lead to a significant reevaluation of migration studies and the conclusions that are drawn from them.

T. G. McGee, Director
Institute of Asian Research
University of British Columbia
Canada
January, 1988

Preface

Migration has long been a well studied and much discussed phenomenon. For many years, studies of migration, and especially of rural-urban migration in the third world, focused on the individual migrant, considering questions such as the psychosocial characteristics of migrants and the way in which they adapted to living in the new, urban environment. More recently, a new perspective has been adopted in some studies, one which considers migrants in their broad social context, including their social relationships not only in the city but also in the rural areas which they have left. This book uses such a two-ended approach, examining the lives and activities of migrants in Dagupan City, a provincial city in the lowland Philippines, and focusing on the ties maintained between migrants and family members residing elsewhere.

This is done through an in-depth consideration of a set of family case studies, which include biographical information on the individual migrant as well as other members of his or her family and data on the type of interactions taking place among family members. These case studies are placed into the larger structural context, including data on urban and regional economic patterns, migration patterns, and features of Filipino culture and social structure that affect migration.

By focusing on families and social networks, within a larger structural context, it is possible to consider the interaction of social, economic, and cultural forces with individual decisions about migration. I suggest that structural forces shape and constrain the activities of individuals and households; at the same time, people respond to the conditions affecting them, make decisions, and take action, following strategies which they choose in terms of their own social and cultural goals.

Overall, migration is a complex process which is part of individual and family strategies for mobility and survival. Furthermore, migrants and those with whom they have links perceive rural and urban areas as part of a single social field within which resources and opportunities, as well as constraints on those opportunities, exist.

This study results from research carried out during a nine-month stay in the Philippines in 1978–79. The majority of that time was spent in Dagupan City, where I met and interviewed a large number of migrants. I selected a small number for the case studies and began to go with these individuals when they visited their home towns and families. Through these visits, I became acquainted with rural people and conditions, mainly in Pangasinan Province, although some of the migrants studied were from outside the province. In addition, I spent a few weeks in Manila where I was able to collect data and documents from government agencies and at universities; these data were essential for helping to examine the broader structural conditions that affect migration.

A large number of individuals, and several institutions, helped make possible the research and subsequent writing. In Dagupan City, my greatest debt is to those I studied, who included me in their activities, introduced me to family and friends, and continued to answer my innumerable questions over a period of several months. I have not identified by name those who form the basis of the case studies of Part 2 of this book and therefore cannot name them here; but clearly, without their willingness to participate and help me, the book would not exist.

Several individuals from Dagupan should be named, however. First, I want to express my gratitude to Josie Gonzalez, who worked with me throughout the research period, helping to conduct interviews and collect other data, while also helping me to understand Filipino culture. Second, Dr. Adoracion Hiquiana provided me and my husband with the urban anthropologist's dream location in the city: a house to live in located just off the plaza, the focal point of a Philippine city. Andrea Muyargas helped make our stay at Dr. Hiquiana's house an extremely comfortable and enjoyable one. Finally, Virgilio and Ely Dumantay included us in many activities of their family and business.

The assistance and support of my husband, Dick Ammann, have been invaluable. He first introduced me to Dagupan, having been there previously as a Peace Corps Volunteer. His friends and acquaintances helped make the research process far easier than it might otherwise have been. During 1978–79 Dick assisted me in my research, while also carrying out his own study of language use among urban migrants. Since then, he has provided me with an important sounding board as I developed the ideas and analysis of this book. He also took most of the photographs used here, although one was taken by me.

As a novice to Southeast Asian studies (my previous research having been in Nigeria), I have been aided immeasurably by Professor T. G. McGee, who helped point out useful theoretical directions for the research, and who has continued to take an interest in it during the long period during which this book has been in process. He agreed to supervise my work as part of a postdoctoral grant, and since he was then in the Department of Human Geography, Research School of Pacific Studies, Australian National University, I spent six weeks in Australia before going to the Philippines. During that time I benefited from discussions not only with Terry McGee but also with others in the Human Geography Department; I am particularly grateful to Professor R. G. Ward, then Head of the Department, for facilitating my stay in Australia.

The period in Australia as well as the research itself were made possible by a postdoctoral grant from the National Institute of Mental Health (NIMH Fellowship 1F32MH 07222-01).

In the Philippines, thanks are due to the Institute of Philippine Culture, Ateneo de Manila University, and its director at the time, Dr. Ricardo Abad, for granting me research affiliation.

The University of Wisconsin-Parkside has assisted in a variety of ways: first, with a leave of absence to take the postdoctoral fellowship and second, with a summer grant from the Committee on Research and Creative Activity in 1980 to begin writing. I am grateful to Marge Rowley, Luella Vines, and Jackie Battersby for providing excellent secretarial assistance. Maps and figures were drawn by student employees at the university's Media Services Department. I would like to thank as well the Southeast Asian Studies Program at University of Wisconsin-Madison for providing a small grant in 1982–83 that helped facilitate library research.

In discussions and presentations during the last several years, a number of people have commented on the ideas discussed here. I have particularly benefited from the comments of James Anderson, Dan Doeppers, the late Donn Hart, and Estellie Smith.

This book is dedicated to my parents, William and Ida Trager, who first stimulated my interest in the rest of the world.

Contents

Figures

Tables

Chapter 1

Introduction

"I came to Chicago last August. I didn't want to come but my family wanted me to, so that they will be able to follow me later. In Dagupan City, I owned a restaurant in the marketplace; here, I am working as a busboy, the lowest paid job in this hotel. I stay in a room by myself. I will petition for my children, and after they come I will return to the Philippines" (Filipino immigrant working in a Chicago hotel, November 1983).

". . . I don't think that migration, the process of being uprooted, necessarily leads to rootlessness. What it can lead to is a kind of multiple rootings. It's not the traditional identity crisis of not knowing where you come from. The problem is that you come from too many places. . . . It's not that there are pulls in too many directions so much as too many voices speaking at the same time" (Salman Rushdie, in an interview in the *New York Times Book Review*, November 13, 1983).

A chance encounter in Chicago led to the first comment quoted above: a middle-aged Filipino man who happened to be from the city where I did research in 1978–79 was working in a hotel restaurant where I was having lunch. He knew people that I had known in Dagupan City, his restaurant was in an area I knew well, and I felt as though we might have met, or very likely seen each other before, during my nine-month stay in the city. Furthermore, his comments on his recent move to the United States reinforced a number of key ideas about Filipino migration and the migration process. He hadn't particularly wanted to come to Chicago but, since he was eligible for U.S. citizenship as a veteran of the Philippine Army from World War II, his family had wanted him to immigrate so that they would have the chance to come later. What he was doing right now was not so important; what was important was the opportunity to be provided to other family members. Clearly, his ties with family at home were of great importance, and the considerable geographical distance between himself and them did not greatly affect those ties. He had not migrated mainly for his own economic reasons but for a variety of motivations, of which long-term economic interests (eventual employment in the United States for his children) were perhaps key. Finally, he planned to return to the Philippines once he had succeeded in fulfilling the goal of helping his family; his own economic and social status were higher there, and he was aware of that.

The current study is primarily concerned with migration within the Philippines, rather than emigration from the country; however, this man's brief comments help to exemplify several major themes of this book. First, there is a need to recognize the complexity of the migration process. That process involves not only the individuals who migrate but also others with whom they have ties. In this man's case, family was clearly paramount in the decision to migrate. In addition, the larger structural context in which movement takes place needs to be taken into account. For him, the structural context of immigration policies and economic opportunities is one that allows for his immigration but not that of other members of his family. Second, the migration process needs to be considered in its specific historical and cultural context. The fact that the migrant or immigrant is Filipino affects the decisions made and activity pursued; consideration of Filipino culture provides a context for understanding some aspects of migrant activities. Third, a question arises as to the way in which those who move perceive their own behavior. Do they think of themselves as migrants, leaving one place more or less permanently to go elsewhere? Or do they see themselves as people who move for a variety of reasons and in a variety of contexts, and who are rooted in and have appropriate behavior patterns for two or three—or perhaps more—different places at the same time? The author, Salman Rushdie, quoted above, suggests the latter; I, too, will suggest that in general those we as social scientists label as "migrants," with the suggestion of uprootedness it carries, do not see themselves in that way. Rather, they move from one place to another with relative ease, adopting appropriate behavior patterns, but at the same time retaining ties and behavior patterns appropriate to the place they have come from.

In this study, these themes are examined through the analysis of case studies of urban migrants in the provincial urban center of Dagupan City, Philippines. Each case describes and analyzes individual migrants within the widest possible social and economic context. They are seen not simply as individuals living in an urban setting, but rather as individuals with social networks reaching back to rural areas as well as out from the city to other cities, and even, in some cases, to other countries. Each case therefore also includes information on others, mainly relatives, not living in Dagupan. The decision to migrate, as well as current and future decisions and activities, are therefore considered not solely with respect to a particular individual, but also in terms of the social context from which he or she comes and to which he still belongs.

The cases are placed in the larger structural and cultural context of the lowland Philippines, particularly the northern part of the Central Luzon Plain, the region where Dagupan City is located and the home of the majority of migrants to the city. The first part of the book examines the structural context, considering the urban and regional economy as well as broad patterns of internal migration in the region. This section also discusses aspects of lowland Filipino culture that play a role in the decisions and activities of migrants. Of particular importance are the role of the family and kinship ties and of reciprocal obligations within personal networks. The second part of the book then examines in detail the specific cases and analyzes the activities of migrants and their families in terms of the larger structural context set forth in Part 1.

The major themes listed above will be elaborated upon throughout the study and will be demonstrated in particular in the analyses of the case studies. These themes encompass a number of other topics. In general, I am suggesting an approach to the study of migration which incorporates structural, cultural, and social network perspectives. The remainder of this chapter discusses this approach in greater detail and describes as well the methods used in the study.

Complexity of the Migration Process

Migration at its simplest may be understood as the movement of individuals from one place to another, on a more or less permanent basis. But migration is not a simple process. It involves not only the individuals who move, but others with whom they have ties—family, friends, employers, etc. What may appear as a single decision of a single individual to move from point X to point Y may in fact be determined by a wide range of prior events and social contexts, as well as by expectations regarding the place to which he or she is moving. Once a move takes place, further complexities enter, which may affect whether or not the migrant should be viewed as a "permanent" resident of his new locale, and hence whether he is a "migrant" at all.

Research on migration has in recent years recognized the definitional, conceptual, and theoretical problems associated with the study of the movement of people from one place to another. For example, Abu-Lughod noted the passing of simplistic notions in the study of migration in which "human beings, like iron filings, were impelled by forces beyond their conscious control" (1975:201) while commenting that theories for dealing with the newly recognized complexities of migration had not been developed.

Recently, however, new conceptual and theoretical approaches have been proposed. These include attempts at refining definitions and concepts of migration, as well as the development of theoretical propositions which, it is argued, will help to advance our understanding of the migration process.

Concepts and Definitions

Studies of migration in the past tended to assume that moves from one point to another were permanent; hence, rural-urban migration meant that a person left his or her rural home to live permanently in a city. This still forms the basis of definitions used in most surveys and censuses (United Nations 1978:1). As empirical research on rural-urban migration in the third world has demonstrated, this is not in fact the pattern always followed. In one of the first such studies, Mayer (1962, 1963) stressed the retention of "extra-town" ties among urban migrants in South Africa. Since then, many others have pointed out the extent to which such ties are maintained, as well as the frequency with which migrants themselves move back and forth between different locales. In the Southeast Asian context, for example, van den Muijzenberg (1973) coined the term *circo-commuting* to describe the pattern of movement of Filipinos who spend part of the year in their village and part in Manila, while Hugo noted the importance of what he called circular migration in Indonesia (1975, 1982).

A result of these studies has been the development of new terminology and concepts which better encompass the extent of movement in which migrants engage. The term *circulation* has been used to refer to those movements that are not permanent, in which there are "reciprocal flows . . . of individuals and small groups between places [with] such movement ultimately [concluding] in the place or community in which it began" (Chapman and Prothero 1983:597–98; see also Prothero and Chapman 1985). It has been suggested that "Third World societies may be increasingly characterized as bi-local populations . . . composed of individuals in constant motion between village and non-village places" (Goldstein 1978:18–19). As a result, there is a need for concepts that allow for understanding movements and behavior patterns involving more than one place, that help in the understanding of the "ambiguity and volatility in people's movements" (Chapman 1978:563).

While notions like circular migration and circulation may help to convey the extent of movement between places, others have suggested the use of more general concepts that include all the varied movements that are found. The most general term here is simply mobility, which, McGee notes "offers more conceptual breadth encompassing all types of geographic, social, and economic mobility" (1978:219). The notion of mobility helps to avoid the necessity of typologizing movements. For example, most studies of migration in the third world focus on rural-urban migration, yet other types of moves take place as well. Although I began the current study by considering the ties retained by urban migrants with rural homes, it soon became apparent that the migrants I was studying did not only move back and forth between rural and urban places, but were also in some cases involved in other types of movement. That is, some members of a single family or household may move to an urban place while others move overseas to engage in international migration. Furthermore, a single individual may engage in a variety of moves over the space of several years. Hence, the general concept of mobility is useful as it does not assume a particular type of move, nor does it imply a certain consequence—such as permanence—of the move.

Implicit in the notion of permanence associated with earlier concepts of migration was also an assumption that a particular move necessarily involved some process of adaptation on the part of the migrant. On the one hand, rural-urban migration implied that a migrant "became urban" or became an "urbanite," with the implication of adopting new life-styles and behavior patterns, while at the same time presumably breaking ties or at least moving away from the views and behavior patterns appropriate in the rural home. As one study after another demonstrated that this frequently did not occur, the notion then emerged that rural migrants remained "peasants" in the cities, maintaining rural behavior patterns and personal ties with others from their rural homes (Mangin 1970; McGee 1973).

The dichotomy of being either an "urbanite" or a "peasant" does not convey the complexity of actual behavior patterns that is associated with the types of mobility in which third world peoples engage. Just as the geographical moves are not necessarily unidirectional, so the process of adaptation is not based on an either/or proposition. Individuals are likely to incorporate ideas and behavior patterns appropriate to a variety of different contexts (cf. McGee 1975). The adaptation process is not necessarily a move away from the old, but it is not simply a retention of rural patterns in urban contexts either. Rather, the process may include incorporation and maintenance of both old and new social ties and behavior patterns.

Current Theoretical Approaches in Migration Studies

At the same time that concepts such as circulation have been introduced to help clarify the varied movements observed among people in third world societies, new theoretical approaches have also been proposed, in the effort to better understand and explain the migratory processes observed. Two very different sorts of theoretical perspective dominate recent literature; a third perspective has also been proposed as providing a link between the first two. These three types of approach may be labeled as: (*a*) structural historical; (*b*) individual decision making; and (*c*) household and social networks.

Two basic, and contradictory, propositions about migration are developed in much of the recent discussion. On the one hand, those using structural perspectives argue that migratory movements are determined by societywide and, in many cases, worldwide, economic forces that cause the conditions in which people move. At the other extreme, those focusing on individual decision making look for the causes of migration at the individual level, examining characteristics of those who migrate and their decision-making processes, and presumably assuming that such decisions are made in an environment relatively free of constraints.

Two very different sorts of analysis result from these differing theoretical viewpoints. Those concerned with structural forces are not particularly concerned with who moves and who does not, and why, but with the broad, macroeconomic conditions of the society in which they move. World systems and dependency perspectives have been particularly of value in these studies, emphasizing how local and regional conditions are determined by larger political and economic forces. In general, a model is used that stresses the impact of penetration of the world capitalist economy on peripheral economies, but the particular aspects of the process that are emphasized vary in these studies (cf. Wood 1982; Portes and Walton 1981). The key feature of modern migration, according to these perspectives, is that it consists of the "migrations of labor, not of people" (Amin 1974:66; Portes and Walton 1981:21). Portes and Walton, in focusing mainly on international movements, emphasize that these movements take place within a single unit, the world-capitalist system, and hence occur "as part of the international dynamics of [that unit]" (1981:29). Meillassoux, on the other hand, takes a perspective that considers two intersecting sectors, the capitalist economy and the non-capitalist, or domestic, economy, wherein the former exploits the latter. In this context, migration, especially temporary labor migration, "preserves and exploits the domestic agricultural economy" (1981:110), so that in the region he is considering (former French colonies in West Africa) labor reserves are created, with domestic relations of production in the rural area and migration for seasonal work in the capitalist sector. Despite their differences, these analyses tend to ignore the people who migrate in favor of the structural conditions causing (or forcing) them to move.[1]

In contrast, those studying individual decision making are concerned with who moves and who does not, and why. Chang, for example, states that a "general theory of migration" must be able to answer the following questions:

"Who are the migrants? Why do they move, stay or return?
How and where do they move?
When do they move?
What are the effects of such actions on the migrants and on others?" (1981:304–6)

Large numbers of surveys have addressed such questions in many regions of the world, usually ending with a list of "push" and "pull" factors in which economic motivations tend to dominate. At present, a major perspective for answering such questions is the use of human capital models, microeconomic models that have as their basic premise "that an individual migrates in the expectation of being better off by doing so" and that "people are motivated by a desire to do what is best for themselves" (DaVanzo 1981:92). With this basic assumption, models are then developed to explain differing patterns of migration in terms of individual decision making, although occasionally families are seen as the decision-making group rather than individuals (Harbison 1981; Findley 1987).

These two dominant theoretical perspectives address entirely different sorts of questions: on the one hand, what are the structural determinants leading to migration; on the other, what are the individual features affecting decisions to migrate. Their one similarity lies in the fact that both tend to emphasize economic forces over others, but at very different levels of analysis.

In response to these opposing perspectives, suggestions have been made for an intermediate position, which would link the examination of structural forces with that of individual behavior. Lomnitz (1976) proposes the study of social networks as a way of analyzing migration, arguing that the social network "represents a middle-range level of abstraction situated between large-scale social structure and the individual" (134). Wood, (1981, 1982) suggests the household as the intermediate unit of analysis, stating that "study of household sustenance strategies, interpreted within an analysis of the socioeconomic and political forces that affect the maintenance and reproduction of the household unit, provides a framework that potentially identifies both structural and behavioral factors that propel population movement" (1982:300). In other words, he is suggesting that examination of the activities of households within their larger structural contexts provides a basis for linking individual behavior to wider political and economic forces.

Both network and household perspectives provide valuable insights into the analysis of migration. The two are similar in providing access to a middle level of social organization, one having reality for individuals in most societies. Social networks, however, provide a broader category of relationships than does analysis of households alone. In most cases, networks include household and family members, but they also point to nonkin and nonresidential ties that may be of great importance. Furthermore, households are simply not a useful construct in analysis of some societies (cf. Guyer 1979, 1981:22–34). On the other hand, as shall be seen below, households do provide a useful unit of analysis, as part of larger networks, for consideration of migration in the Philippines.

These middle-level perspectives invite dangers of their own, however. On the one hand, analysis can simply be transferred from the study of individual decision making to that of household or network decision making, with the focus on the same set of questions noted above for microeconomic studies. On the other hand, these units can be seen simply as units to be propelled about as a result of structural forces, without consideration of the way in which their own decisions shape their activities. Finally, none of these perspectives examines the cultural context in which migration takes place and the ways in which that, too, may help shape the activities and behavior of individuals and larger social units.[2]

Perspective of This Study

In this study I am primarily interested in the activities of a set of urban migrants and other members of their families and social networks with whom they are in contact, regardless of where they reside. My approach, then, is basically along the lines advocated by Lomnitz (1976) and Wood (1981, 1982) in focusing on an intermediate level of social organization. At the same time, I am concerned with placing these migrants and their families into the broader social structural and cultural contexts in which they exist, to see how their decisions and activities are constrained and shaped—but not determined—by the larger context. I am suggesting, in other words, that structural forces shape and constrain the activities and decisions of individuals and households, and that we therefore need to examine those forces. Likewise, cultural values operate to affect the ways in which people behave. Decision making, in other words, does not operate in a constraint-free environment. However, people do respond to the conditions affecting them, make decisions and take action, following strategies that they choose in terms of their own cultural and social goals. Hence, particular behaviors observed may be seen as the outcome of strategies followed, but decisions regarding those strategies are made by individuals and groups in particular social and cultural contexts.

Such a perspective has a number of implications. First, examination of the structural context, focusing in particular on the regional and urban economy, provides an understanding of the situation of particular migrants and their families. In the rural, rice-growing region of Central Luzon, where this study takes place, a large majority of farmers are poor and unable to sustain themselves and their families through farming alone; still other rural people have no access to land at all. Urban migration of family members represents one way to obtain access to other resources. However, not all migrants come from the poorest families. Given the social class structure of the Philippines, there are also migrants from middle- and upper-class backgrounds. Their activities and strategies, like those of people from poor backgrounds, need to be placed in the context of the situations from which they come and of the opportunities available to them. This study includes families from varying socioeconomic backgrounds, and examines the differing strategies of these people within the broader structural context, considering both strategies that essentially are oriented to subsistence and maintenance at a basic level and other strategies that are oriented to some degree of social mobility.

While the economic context within which migration takes place is important in shaping the strategies pursued and the behaviors observed, it is not the all-determining factor. Cultural values, too, play a role in shaping the activities of migrants and others to whom they are close. In the Philippines, two particular concerns stand out: (1) the role of the family and family obligations and (2) the position of women in the society. A considerable proportion of migrants in the Philippines are women. Questions have been raised as to the reason for this; I will suggest that Filipino cultural values regarding the roles of males and females help to provide a basis for understanding this pattern. Second, and perhaps more important, ideas about the family and family relationships are of great importance in understanding the behavior of migrants, especially the extent to which ties are maintained among family members living in a number of different places. Great emphasis is placed on reciprocal obligations both within the family and in other personal alliances. In this study, we will see the extent to which migrants accept those obligations and engage in activities that reinforce existing social ties.

Ultimately, however, this is a study neither of economic conditions in the Philippines nor of Filipino culture. It is, rather, a study of a set of people who have migrated to a particular city and of their lives and the lives of those closest to them. Only through in-depth study of particular individuals and their networks can we come to understand the reasons for particular behaviors observed, and perhaps most important, the way in which those involved see their own decisions and activities.

Each case study begins by focusing on an individual who has migrated to Dagupan City. That individual is then seen in his or her immediate social context—friends, co-workers, etc. in the city, and family and others in the rural home or elsewhere. Focused life histories are used to point out key events in the life of the migrant and of the others who have been important in decisions that were made. These life histories focus in particular on decisions concerning education, employment, and migration. Family networks are discussed at some length and, in particular, the maintenance of ties between those in Dagupan and those elsewhere. In most cases, these include the giving of monetary remittances, which are used in various ways by those at home. In some cases, the remittances are essential for family subsistence. In others, they are used for investment either by the migrant herself or by other family members. To the extent possible, the case studies incorporate the views of the individuals themselves about their activities. Thus we see that in some cases, those we have labeled migrants see themselves as still having their "home" with their family in the rural area, while others are more permanently tied to city life although still maintaining links with the rural place. In all cases, movement back and forth takes place with relative ease, even in situations where the language spoken differs from place to place.

Migration and Rural–Urban Links: Are Migrants Migrants?

From the case studies emerges a portrait of a set of people who pursue a variety of strategies in attempting to deal with situations in which they find themselves and in terms of their own cultural values. I have labeled those who have moved to Dagupan City as migrants and have focused on their relationships with others, particularly with those family members remaining in the rural area. Certainly these individuals are mobile; in many cases, they have moved more than once although most are still relatively young. On the other hand, other family members now living at home are also quite mobile; they may have lived elsewhere at some time in the past, and most engage in visiting or other activities that require moving about from place to place. We find families—including husbands and wives—that are quite widely dispersed geographically and yet which maintain regular ties, seeing each other frequently and giving money and other assistance to one another. We find, furthermore, that some of those who have moved to the city on a more or less permanent basis see themselves as still having their "home" where their family resides. To what extent, then, are these people "migrants" and are the links they maintain "rural-urban" links? From the perspective of the social scientist studying them, they have moved and may be counted as migrants. In addition, the place where they now live is clearly an urban place while that they left is clearly rural. Yet they do not necessarily see themselves in this light. Rather, they see themselves as people who have responded to particular situations and particular opportunities; at the moment, that may mean living in an urban locale, but in future, there may be other opportunities which involve further moves, perhaps to another city, perhaps to a rural locale.

By arguing this, I am not saying that there is no difference between rural and urban places or that those who move don't recognize those differences. Certainly they do. Nor am I saying that they just remain "rural" people who happen to be living in the city at the moment. Rather, I am arguing that the key fact for them is not rural–urban *migration* but rather, where within a field of opportunities open to them and within the constraints imposed by their position in society, they may find resources—social and economic—that allow them to sustain themselves and their families, and in some cases, to engage in some degree of socioeconomic mobility. From this perspective, rural and urban places are part of a single social field within which, over time, there may be considerable movement, not only between one village and a particular city, but between a number of such places. Similarly, within a single family we find individuals in a number of different places at a single point in time; in some families, we even find members overseas, which is certainly not part of the available resource field open to all.

As people move among a variety of places, they adopt behavior patterns appropriate to the place in which they are living and working while still retaining patterns appropriate for other places. Hence we find young women working as salesgirls in an urban store who go home on weekends to help with household and farm chores. In some cases, these transitions involve not only different social contexts but different linguistic contexts as well; one case considers a young woman who uses one language at home and two to three other languages in Dagupan.

Migration and associated behavioral changes have usually been seen as problematic. Attention has focused in general on the question of *why* people move, implying that they would always stay put if possible. While the why question remains of interest, perhaps too much emphasis has been placed on it. In a situation where movement is relatively easy, where it is possible to maintain ties over distances, and where resources are often *not* available in the home area, it is perhaps not surprising that individuals and families follow strategies that require geographical movement while continuing to see themselves as part of units based in rural homes.

Methods

The primary methods used in the research were basic anthropological ones—observation, unstructured and structured interviews, a lot of visiting with people at home, at work (when possible), and when they visited friends and relatives, both in Dagupan and in their hometowns. In addition to those whose lives I focused on for the case studies, there were many others with whom I talked and who contributed in various ways to my understanding of rural-urban migration. In addition, an interview schedule was used to survey a sample of 176 migrants. The interviews focused on migration and work histories and on the maintenance of ties and giving of remittances.[3] Government censuses and surveys, as well as survey data collected and analyzed by others, provides the basis of much of the analysis of urban and regional structural conditions discussed in Part 1.[4]

Essentially, this is a study of migration at the level of individuals and families, placed into a broader structural context. Therefore, I placed most of my emphasis on individual life histories and family case studies, as it seemed to me that these methods provide insights into the complexities of the migration process as it is experienced by individuals and families. Life histories and family case studies are two related approaches used by anthropologists to collect and analyze extensive and detailed data on selected individuals and families. Life histories in anthropology date to the 1920s; in recent years, they have been part of a move to "person-centered" ethnography (Langness and Frank 1981:1). To some extent, they were seen in the earlier period as primarily a method for data collection, and were largely nonanalytical. More recently, life histories have been used not merely as a data collection method, but also as a set of data for analysis. Two types of analytical approaches have been particularly important: first, the use of life histories to understand the relation of the individual to his or her culture, in particular the relationship between individual psychology and cultural values and ethos (Langness and Frank 1981:64–69); and second, examining life histories in relation to social change.

Perhaps the best example of this latter approach is Mintz's study of a Puerto Rican sugarcane worker ([1960], 1974). Although most of the study consists of the individual's own story, Mintz examines the social and cultural context in which that individual has lived. As he points out,

> [Taso] is not an "average" anything—neither an average man, nor
> an average Puerto Rican, nor an average Puerto Rican lower-class
> cane worker. He has lived just one life and not all of that. He
> doesn't think of himself as representative of anything, and he is
> right. His solutions to life's problems may not be the best ones,
> either, but he seems satisfied with his choices. I have tried to put
> down his story in the context of what I could understand about the
> circumstances under which he lived and lives. (1974:11)

In other words, the value of a detailed life history is to see how an
individual has lived and experienced the social and cultural changes that
have affected his society. At the same time, however, the understanding
of an individual life can aid in understanding those broader social and
cultural processes. Mintz expresses this goal as follows:

> When I wrote this book . . . my main objective was to make avail-
> able a rural proletarian's account of the experience of "westerniza-
> tion" . . . in an agrarian, insular subtropical setting. While I sought
> to deal with the particular, local and individual in this instance, it
> did not escape me that, throughout Africa, Asia and Latin America,
> anthropologists were busily studying "tribal" peoples, while
> largely ignoring those who were being subjected to what were
> common and widespread processes of this kind. Thus I was dealing
> with a single case; but I believed it had extremely wide relevance in
> the modern world. (1974:xii)

Individual biography or life history provides an individual's own
"personal document" of the decisions he or she has made and the activities he has engaged in. With regard to the study of migration, such
personal stories can help in understanding how individuals perceive and
act on the social structural and cultural forces that affect them.

Closely related to life histories in anthropology are family case studies.
While some anthropologists focus on the biography of single individuals,
others have looked at sets of individuals within family groups, collecting
life histories from a number of family members as well as observing
family interaction. Oscar Lewis's studies of families in Mexico, Puerto
Rico and Cuba are probably the best known of such family studies but
are largely descriptive (Lewis 1959, 1961, 1964, 1965; Lewis, Lewis, and
Rigdon 1977). Aronson (1980) has used family studies as the basis for an

analysis of social and cultural change among migrant Ijebu Yoruba living in the city of Ibadan, Nigeria. His goal is to balance the personal and particular with the social and general, in the effort to understand "how real people continually create and are continually affected by the no less real social and cultural forces around them" (1980:xix).

Family studies and life histories, then, are forms of personal documents; their great value is not simply as a method of data collection, but more importantly as the basis for analysis of the ways in which individuals and families experience the broader social and cultural forces affecting them. What is key in these approaches is that they provide, in the first place, rich, detailed data. Life histories provide details of an individual's experiences, while family studies provide detailed observations of family activities and interactions. Often, experiences and activities that might not be seen as inherently important by the outside observer may be seen as important by the individuals involved. This leads to the second major point regarding the value of such approaches: they help in providing an insider's account, although ultimately that account is shaped by the ethnographer who presents the life history or family study.

The analysis resulting from the use of detailed life histories and family case studies is very different from approaches that use residence histories as the basis of statistical analysis. Residence history analysis has been advocated as a methodology for studying migration patterns (Balan et al. 1969; Pryor 1979). However, statistical residence history analysis reduces individual activities to statistical patterns and hence loses what is the essence of life histories—the richness and complexity of lives as they are lived and experienced by the migrants themselves. If we are interested in understanding the complexity of migration, statistical analyses alone will not provide us with the sort of data necessary for examining such issues as the decision-making process within families that lead to migration of specific individuals, or the later activities and decisions that follow migration, including continued interaction between family members and strategies for adaptation to the new locale. Statistical analysis of residence histories helps to point out patterns of movement—e.g., circulatory movements between rural and urban areas—but can not provide any significant insights into how those moving, as well as those not moving, perceive and describe their own activities or why they have undertaken them. In other words, the goal of the approach used here, of using life histories and family case studies to obtain and analyze detailed data on relatively small numbers of people, is quite different from the goal of those concerned with statistical analysis of residence histories, even though the terminology may seem similar.

In doing the case studies discussed in Part 2, a variety of types of data were collected. I interviewed the migrant members of the family, collecting life history data as well as other information. Since several of the migrants were quite young, they did not provide lengthy life histories, but were able to tell me about their activities prior to migrating and the context of the decision to move to Dagupan. I also interviewed family members living in the rural home and elsewhere, again collecting life history data from them when possible. In addition, I observed the migrant member of the family in his or her work setting, in living quarters, and on social occasions. I also went with the migrant when he or she visited at home, and in several cases was able to stay with families for short periods of time. Unlike family studies carried out in one location (e.g., Aronson 1980), I was not able to carry out detailed observations of all the day-to-day activities of the family, but rather observed on several occasions and obtained other data through lengthy, open-ended interviews and discussions on a wide range of topics.

Family and life history data can provide the basis for examining the links between individual behavior and larger social and cultural context. When we consider individual migrants whose parents are tenant farmers, for example, we can begin to consider the decisions and strategies of such families within the larger context of the situation of rice farmers in the lowland Philippines. Or, in the case of a young girl working as a domestic servant, whose parents are landless, we can see the importance of her income as part of the total income of the family and understand this in terms of the situation of landless rural Filipinos. It is not that any particular migrant or his family is "typical" or "representative" of others, but they do exist in particular historical and cultural circumstances, which affect their decisions and interactions, just as such circumstances affect others in their society. The detail and richness of data obtained through such an approach can provide analytical insights into the complex behavior of individuals and families in situations of social change.

The Philippine Context

Recent events in the Philippines have attracted a great deal of attention, especially since the February 1986 "People Power" Revolution, which resulted in the coming to power of President Corazon Aquino. Most discussion has focused on political developments (e.g., Villegas 1987), although economic issues have also received some attention. For example, an August 1987 report in the *Far Eastern Economic Review* suggested some improvement in macroeconomic conditions while recognizing the existence of many continuing problems (August 6, 1987). There is, however, little if any evidence to suggest improvement in the lives of the majority of ordinary Filipinos. When this book was researched in the late 1970s, there was considerable evidence of an overall worsening of socioeconomic conditions, particularly for rural people. The situation deteriorated further during the early 1980s. It is still too early to know if Aquino will be able to carry out reforms that will lead to significant improvement, especially in areas such as land reform.

A recent *New York Times* article quotes a Filipino farmer as saying "If you depend on the land, it's never going to be enough" (October 18, 1987). This viewpoint is similar to that of the individuals and families studied in this book, who in response to the constraints and opportunities of the socioeconomic conditions in which they find themselves, seek out and follow a variety of strategies, which they choose in terms of their own social and cultural goals. The analysis of these strategies, within a broader structural context, helps provide us with an understanding of migration and rural-urban linkages that has implications not only for the Philippines but also for an understanding of similar processes elsewhere.

The Urban and Regional Context of Migration

Part 1 examines the context and setting in which migration to Dagupan City takes place. Any particular move of any particular migrant occurs within a context of opportunities and constraints affected by existing economic, political, and social realities. While behavior is not necessarily *determined* by any one of these, discussion of them provides an understanding of the structural framework in which migrants and their families operate.

Studies of broad socioeconomic conditions in the Philippines in the 1970s painted a picture of relatively good economic growth rates accompanied by vast inequalities in income distribution (International Labor Organization [ILO] 1974:13; Fields 1980:219–24). At the same time, inflation was increasing rapidly, and the number of people considered to fall below a measurable index of poverty ("poverty threshold") was also increasing (Tan and Holazo 1982; Abrera 1976). In recent years the overall economic situation has worsened. Within this broad context, there is great variation between regions of the country and between rural and urban areas (Castillo 1977), ranging from the "Makati nexus"—the modern commercial area of Metro Manila—to the poorest areas of the mountains of Northern Luzon and the Eastern Visayas.

Because of the great variation within the country, my discussion will focus on the region where Dagupan is located, and from which most migrants to the city come. This region can in broad terms be referred to as Central Luzon; this is not an administrative region, but refers to a set of common geographic, economic, and social features (see fig. 1 and discussion in chap. 3). It is a predominately agrarian region, with rice as the major crop. Although nonfarm occupations are increasingly important, ties with rice farming and with rural areas are still central concerns to the vast majority of people.

Chapter 2 discusses Dagupan City itself and the role it plays in regional affairs. Chapter 3 examines regional economic conditions, using

19

data from both Pangasinan Province and from the larger Central Luzon region, while chapter 4 is concerned with migration patterns in the region. Chapter 5 provides a brief discussion of the sociocultural context in which migrants are operating.

The period referred to in these chapters is the late 1970s; the field research in Dagupan was carried out in 1978–79, while census and other statistical sources from the mid and late 1970s provide data on the regional socioeconomic context.

Chapter 2

Dagupan City

At 4 o'clock in the morning, the buses begin arriving on the main street in front of the plaza. From towns in the province—Alaminos, Lingayen, Malasiqui—they carry people with bundles, coming to sell fruits and vegetables in the city. The sellers set up makeshift stalls in front of the post office and the bank and spread out their tomatoes, green mangoes, and other produce. Already established in front of the small marketplace are the fish sellers, who began work at 2 A.M., buying fish from the boats that came in the night before and from the wholesalers who trucked fish in from Manila. Interspersed between fish and vegetable dealers are the street vendors, selling cigarettes, *bibingka* (pancakes), *balut* (duck eggs) and other necessities for the early-morning customers. *Pan de sal* sellers move among the others, calling attention to their hot rolls with the penetrating sound of horns.

As the city awakens, customers arrive: school teachers buying fish for the day before going to work, housemaids getting the morning supply of *pan de sal*, bus passengers picking up a snack of *bibingka* before boarding a bus for a nearby town.

By sunrise at six, most of the sellers have disappeared. The area in front of the post office is empty and someone is sweeping the post office steps. Guards appear in front of the supermarket just down the street. Buses move in and out, discharging passengers and reloading, with a boy calling out the destination to all, trying to encourage them to take his bus.

Soon, most of the residents of Dagupan City are going about their daily business. The stalls in the large enclosed marketplace, known as the Supermarket, begin to open, and customers arrive. The small shops along the main street, selling clothing, records, groceries, and providing services such as hairdressing and eyeglasses, are open as well. Children get ready for school, while their mothers and fathers go to work. Some work in offices in the center of town. Others are employed at stores or sell in the market. Many have fashioned their own small means of earn-

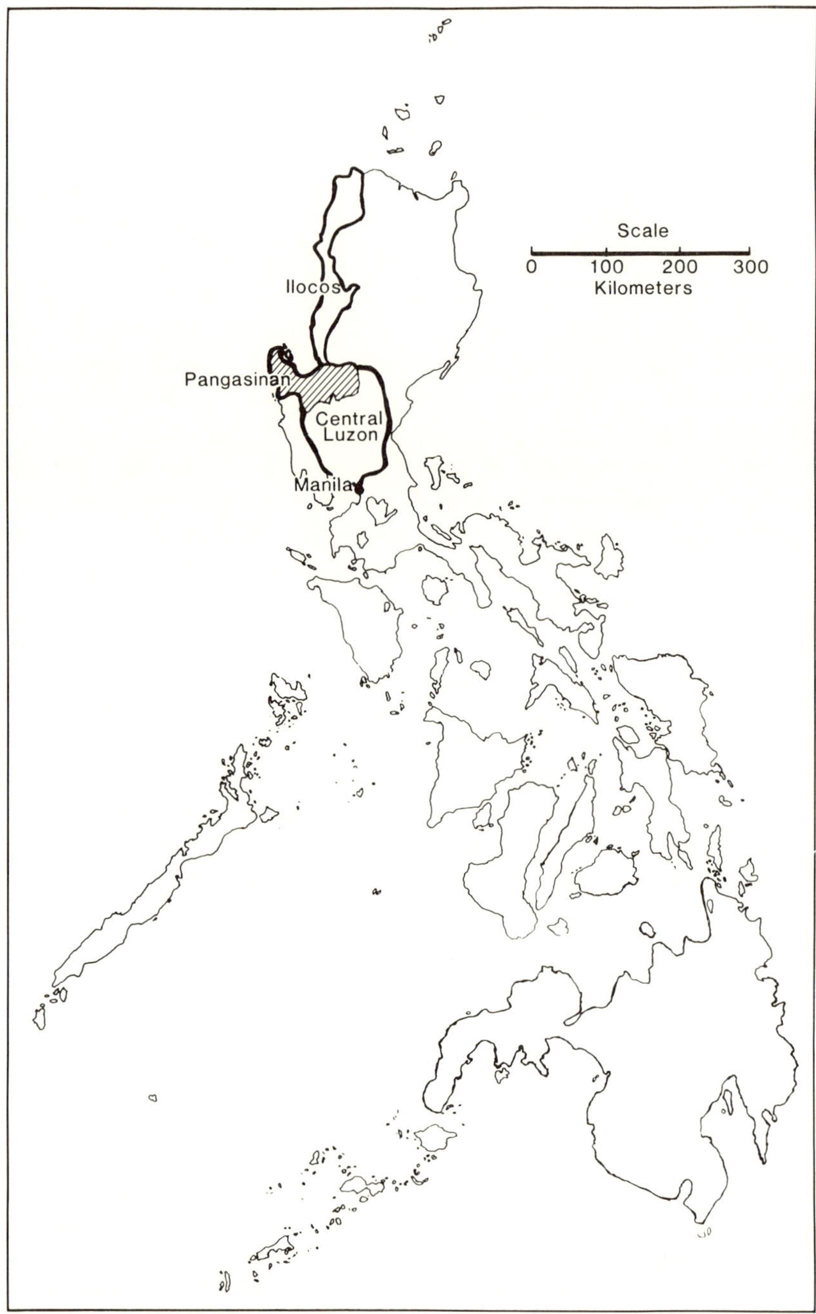

Fig. 1. The Philippines. This map outlines the boundaries of the
geographic regions most commonly thought of as Ilocos and Central

ing a living—vending ice cream or peanuts, creating kerosene lanterns out of old jars and tin cans, pushing carts loaded with goods to the market for a trader.

Throughout the day, the streets and sidewalks are crowded. Jeepneys (jeeps converted into minibuses) go back and forth from the *poblacion* (town center) to the outlying barrios, while tricycles (motorcycles with side cars) take passengers from place to place in the town center. Street vendors and hawkers crowd the sidewalks—women selling fruit juice and peanuts, men selling lottery tickets. At midday and in the early afternoon, the streets are quieter as people stay indoors to escape the midday heat.

By late afternoon, the streets are active again, as the early-morning process reverses itself. Schools and stores close, people go home from work, commuters flag down the buses that will take them back to the nearby towns, and the vegetable and fruit sellers move back out of the marketplace onto the street, hoping to make sales to those returning home from work who think they will get a bargain by buying late in the day. *Bibingka* and *balut* vendors reappear and are out until 11 P.M. or later, to catch the late passersby. By two in the morning, the cycle begins again, as the fish arrive from Manila and the wholesalers take charge of selling them to the vendors who will later appear in front of the post office.

Throughout the day and much of the night, the *poblacion* of Dagupan City is active. It is the center not only of a city of 100,000, but also of a province with a population of 1,520,000. Located on two rivers and just a few miles from the coast, the city has become the major urban center in Pangasinan Province (fig. 1). Like other cities in the Philippines, Dagupan contains a commercial core known as the *poblacion*, in which are located most stores, the cathedral, city and other government offices, and the plaza (Hart 1955). In addition to the *poblacion*, there are twenty-seven other *barangays* or *barrios* in the city, most of which are primarily residential. While all of the barrios in Dagupan are officially classified as "urban" by the census,[1] in appearance some would seem to be no differ-

---

Luzon, including the province of Ilocos Norte, Ilocos Sur, and La Union in Ilocos, and the provinces of Pangasinan, Tarlac, Nueva Ecija, and Pampanga in Central Luzon. These boundaries do not coincide with regional administrative areas currently in use in the Philippines (see chap. 3, note 1).

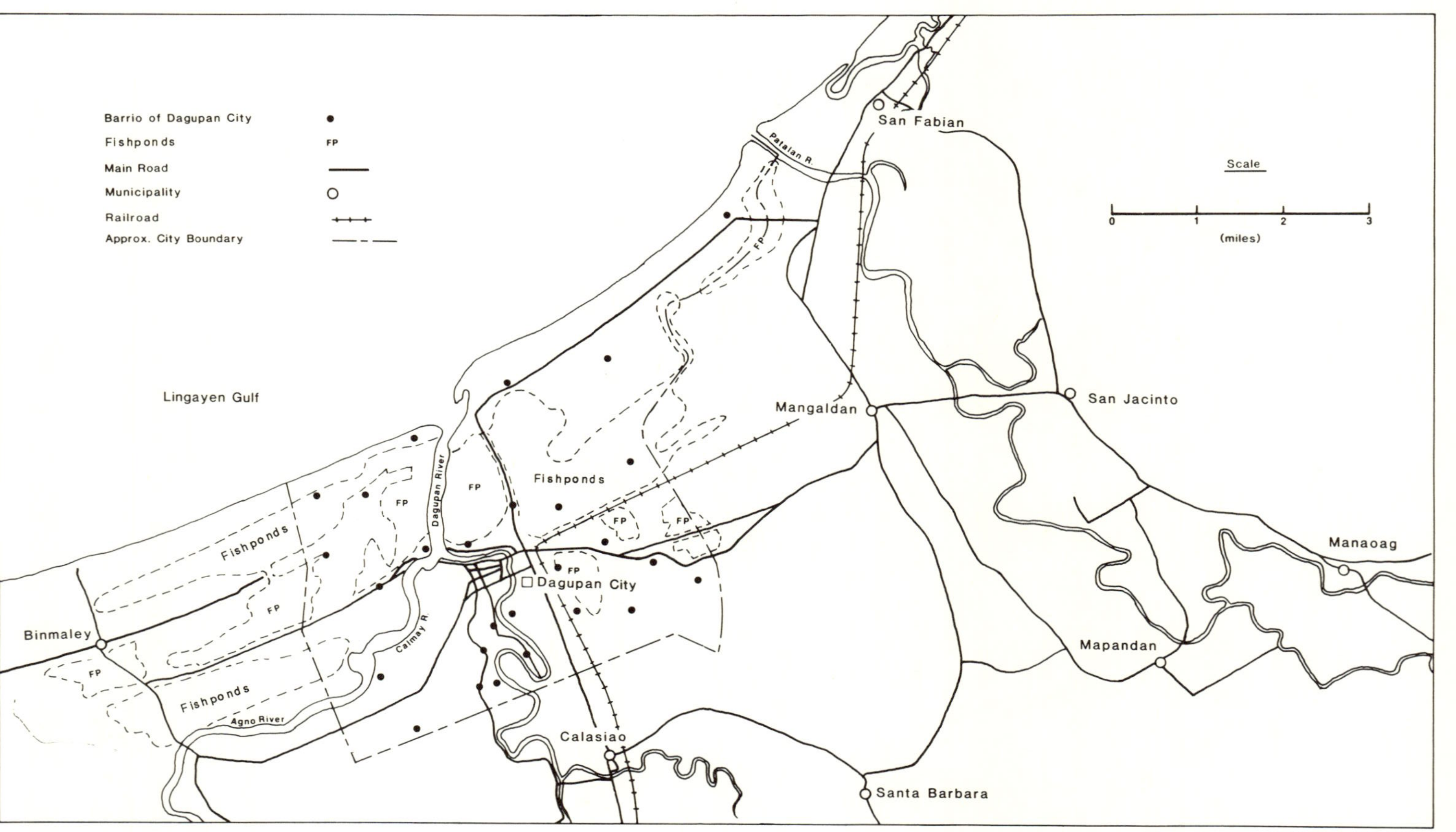

Fig. 2. Dagupan City and surrounding municipalities

ent from rural barrios in neighboring towns. For example, the territory of the city includes several island barrios that are largely fishing communities (see fig. 2).

In the outlying residential barrios the houses are mainly built of bamboo or of nipa palm and thatch, as are houses throughout lowland Luzon. In some suburban barrios, expensive subdivisions have been developed, with concrete houses, gardens surrounded by walls, and other signs indicating the residences of the rich. In the *poblacion*, the largest structures are the modern cathedral and the new luxury hotel, with its revolving restaurant overlooking the tin roof of the marketplace. The commercial buildings along the main street, many of which are owned by Filipino Chinese (Doeppers 1971:134), are two and three stories, with stores below and offices or living quarters above. Lower, more modest structures are squeezed between the stores and the river. Not visible from the main street, they include houses and small warehouses. The Supermarket, an enclosed marketplace, takes up an entire block. Inside, it is a maze of narrow corridors with cement floors and poor drainage, providing access to hundreds of individually operated shops, which sell everything from sausages and fish to vegetables to cloth and clothing. Across the street from the Supermarket is a smaller marketplace, where groceries and vegetables are sold. Fishing boats bring their catch to a dock on the other side of the river from this market; the fish are then brought across the river in small boats for resale to vendors.

Not all of the *poblacion* is devoted to commercial activities. Some of the buildings facing the plaza are residences, still owned by some of the prominent families of the city, although many of the family members have moved to the subdivisions or to Manila. Behind the main streets are interior areas containing slum and squatter settlements, with houses constructed of discarded building materials. Some of these settlements spread out over the river; others are on swampy land formerly used as fishponds. Many migrants to the city live in these settlements or in boarding houses that rent out rooms to individuals and families.

Historical Background

Dagupan City is the major urban center in Pangasinan Province as well as the major city in the northern part of the Central Luzon Plain. A prehispanic settlement was located there (Doeppers 1971:72) when Augustinian missionaries arrived in 1590. In 1720 the settlement was named

Dagupan (Polido 1971). With its coastal and riverine location, Dagupan became important in trade between Pangasinan and Ilocos (Basa 1972:5; Doeppers 1971:74).

In 1885, its commercial activity was described as follows:

With the arrival of the northeast monsoon mercantile enterprises begin. The port of Dagupan becomes filled with pontines and other craft serving coastal traffic, which carry the goods to Manila. In this period there is much movement up until . . . June and July when the wet season commences and traffic is paralyzed, and the boats depart, seeking shelter until the return of the fair season. (Carrozal 1886, quoted in McLennan 1973:107)

After the establishment of the railroad between Manila and Dagupan in 1894, Dagupan's importance as the region's commercial center increased (Doeppers 1972). A 1901 description stated:

During the period of the disposal of the rice harvest, there is much traffic at the railway station, and so for a space of 6 months, one sees a succession of miles and miles of carts forming upon it [the bridge] during the busyest [*sic*] hours in two uninterrupted lines both coming and going. Without fear of contradiction I am able to attest that except for Manila's bridges, there is no other which, during the course of the year, pass as many people, carriages, carts, coaches, horses and merchandise as this Pantal bridge, which is located in Dagupan in the heart of the port of disembarkation for ships and steamboats. (Flormata 1901, quoted in McLennan 1973:136)

Throughout the period of the late 1800s and early 1900s, Dagupan was a center not only for commercial activities of Pangasinan Province, but also a transport center for much of the northern part of the Central Luzon Plain. A novel by Edilberto Tiempo describes a journey in about 1919 in which the characters travel four and a half days on horseback across the mountains and through eastern Pangasinan to Dagupan, where they take the train to Manila (1972:49).

The establishment of a major bus company, Pangasinan Transportation Company (Pantranco) in 1917 increased further the importance of Dagupan as a commercial and transport center. During the early 1900s the city's major commercial role shifted from being an assembly point for exports such as rice to being a distribution center for manufactured products from Manila (Dannhaeuser 1983:17).

Contemporary Role in the Region

Dagupan's continued importance within the province is evident on a number of measures—as a population center, as a center of educational and health facilities, as a locale for government offices, and most importantly, as a transport and commercial center.

Dagupan is one of two "chartered cities"[2] in the province. The other, San Carlos City, has a population equal in size to that of Dagupan but a much lower population density, and a number of barrios within its city limits are classified as "rural." Dagupan is, therefore, the only fully urban center in the province (see fig. 3).

Although the town of Lingayen is the provincial capital, many government offices are located in Dagupan. Regional branches of national agencies such as the Bureau of Fisheries, Department of Labor, and about twenty others have their offices in Dagupan, making it a center for a variety of governmental activities and employment. Many of the middle income migrants to Dagupan work in these agencies.

Dagupan is similarly a center for educational and health services. Three large colleges are located there—University of Pangasinan, Luzon Colleges, Lyceum Northwestern—as well as a number of vocational schools. As in other provincial colleges throughout the country, the quality of education is not equivalent to that in the better Manila institutions, but, for many students, these schools provide the only access to higher education and hence to the possibility of social mobility through education. As a result, they attract students not only from within the province but also from other provinces in Central Luzon; many migrants first come to the city as students.

Eight private hospitals and one public hospital, as well as a number of clinics, are located in the city, far more than in other towns and cities of the province. These have brought a large number of medical professionals to the city; professionals, mainly in medicine, make up one-third of the sample of upper-class household heads studied by Doeppers in 1969 (Doeppers 1971:237).

Dagupan continues to be largely a commercial center, as it was in the past. In the mid 1970s there were over 2,100 commercial establishments

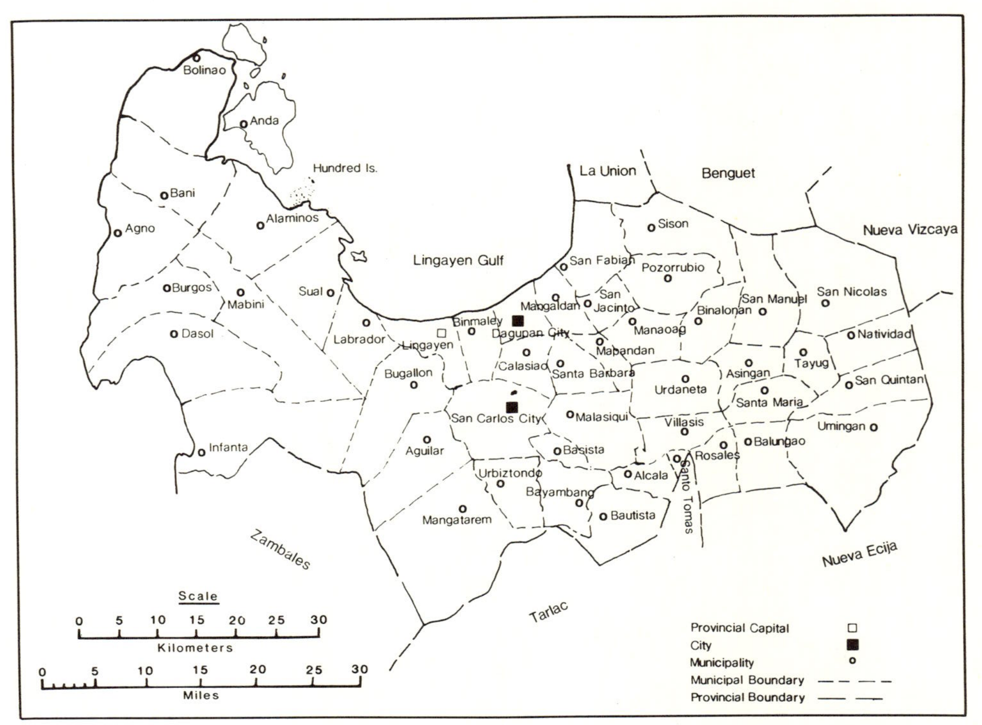

Fig. 3. Province of Pangasinan

and twenty-one banks (Dagupan City n.d.a). Many of these establishments, especially those in retail trade, are small shops, located both inside the marketplace and on the main streets of the *poblacion*. Nevertheless, these shops, as well as the more prominent establishments such as banks and the American-style supermarket that opened in 1979, provide employment for considerable numbers of people. The central commercial district of the city is dominated by Filipino Chinese, although the proportion of Chinese-owned stores varies with the specific locale and the type of goods sold (Doeppers 1971:162–63). Within the marketplace, on the other hand, most establishments are Filipino-owned.

Dagupan's importance as a commercial center is best measured by its role in the distribution of goods entering the city from elsewhere. Dannhaeuser's study of the distribution of grocery goods shows that the commercial hinterland of the city includes many of the surrounding towns; he estimates that the city's trade hinterland extends five thousand square kilometers and includes more than one million people (1980:160). Many Manila-based companies have made Dagupan their center of distribution not only for Pangasinan but also for the entire northern part of the Central Luzon Plain and for the mountain areas to the north. As a result, sales agents for those companies make Dagupan their home base, from which they travel west to Zambales, east to Isabela, and north to Benguet. Pharmaceutical companies, in particular, use a large number of sales agents who are based in Dagupan (Dannhaeuser 1983:111–20).

The city also plays an important role in fish distribution. There are two sources of fish traded in Dagupan. Those caught in local waters by Dagupan-based boats are sold locally and are also shipped out to cities elsewhere. Many other fish, especially those which are processed as smoked fish and for *bagaong* (a fish condiment) are trucked to Dagupan from the large ports in Rizal Province, south of Manila. In Dagupan, wholesalers resell them to local vendors and processors as well as to vendors from other Pangasinan towns (interview with Tony Reyes, fish wholesaler, March 27, 1979).

Facilitating Dagupan's place as an important commercial center is the extensive transport system which provides access to most other major cities on Northern Luzon as well as to the smaller towns in the province. In addition to the train, five bus lines provide service between Dagupan and other large cities. Two of these, Pantranco and Dagupan Bus Line, primarily run between Dagupan and Manila, with better than hourly service; Pantranco also goes east to Nueva Ecija and the Cagayan Valley and north to Baguio. Of the others, one provides daily service to Santa Cruz, Zambales, the province to the west; and two provide service to the Ilocos provinces to the northeast. These buses carry large numbers of passengers. On a midweek day in January when travel was relatively light, more than twenty-five hundred passengers traveled on Pantranco buses running from Dagupan to Manila, and a slightly larger number from Manila to Dagupan (Pantranco records 1979).[3]

Within the province, transport is provided by minibuses and jeepneys running from Dagupan along each of the main roads leading out from the city. The fare is relatively low (e.g., thirty centavos to Calasiao and seventy-five centavos to Lingayen in 1978–79) and the buses run frequently to the nearby towns. Traffic is heavy in both directions, with commuters and shoppers coming into the city and with others, such as market vendors going to sell in periodic markets, going out from the city. Several thousand people travel in each direction every day.[4] On weekends migrants living in Dagupan use these buses to go home for visits, and when they can't go home, they send messages home by way of the drivers and conductors.

Urban Jobs and Incomes

As might be expected from the preceding discussion, the employment structure of Dagupan is heavily dominated by commercial and service occupations. There is little industry in the city, or elsewhere in the province for that matter.

Tables 1 and 2 present census data on the employment and industrial structure of urban areas of Pangasinan in 1975; with nearly one-third of the total urban population of the province, these data may be taken as indicative of the structure in Dagupan as well.[5]

Industry in the Philippines is highly concentrated in the Metro-Manila region, with some development of industry in the Visayas and Mindanao (World Bank 1980). The lack of industry north of Manila is apparent in the statistics on Pangasinan: only 10.7 percent of the urban population is employed in manufacturing. Of those in this sector, 20 percent are employed in food-manufacturing industries while 30 percent are employed in industries manufacturing shoes and clothing; the remainder are scattered in a variety of other manufacturing enterprises. Such industry as exists in Dagupan is small scale and includes several noodle factories, a *bacayo* (coconut candy) factory, and a number of cottage industries employing small numbers of people and making products such as candy, baskets, and furniture. In 1976, 166 cottage industries in Dagupan employed a total of 451 people (Pangasinan Development Staff 1976). Further evidence of the small-scale character of industry in Dagupan is provided by the fact that 41 percent of those in manufacturing occupations are working on their own without any paid labor (Philippines [Republic] National Census and Statistics Office, 1975b: table 12).

In contrast to the manufacturing sector, agriculture, commerce, and services make up a large proportion of the employment opportunities in urban Pangasinan. In Dagupan, most of those employed in primary sector occupations are fishermen living in the coastal barrios; they are essentially subsistence fishermen and are among the poorest segments of Dagupan's population (Dagupan City n.d.b).

Of the 18.1 percent in the commercial sector, more than 80 percent are

TABLE 1. Occupations of Urban Population Ten Years and Older in Urban Pangasinan, 1975

Gainful Occupation	Number	% Gainfully Employed	Males	% Gainfully Employed Males	Females	% Gainfully Employed Females
Professional, technical	10,029	13.6	3,815	7.8	6,214	25.2
Administrative, executive, managerial	1,472	2.0	1,135	2.3	337	1.4
Clerical workers	4,875	6.6	3,078	6.3	1,797	7.3
Sales workers	12,617	17.1	5,781	11.8	6,836	27.8
Farmers, fishermen	14,033	19.0	13,419	27.3	614	2.5
Miners and related	222	0.3	214	0.4	8	0.03
Transport and communication workers	5,314	7.2	5,202	10.6	112	0.5
Craftsmen, production workers	11,165	15.1	8,996	18.3	2,169	8.8
Service, sports	9,875	13.4	3,715	7.5	6,160	25.0
Stevedores and related	2,698	3.7	2,564	5.2	134	0.5
Not elsewhere classified	1,475	2.0	1,238	2.5	237	1.0
Total gainfully employed	73,775	100.0	49,157	100.0	24,618	100.03[a]

Source: Philippines (Republic) National Census and Statistics Office 1975b: table 9.
Note: Total population, 201,378; males, 95,878; females, 105,500
[a]Percentages may not total 100 due to rounding.

engaged in retail trade. Furthermore, a large majority in this sector are self-employed (Philippines [Republic] National Census and Statistics Office, 1975b: table 12), indicating a predominance of small-scale, informal sector activities.

The largest sector is the service sector, accounting for fully 35.9 percent of all employment in urban Pangasinan. However, this sector includes a wide variety of types of occupation ranging from personal services (33.6 percent of the total in services) to government (20.8 percent) and community services (32.7 percent). The composition of the service sector becomes more clear from an examination of the occupations shown in table 1. The government and community service categories include many of the professional and administrative occupations. For example, teachers and professors (9.3 percent of all gainfully employed) and health personnel are included here. Occupations in domestic service, such as housekeepers, cooks, and maids, also are part of the service sector and account for 8.7 percent of all urban employment in the province (Philippines [Republic] National Census and Statistics Office 1975b: table 9).

The employment statistics show a number of important differences in the types of employment available to males and females in urban areas of Pangasinan (see table 1). For females, there are essentially three occupa-

TABLE 2.   Population Ten Years and Older, by Industry, in Urban Pangasinan, 1975

Industry	Number	% of Total	Male	% of Males	Females	% of Females
Agriculture, hunting, forestry, fishing	14,158	19.2	13,504	27.5	654	2.7
Mining, quarrying	236	0.3	222	0.4	14	0.06
Manufacturing	7,923	10.7	5,618	11.4	2,305	9.3
Electricity, gas, water services	295	0.4	275	0.6	20	0.08
Construction	3,829	5.2	3,768	7.7	61	0.2
Commerce	13,344	18.1	6,349	12.9	6,995	28.4
Transport, communication, storage	5,332	7.2	5,172	10.5	160	0.6
Services	26,464	35.9	12,535	25.5	13,929	56.6
Industry, not adequately described	2,194	3.0	1,714	3.5	480	1.9
Total all industries	73,775	100.0	49,157	100.0	24,618	99.9

Source: Philippines (Republic) National Census and Statistics Office 1975b: table 10.

tional categories in which they participate heavily and, to some extent, dominate. These are (1) professional occupations (25.2 percent), especially professors and teachers, in which 20.9 percent of all employed females are employed; (2) sales workers, accounting for 27.7 percent of all employed females and (3) services (25 percent), especially housekeepers and maids, accounting for 21.6 percent of all female employment. Males, on the other hand, are spread more widely over a number of different occupations. One category of some importance in providing employment for males is that of transport and communication workers; 10.6 percent of employed males fall into this occupational category, of whom 80 percent are drivers on road transport, including bus, jeepney, and tricycle drivers (Philippines [Republic] National Census and Statistics Office 1975b: table 9).

With the exception of government employment and teaching positions, the occupational structure outlined here provides jobs primarily in sales and a variety of services; most in these occupations are self-employed or work in very small enterprises. Such an employment structure is typical of what is found in urban areas of the Philippines in general. In recent years, there has been a decline in self-employed and family labor in agriculture, while at the same time, there has been an increase in self-employment and family employment in a wide variety of small-scale enterprises (ILO, 1974:177–84).

Both migrants to Dagupan and natives of the city work in the types of jobs indicated here. As shall be seen in chapter 4, there seems to be relatively little distinction among the occupations in which migrants are employed and those employing Dagupan natives.

Income data for Dagupan are meager, but what is available indicates a pattern that could be anticipated from the preceding discussion of the occupational structure. Incomes for most of the population are low, while a small percentage has high incomes. Table 3 summarizes data collected in a 1976 household survey by the City Planning and Development Staff of Dagupan. The data refers to income of the family head, not to that of the household; actual incomes of families and households are likely to be somewhat greater, as many households have more than one income-earning member. According to this data, more than 43 percent of household heads earn ₱200 or less per month, or an annual income of ₱2,400–3,600 or less, while 9 percent earn more than ₱500 a month, or ₱6,000 a year.[6]

This data can be compared with national and provincial income dis-

TABLE 3.   Monthly Earnings of Family Heads
in Dagupan City, 1976

Monthly Earnings	Number	Percent
₱200 or less	5,945	43.9
₱201–300	2,766	20.4
₱301–400	2,204	16.3
₱401–500	1,411	10.4
Over ₱500	1,226	9.0
Total	13,552	100.0

Source: Dagupan City 1976 (Socioeconomic Profile of Dagupan City).

tribution data. Castillo provides 1971 data, in which she divides the population into low income (₱3,000 and below a year), middle income (₱3,000–₱5,999) and high income (₱6,000 and above). Table 4 compares her data for the country and the province with that for Dagupan, showing that a large majority in both city and province are in the low-income category. However, there is a larger proportion of middle-income families in the city than in the province as a whole.

Middle income is a rather arbitrary concept, however. It is perhaps more realistic to consider how much money is needed for a basic standard of living. Abrera (1976) and Tan and Holazo (1982) have examined this issue by attempting to define the minimum needed to provide "nutrition, shelter, health, and education requirements for the survival of the

TABLE 4.   Income Distribution in the Philippines, Pangasinan Province, and Dagupan City

Annual Income	Philippines (1971) % Families	Pangasinan Province (1971) % Families		Dagupan City (1976) % Household Heads
Low income (₱3,000 and below)	59.0	78.1	(₱3,600 and below)	64.2
Middle income (₱3,000–5,999)	25.0	9.8	(₱3,601–6000)	26.6
High income (₱6,000 and above)	16.0	12.1	(Over ₱6,000)	9.0

Source: For the Philippines and Pangasinan Province: Castillo 1977:I, 8–9 (1971 data). For Dagupan City: Dagupan City 1976.

entire family" (Tan and Holazo 1982:118). Abrera has found that 41 percent of families in the country, or about three million persons, were unable to meet the food threshold, an index of the minimum needed for adequate nutrition (Abrera 1976:244). The incidence of poverty—or the number falling below the threshold—varies from one region of the country to another. Tan and Holazo estimate that ₱3,688 per year was needed for a family of six in Central Luzon, including Pangasinan, to be above the poverty line; according to their calculations 37.8 percent of families in the region were below this line in 1975, an increase of 7 percent from 1971 (1982:112–15).[7]

In Dagupan, then, we find an economic structure characterized by service and sales occupations, considerable self-employment, and relatively low incomes. Wage labor is mainly located in the service sector—especially domestic service—and in commerce. Unlike Manila or a few medium-sized cities where industry has located, such as Iligan (cf. Ulack 1975), Dagupan has little industry.

Dagupan is in many ways quite representative of secondary cities (Rondinelli 1983:115–70) in being primarily a center of commerce and transport for the surrounding region and, as a result, in having strong links with the surrounding hinterland. Such cities are often ignored in studies of urbanization and migration, as they seem less important in these processes than the enormous metropolises such as Metro Manila. Clearly, the latter attracts the largest number of migrants and plays the dominant role in the urbanization process of the country (cf. Pernia 1977). Yet smaller cities also attract migrants, and play important regional roles. The highly developed commercial and transport sectors affect the surrounding rural hinterland from which most migrants come, and at the same time, provide many of the jobs open to those migrants who move to the city. In the next chapter, we focus on the rural economy of the region, examining the rural context from which migrants come and to which they retain strong ties after migration.

Chapter 3

The Rural Region: Rice, Employment, and Household Incomes

In the Philippines as a whole, large numbers of people live at or below minimum standards of living. Although the rice-producing region of Central Luzon is one of the "richer" sections of the country, that does not mean people there are well-off on an absolute scale. As an International Labor Organization study pointed out, "The worsening income distribution was not so much because the relatively rich regions of Central Luzon and Southern Tagalog were growing faster than the average, but rather because more families in the poorer regions were falling into lower income groups" (ILO 1974:9). For many in Pangasinan Province and the Central Luzon region in general, a major issue is survival—how to obtain enough income to feed and provide necessities for their families. Others, including many classified as middle income, do not live at the margins of existence, but are in a situation in which they are attempting to increase family incomes, at least minimally. For all, migration represents a possible strategy that may provide access to income and other resources.

To understand the economic context in which migrants to Dagupan are operating, it is necessary to consider the agrarian economy of the region.[1] This chapter examines the rural rice economy, employment patterns in the rural areas, and sources of household income for farm families. It also considers data on education and socioeconomic mobility.

The regional economy is complex and changing. Rice-producing areas such as Pangasinan and other Central Luzon provinces have long been part of and influenced by national and global economic forces (cf. McCoy and deJesus 1982:10). Rural and urban stratification patterns have developed and changed over time; contemporary Filipino families operate in contexts of historically generated patterns and current dynamics. Migrants to a city such as Dagupan include poor and relatively wealthy; individuals from landless, tenant, and landed families; those whose homes are in rural barrios and others from *poblacions* and urban centers. These patterns of migration cannot be *explained* by simply referring to the rural economy and the rural class structure. Rather, the goal of the present chapter is to examine the contemporary economic structures that provide the context in which individuals and families—at various class levels and from various backgrounds—operate.

A historical perspective is helpful in accomplishing such a goal. As recent regional histories demonstrate, local and regional dynamics are varied and have been greatly influenced by external forces and internal responses to them (cf. McCoy and deJesus 1982). The first section of this chapter therefore considers the way in which rice farming expanded and became commercialized in the nineteenth century in Pangasinan and Central Luzon. The rest of the chapter examines the contemporary economic situation, focusing on the complexities of land tenure and stratification patterns; on the diversity of income sources of rural households; and on the possibilities for education and mobility as they differentially affect portions of the population.

From this examination, it becomes clear that rural households are tied into and dependent upon the national economy in a variety of ways and that many cannot support themselves through farming alone. The rural sector "has been less and less able to provide sufficient opportunities for productive employment" (ILO 1974:25). In this context, urban migration becomes one means by which farm families can obtain additional income. Urban and rural areas are, in other words, part of the total "resource field" (van den Muijzenberg 1973:152) available to the population.

Rice in the Regional Economy

Rice farming is "the single most important economic activity in the Philippines" (World Bank 1976:100), and the Central Luzon Plain is the premier rice-growing region in the country. In Pangasinan, 96 percent of the farms produced *palay* (unshelled, or paddy, rice) in 1970; total *palay* production was 5,780,175 *cavans*.[2] This was valued at ₱142,424,844, which was 73.8 percent of the total value of all crop production in the province (Philippines [Republic] National Census and Statistics Office 1975a:xxiv).[3]

In discussing the rural economy of Pangasinan, we are therefore concerned primarily with rice farming and rice farmers. Rice farmers today are part of a complex, commercialized system, in which farmers both sell and buy rice, hire labor, and work for wages themselves. Further, while nearly everyone is tied to the rice economy in some way, not all are involved as farmers or producers; there are an increasing number of landless workers, working as wage laborers on farms, and there are, as well, many middle- and upper-class families who own land and receive income from it but who do not participate in any way in productive activities on the land.

Development of the Rice Economy

The commercialized system of agriculture began developing in the nineteenth century, when rice became an export crop. Sual, a Pangasinan town that is today a small town on the coast, was one of the leading ports for exports to China, reaching its peak about 1860 (McLennan 1973:84). As noted earlier, Dagupan became an important commercial center during this period, first in coastal trade and later in the trade by rail and roads (McLennan 1973:130–31). By the end of the nineteenth century, rice was no longer exported to foreign markets, but Pangasinan became the major supplier to Manila and to the Ilocos coast to the north, which had become a rice deficit area as a result of an emphasis on tobacco production. Pangasinan continued to be the major supplier of rice until the 1920s, when it was replaced by Nueva Ecija (McLennan 1973:400).

In the 1800s, rice production increased primarily as a result of expansion in the amount of land cultivated. By 1870, 49,000 hectares were reported to be under cultivation, with a peso value of exports estimated at ₱678,200 (McLennan 1973:389). In the early 1900s, the number of hectares under cultivation continued to expand (e.g., 67,000 hectares in 1902; 179,000 hectares in 1920), as did the amount of rice produced (McLennan 1973:403).

In addition to the demand for rice from China, and later from Manila and the Ilocos coast, a major impetus for the expansion of production resulted from internal migration within the province and region, leading to settlement of the interior. Prior to the nineteenth century, most settlement in the region continued to be along the coast and major rivers, as it had been in the pre-Hispanic era. Starting around 1815, people from Ilocos began to migrate to the interior of Pangasinan and later to Nueva Ecija, leading to major changes in settlement and land tenure patterns (McLennan 1973:139). (See chap. 4 on migration for more details on this movement.) In Nueva Ecija, the ultimate result of these movements and of changes in land ownership patterns was the development of a system of wet-rice monoculture on large haciendas (McLennan 1982). Such a system did not develop in Pangasinan, except in the far eastern part of the province, bordering on Nueva Ecija.

In Pangasinan, there were more small-holders than elsewhere in the region, and more diverse crop production. The dominant pattern of landholding was the *kasamahan* system of share tenancy, where the landowner divided his holdings into small farmsteads that were cultivated by peasants in exchange for a portion of the crop (usually one-third to one-half of the crop). Sharecropping arrangements often resulted from the need for credit on the part of the peasant, who gave up his land in order to pay debts, and then cultivated his former land as a *kasamahan*. In Pangasinan in 1903, there were 16,461 share tenants (Bureau of Commerce and Industry 1922). By 1939, there were 26,530, representing 30.6 percent of the total number of farm operators. The percentage has remained relatively constant since then, with censuses showing 34.3 percent in 1948 and 33.4 percent in 1971 (see table 5). In having a relatively large proportion of small-holders, Pangasinan has continued to differ from neighboring provinces. At the same time, farm size has remained small throughout the period, with more than 80 percent of the farms in both 1939 and 1971 under 3 hectares (Philippines Commonwealth Commission of the Census 1939: table 5; Philippines [Republic] National Census and Statistics Office 1975a: table 5A).

As rice production increased, there was a need for more labor in the

TABLE 5. Tenancy of Farms in Pangasinan Province, 1939, 1948, and 1971

Tenancy	1939		1948		1971	
	Number	Percent	Number	Percent	Number	Percent
Owners	33,450	38.6	32,000	34.3	31,112	34.8
Part owners	24,444	28.2	21,331	22.9	19,976	22.4
Share tenants	26,530	30.6	32,012	34.3	29,808[a]	33.4
Share-cash tenants	715	0.8	496	0.5	—	
Cash tenants	1,465	1.7	715	0.8	228[a]	0.3
Fixed amount of produce	—		—		3,521[a]	3.9
Other tenants	—		6,734	7.2	1,250[a]	1.4
Other forms of tenure	11	0.01	34	0.03	3,437	3.8
Total farmers	86,615	99.9	93,322	100.03	89,332	100.0

Source: 1939 Philippines (Commonwealth) Commission of the Census 1939: table 2.
  1948 Philippines (Republic) Bureau of the Census and Statistics 1952: table 5.
  1971 Philippines (Republic) National Census and Statistics Office 1975a: table 6A.
[a]Total tenants for 1971 = 34,807 (38.9%).

central plain area. In the late nineteenth century, seasonal migration from the Ilocos coast began, with Ilocanos coming to Pangasinan to work in the harvest in return for one-fifth of the crop. According to one description,

> Every year, when the rice is ripe, hundreds of Ilocanos come to Pangasinan to help in the harvest. Some of them come in the sailing vessels that carry salt to Dagupan, and others walk with their families even from Ilocos Norte. After the harvest most of them take their share of the crop and go back with it to their towns but some remain and make new homes. (Miller and Polley pp. 39–40, quoted in McLennan 1973:252)

Those who remained were among the continuing flow of migrants to Pangasinan and later to Nueva Ecija, discussed in chapter 4.

Finally, commercialization of the rice economy was part of the overall expansion of the internal commercial economy. Internal commerce began to develop in the eighteenth century with the evolution of networks of periodic markets; the town centers established by the Spanish began to become economic as well as religious centers. Pangasinan supplied not only rice but also salt, sugar, oil, and dried fish to other regions such as Ilocos, Cagayan, Nueva Ecija, and Pampanga (Cortes 1974:137). Much of the early trade was along coastal routes and inland waterways, particularly along the Agno River. In the nineteenth century, the largest market in the province was reported to be the weekly market in Calasiao (McLennan 1973:108–9). Lingayen became a major port, as did Sual for a brief time. As we have seen, Dagupan later replaced Lingayen as the major commercial center, especially after the railroad was built and road transport displaced water transport.

In addition to commerce, some light industry developed in Lingayen and Dagupan. Lingayen was a boatmaking center (Cortes 1974:139), while elsewhere there were sugar mills, nipa wine and coconut oil producers, and small weaving industries. In 1886, Carrozal described the role of Dagupan in the local economy as follows:

> Dagupan is almost the only town where there is commerce; all goods of the province flowing through this port. The strongest merchant house in Dagupan is an English firm, Heald and Company, its boats carrying as cargo the produce of the province. Al-

most all the purchases are made by middlemen who collect the
produce of farmers, to whom they make advances. Money passes
through a multitude of hands before reaching the producer. The
exportation of rice, sugar cane, etc. is made through Dagupan,
where all the products of the province, and much of that of Nueva
Ecija and Tarlac, collect. (Carrozal 1886, quoted in McLennan
1973:135)

Land, Stratification, and Employment:
Contemporary Patterns

As the rural economy commercialized and as differentiation among rural
residents developed, complex social patterns emerged based on the ten-
ant-landlord relationship:

A well established system of patron-client relations came to exist
between the landowner and his tenants. In exchange for a share of
his crop [usually one-half], labor on demand, and social deference,
the tenant could legitimately expect a supply of seed rice, the use of
draft animals, loans of rice at no interest during periods of scarcity,
loans of cash—often at usorious interests—and gifts and personal
attention at times of birth, baptism, marriage, sickness, and death.
Other ties, noneconomic in nature, also bound the landowner and
tenant together. The landlord depended on the political loyalty of
his tenants at election time and in return served as a powerful
intermediary on their behalf in dealing with state authority and as
an adjudicator and mediator in local disputes. (Vreeland et al.
1976:285)

While this description provides an accurate picture of land tenure relations in the past, it is no longer sufficient to portray the complexities of
rural stratification or the types of relationships existing between those in
different strata. While share tenancy remains the predominant characteristic of rice farming areas, patron-client ties have tended to break down
in recent years. Landlords and tenants are not homogeneous groups, and
there are many who both own their own land and are tenants on the land
of others. Furthermore, the division into landlord and tenant categories
omits an increasingly important category of rural people—those with no
access to land at all.

As we see in table 5, 34.8 percent of farms in Pangasinan in 1971 were farmed by owners and 38.9 percent were farmed by tenants of one type or another; another 22.4 percent were farmed by part owners, meaning that they both own land and are tenants on the land.[4] Of the share tenants, 77.2 percent report sharing the produce on a fifty–fifty basis, while 16.3 percent share either on a forty–sixty or thirty–seventy basis (Philippines [Republic] National Census and Statistics Office 1975a: table 57).

Regardless of tenure status, many rice farmers "are in the process of becoming farm managers/supervisors rather than actual tillers of the soil" (Castillo 1977:I, 151). In other words, rice farmers now hire others to carry out much of the farm labor, including plowing, planting, weeding, and harvesting. Rather than using family labor, a farmer who can afford it "will limit his farming activities to supervising, watching his carabao and water control" (Castillo 1977:I, 152). All the other work will be done by hired labor. In Pangasinan, in 1971, 36.4 percent of farms reported that at least some laborers were hired; 25 percent reported that most of the labor was done by hired workers (Philippines [Republic] National Census and Statistics Office 1975a: table 43).

Those who are hired to work on farms include farmers themselves, farmers' children, and landless rural workers. This suggests another way in which farmers and farm families are not simply "tillers of the soil." Rather, they form a portion of a wage-labor pool available for hired labor on farms. Furthermore, many of these farmers work not only on other farms but also at other, nonagricultural wage labor jobs. Studies in the early 1970s showed that about half of all rice farmers are part-time farmers. This is true in all tenure groups; regardless of tenure status or whether they own their own farms, rice farmers tend to be employed at jobs other than farming their own farms (Castillo 1977:I, 151). In other words, it cannot be assumed that people who own or are tenants on rice land are dependent exclusively on farming for their livelihood, nor can it be assumed that they are the ones actually doing the farming on their land.

Landless rural workers form an increasingly large portion of the labor pool in rice farming areas. These are people working in rural areas but with no clear rights to either own or operate the land.[5] Weeding and harvesting are the major tasks carried out by landless workers. In some areas, as land has become increasingly fragmented, specific plots of land are contracted for by landless workers. They do the weeding on these plots without immediate payment, and are then given exclusive right to harvest the crop on their weeded portions, in return for a percentage share of the harvest (one-sixth or one-seventh of the harvest) (Ledesma 1978).

Ledesma's study of two rice farming villages, one in Nueva Ecija and the other in Iloilo, shows that those with access to land, both as owners and as tenants, earn three or four times more income than do landless workers, and are in general better off (1978:13). He finds that household heads in landless worker families spend more time working on rice farms than do rice farmers themselves, and that other household members work on the farms "four times more than their counterparts among rice farmers" (1978:11). As a result,

> children of rice farmers have more opportunities to finish their schooling, some reaching the high school and college levels. On the other hand, children of landless workers, . . . are more pressed to work in the fields, and to forego schooling for the time being or even completely. (1978:11)

As increasing differentiation has taken place within rural communities, the complexity of rural stratification has increased, leading to considerable diversity in the peasantry (Kerkvliet 1980:17). Rural landless workers tend to be at the bottom, as they are dependent on farmers for employment and as their incomes tend to be significantly less than the incomes of others. Tenants themselves do not form a homogeneous group; some are considerably better off than others, and have become primarily farm operators rather than farmers. Landlords, too, differ from one another. In the rice-farming areas, such as Pangasinan, there are relatively few very large landlords. The majority have plots of land under seven hectares and therefore have not been affected by the most recent agrarian reform laws.[6] On the other hand, even these small landholders are different in important ways from owner-operators and from part-owners. Most landlords are absentee owners, and are not cultivating their own land, although they may still earn a significant portion of their income by receiving their share of the produce from their tenants (Grace 1977).

In a study published in the early 1960s, Anderson pointed out the considerable status differentiation in a single Pangasinan barrio, arguing that differential status was based primarily on access to land (1964:175).

He distinguished four status groupings: (1) medium landlords, who live in the *poblacion* or in Dagupan City and who do not farm their own land; (2) small owners, owner-farmers and owner-tenants; (3) tenants, whose "share of the produce of the land is usually insufficient to support the family by minimum local standards, without supplementary activities or earnings" (1964:178); (4) laborers, agricultural workers, underemployed and unemployed. In addition, some families are mainly dependent on salary from non-agricultural employment, such as school teaching, and others depend largely on income earned outside the barrio, including those having income from family members working outside the Philippines (1964:176–80).

Other studies have stressed differentiation even within the types of status groups outlined by Anderson. For example, van den Muijzenberg has shown that the change from share tenancy to leasehold arrangements in some regions led to a distinction between "strong" and "weak" tenants (1975). As a result of the Land Reform Code of 1963, many tenants became leaseholders, paying a fixed rent and, in the process, cutting themselves off from the landlord as a source of credit. However, others remained share tenants and were rewarded by the landlords for their loyalty. Since the leaseholders could no longer obtain credit from the landlords, they began to turn to the other tenants for loans. Ultimately, "the weaker tenants accumulated debts until . . . they were forced to sell their 'right of tenancy' . . . to the moneylending tenants" (van den Muijzenberg 1975:149).

The contemporary complexity in rural Central Luzon is still greater than indicated by these studies however. In examining standards of living and sources of livelihood in a single village in Nueva Ecija, Kerkvliet has categorized households into eleven occupational categories and six standard of living categories (1980). Most households—from the poorest to wealthiest—have two or more sources of income. Occupational categories and standards of living categories crosscut one another; for example, impoverished households include those depending on agricultural labor as well as some farm households. Yet farm households own land, and employ agricultural workers, thus being in situations of potential conflict with the workers. Similarly, those able on occasion to extend credit to others are often at similar standards of living with those to whom they lend. As a result of such class complexity and of the interdependent relationships among village households, Kerkvliet argues, people do not generally see themselves as members of a particular "class" in opposition to other "classes" in the community. Yet there are significant differences in standards of living and there is certainly awareness that some are better off than others.

Division of the rural population into a set of classes or subclasses tends to present a static view of the current situation. Yet many aspects of the current picture are relatively recent developments. The present situation must be seen as a dynamic one, with changes and elaborations of the basic structure of rural society resulting from other changes that have occurred in recent years. Foremost among those have been the introduction of new rice technology and attempts at land reform. Although land reform laws have ostensibly been focused on getting "land to the tiller," it is rather questionable the extent to which this has or will happen, given the fragmentation of land ownership that already exists, the relatively small amounts of land held by landlords in rice growing areas, and the complexities of a situation where much of the work is already carried out by hired labor.

On the other hand, new rice technology was introduced in the 1960s and there have been ongoing studies since that time of its effects. While overall rice production has increased in the country, there have been questions raised regarding the increased need for fertilizer, insecticide, and so forth. (See Castillo 1975 for a comprehensive discussion of the effects of new rice technology.)[7]

Another way of viewing the dynamics of the rural scene in Central Luzon rice-growing areas is to ask what kinds of activities the rural population is engaged in. In other words, once we recognize that many rice farmers are only part-time farmers, that many rural households are landless, and that landowners are often absentee landlords, we need to consider the ways in which these people and members of their households earn income. We need, in other words, to examine the total resource field available for the rural population. One way to consider this is to examine various income sources available to rural households.

Rural Households and Their Incomes

Rural Filipino households depend on diverse income sources. Household heads and other household members engage in a variety of strategies to obtain income, both within the rural area and outside it.[8] Sources of income include rice farming; agricultural work on the land of others; nonagricultural work in the rural areas; nonagricultural work elsewhere;

and transfers in the form of gifts and remittances. The number of sources exploited by a particular household tends to vary with age of household head and size of the household, i.e., whether or not there are adult children who contribute income (Fegan 1979:461).

Rice farming remains the most important source of income for farm households (cf. Hayami et al. 1978; Nicholas 1977). While most rice farmers keep some of their own produce, they rarely are able to keep enough for their total consumption for the year. Rather, they usually sell most of their crop right after threshing. This means that later in the year they must buy rice for their own consumption. Overall, many are net purchasers of rice (Castillo 1977:I, 155–56). Regardless of tenure status, most rice farmers both sell and buy rice. By selling rice, they are able to meet their needs for cash and pay off debts. As a result of this situation, rice farmers are affected by government price support policies at both ends—when they sell, and again when they buy. In 1978–79, for example, the market price of rice was increased. As this was done several months after the rice harvest, farmers who sold rice after the harvest were forced to buy it at a higher price later. Even when this does not occur, farmers report having a scarcity of food in the months before the harvest (Castillo 1977:I, 156). In other words, although rice is a source of income for farmers as well as a food, the production of most farmers is not enough to either provide them with sufficient rice for the year or with sufficient income to be able to purchase rice as well as other necessities.

In addition to income from the rice they produce, rice farmers work as agricultural labor. For example, in a Laguna village in Southern Luzon, 43 percent of the total income derived from rice farming and another 28 percent from outside employment, much of which was work on rice farms in the village (Hayami et al. 1978:49–50). Farmers and members of farm households are hired to help with planting, weeding, and harvesting; often they are paid with rice rather than cash (Fegan 1972:137–38). In general, this work can be fit into the work that farm families do on their own land.

Nonagricultural work in the rural area can also be an important source of income; in one barrio in Manaoag, Pangasinan, 50 percent of the households reported nonfarm employment as a source of income (Nicholas 1977). The types of jobs engaged in are basically informal sector occupations, such as sales, tricycle driving, and handicraft making. Tricycle driving and retail trade in the *poblacion* or other nearby town centers seem to be particularly prominent; in Gapan, Nueva Ecija, tricycles tend to be owned by a farmer and operated by him or by his son while the farmer farms full time (Gibb 1974:140).

The only significant amount of rural manufacturing is in those industries labeled cottage industry, which include dressmaking and tailoring, bamboo crafts, ceramics, furniture making, and food industries. According to the National Cottage Industry Development Authority (NACIDA), in 1977 there were 2,722 NACIDA registered cottage industries in Pangasinan and 6,338 nonregistered ones, employing a total of 23,250 people (NACIDA 1977:142–43, 227–29). Presumably, some of these employees would be members of farm households, although it should be noted that these figures include urban cottage industries as well as rural ones.

Finally, a category usually treated as residual is of great and probably increasing importance to rural households. This is the category of "transfer" income, or "gifts, support, assistance and relief." According to Castillo, 33 percent of families in Central Luzon in 1971 depended in part on such income (1977:I, 107). For landless workers, transfer incomes may be particularly important (Hayami et al. 1978:50). For the most part, such income consists of money remitted by family members living and working elsewhere, although it may also include money from relatives living in the barrio. Family members remitting money may be temporary migrants who leave other family members behind in the barrio (Anderson 1972). As we shall see in examining the case studies, such remittances may include food and other material items as well as money, and they can make a substantial impact on total family income.

Education, Work, and Mobility

As indicated in the previous section, the necessity for a household to have diverse sources of income may lead to migration of one or more family members. At the same time, families frequently invest in the education of their children, with the goal of seeing them able to establish themselves at a better level, with a white-collar job if possible (cf. Fegan 1979:413–16). To what extent does migration represent simply geographical mobility, or is occupational and status mobility also taking place? And what role does education play in this process? To consider these questions, it is useful to examine not only the evidence regarding education and occupational mobility, but also to look at differential

A commercial/residential area of Dagupan City

Dagupan City, squatter housing near fishponds and commercial buildings

Street vending in front of Dagupan's central plaza

Cloth vendor in the Dagupan marketplace

Interior of a store in Dagupan City

Children preparing corn for roasting and sale

Making candy at a Dagupan cottage industry

Fishponds within Dagupan City limits

A rural house in Pangasinan Province

Planting rice

Rice fields in Pangasinan Province

effects for different portions of the population, including the varying opportunities for males and females.

Most Filipinos place a great deal of emphasis on education; parents want their children to go to college, if possible, and tend to view sending children to college as a sort of investment for the future. The hope is that once they have higher education their job opportunities will be better. This goal is expressed in the enrollment shifts that have taken place; whereas in the past teacher training courses had large enrollments, now more students are studying health occupations such as nursing and medical technology. This seems to be related to job and income opportunities in the fields, especially with a chance to go overseas to work in the medical fields (cf. Castillo 1977:III, 680).

Studies of the relationship between income and education and of intergenerational occupational mobility indicate that there is some statistical basis to the goals of students and their parents. There is good evidence that amount of education correlates well with income; the higher the level of education attained the lower the incidence of poverty (Castillo 1977:III, 647). Of course, people from higher income groups have more opportunity for better education than do those from lower income groups. Therefore, sons of individuals in elite occupations tend to have access to higher education and are then likely to follow in their father's occupational footsteps (Bacol 1971:206). People from lower socioeconomic strata such as tenants and farm laborers are less likely to be able to obtain a college education, but among those few that do, most move into higher occupational strata than that of their fathers (Castillo 1977:III, 683).

Overall, there is considerable rigidity in the Philippine occupational structure; more than half the sons remain in their father's occupations, and such vertical mobility as occurs is generally of short distance. That is, there is some movement from farm origins into manual occupations, but movement from farm or manual occupations into white-collar positions is difficult (deGuzman 1975:12). For sons from high social origins "occupational success is positively correlated with education," but for those from low social origins, education "does not necessarily remove the obstacle to mobility rooted in social background" (Bacol 1971:206–7).

One result of the emphasis on education coupled with limited mobility has been a sort of inflation in educational requirements. College degrees have become a requirement for relatively low-level jobs (ILO

1974:312). This is evident in some of the case studies in Part 2, where we shall see that individuals working as salesgirls were required to have college degrees to be considered for the job.

Differential employment opportunities exist for males and females. As we have seen in the preceding chapter, jobs for females in Dagupan, as in other urban areas, are basically in three occupational categories: sales, domestic service, and teaching. Males, on the other hand, are found in a larger variety of urban occupations, including production, sales, and transport. At the same time, many more men remain in agricultural work than do women. In the country as a whole, 62.7 percent of males were in agriculture in 1975, whereas participation of women in agriculture has decreased from 41.8 percent of the female labor force in 1956 to 34.4 percent in 1975 (Castillo 1977:I, 78).

In rural Pangasinan Province, 71.3 percent of the males are in farming, fishing and related occupations, compared to 22.7 percent of the female labor force (Philippines [Republic] National Census and Statistics Office 1975b: table 9). Other occupations for females in the rural area include crafts (21.6 percent), sales (19.2 percent), services (15.5 percent) and the professions (14.4 percent). Overall, however, women constitute only 18 percent of the rural labor force of the province, compared to 33 percent of the urban labor force.

These figures suggest some of the differences in employment opportunities that exist for males and females. There are relatively few opportunities for women in rural areas, whereas a number of occupations are open to them in urban areas. These include both those at low status levels, such as domestic service, as well as professional jobs such as teaching. Therefore, it is frequently the case that while young men in a household may stay in the rural area to do farm work, young women will migrate to an urban center for a job. Furthermore, where possible, families try to obtain education for girls so that they may get better jobs. This pattern is apparent in the case studies: in one family, two daughters have college degrees in primary education while a third daughter is in college; in another family, a son is farming while the daughter, having attended a secretarial school, works as a salesgirl. The implications of differential opportunities, both in terms of sex and in terms of education and other socioeconomic factors, will be discussed further; of particular interest are the implications for migration of young women and for family and household organization.

Sex and education differentials affect the rather complex relationship between geographical mobility and occupational mobility. Overall, there is relatively little upward social mobility. When an individual migrates, his or her goal—and that of the family—may be to achieve a degree of upward mobility, but the reality may be quite different. Examination of families at various socioeconomic levels, as is done in Part 2, helps to demonstrate some of the complexity: family members of both better and less well-off families are involved in diverse strategies, of which migration is one. For some, migration is simply a means to help other family members continue to survive, and represents horizontal mobility, both for the migrant and his or her family. For others, migration may mean a measure of upward social mobility, at least for other family members, if not for the individual; for example, the migrant may support the college education of a sibling. And for still others, there may be a considerable degree of both geographical and social mobility. However, this last possibility is mainly open to those starting out at higher socioeconomic levels.

The case studies help to demonstrate the ways in which households and families pursue diverse strategies in attempting to exploit various niches in the economic system, as well as some of the ways in which the wider economic system places constraints on the possibilities open to families and households.

Chapter 4

Migration Patterns: The Philippines, Pangasinan, and Dagupan City

Many studies of migration focus on the urban poor, just as many studies of the urban poor focus on migrants. In this study, I was interested in considering migrants from a wide range of socioeconomic backgrounds, not just the poor. Two of the first questions I had to confront in doing the research were who are the migrants in Dagupan and how should I go about finding them?

In early conversations with people I met in Dagupan—school teachers, professionals, workers in city government—I soon found that they had preconceptions of what a "migrant" is, or should be. For example, I was told that if I wanted to study migrants I should go to Manila, because that is where all the squatters are. Others said that the only migrants in Dagupan are successful business people and professionals; in fact, they said that most of the wealthy people in the city come from other places and do better than locals. An employee in the city planning office told me that the "poorest of the poor," with whom his office was supposed to be concerned, are all Dagupeños. After some time, some of the reasons for these perceptions became apparent. It is true that many of the successful businesses, although certainly not all, are owned by people who came to Dagupan from elsewhere in the country, and of course a significant number are owned by Filipino Chinese. It also became apparent that if a person was originally from another Pangasinan town, and spoke Pangasinan, then he or she was often not perceived as a migrant to Dagupan. I got responses such as "Oh, yes, of course she grew up in Santa Barbara [a nearby town] but she has lived here in Dagupan for many years." Further, in some cases, there are city regulations which encourage an individual to say that he is "from" Dagupan; for example, in order to register as a tricycle driver an individual must be a resident of the city. Despite such initial responses, I began to find migrants in Dagupan, and to find them at all socioeconomic levels. A sample from

my fieldnotes indicates the wide range of conditions in which people
who can be identified as "migrants" live:

> I went with —— to Herrero Street. We found a friend of his
> who said that his mother owns some land where migrants are
> living. After some discussion, he took us to the place. It's on the
> left side of the street. From the street, you see one building which is
> used as a storage area for cardboard cartons. Behind this is another
> building which they said used to be a warehouse for *bagaong* (salted
> fish sauce), up until about ten years ago. The front of the building
> still looks like a warehouse—a blank cement wall and tin roof.
> Around on the side, through a narrow dirt path, are entrances to
> the rooms. Each room is about four by eight; there are about six
> rooms on each side. Each room is literally a hole in the wall—there
> are no windows, just a door facing out on the passageway. There is
> a toilet at one end of the passage. According to the woman who
> owns the place, there are eight families living there; each has been
> there for about one year. One man works as a pushcarter. One of
> the women is a hospitality girl [prostitute] but is not working now.
> . . .
>
> In the afternoon (of the same day) I went to find the house of
> Mrs. ——, whose name had been given to me. It's in one of the
> new subdivisions, off the road to Lingayen. To get there, we went
> through an area of old wood and *nipa* houses, some in pretty poor
> condition, and then arrived in the subdivision, with new, painted
> cement houses, each with a garden and fence around it. We stopped
> to ask one of the boys playing outside the way to Mrs. ——'s
> house; he directed us around the corner to a cul de sac, and told us it
> is the largest house in the subdivision. Inside, I only saw the living
> room, which is filled with overstuffed furniture—*sala* (living
> room) set, chairs, a long bench—covered in a bright yellow print.
> Beyond the house are fields; Mrs. —— owns the neighboring lot
> as well. Her husband is working overseas.

The people living in the warehouse and Mrs. —— are all migrants
to Dagupan; Mrs. —— is involved in the migration process in another
way as well, as her husband has gone abroad to work. In fact, this largely
explains her ability to have built such a large and imposing house. These

two living situations represent extremes; most migrants in Dagupan live neither in abandoned warehouses nor in enormous houses. But migrants may be found in just about every type of housing situation and in a wide variety of occupations.

This chapter provides the context for examining the case studies of migrants to Dagupan. It examines historical and contemporary migration patterns in the Philippines and the role of Pangasinan Province and Dagupan City in those movements. Although it has been argued that migration is not necessarily an easy process and that most people prefer to stay than to move (Simkins and Wernstedt 1971:76–77), Filipinos have been migrating from one place to another in considerable numbers at least since the early 1900s and probably before that. In fact, much of the nation's history has involved movements to frontier areas (Peter Smith 1977:121). Certainly specific patterns and reasons for moving have changed over time. But the current dominant pattern of rural-to-urban movements should not be viewed as something entirely new for rural Filipinos.

Until recent years, data on migration has been limited for the most part to what can be gleaned from censuses; a number of studies have examined statistical patterns of migration by comparing population between census intervals (e.g., Nava 1959; Pascual 1966). From such studies, general patterns regarding numbers of migrants, direction of movement, and characteristics of migrants are available. The first part of this chapter reviews those patterns, both historically and at the present time. The second part of the chapter focuses on Pangasinan Province and Dagupan City, to consider their role in historical and contemporary migratory movements, and ends by again considering the question of who the migrants to the city are.

Broad Patterns of Migration

In 1970, about 14 percent of all Filipinos resided in municipalities different from where they resided in 1960, or from where they were born if they were born after 1960. More than half of these migrants had moved across regional boundaries (Flieger, Koppin, and Lim 1976:10). Moreover, of all Filipinos who were 15 years or older in 1973, 35 percent had moved at least once since birth (Pernia 1975:2). Filipinos are, in other words, a relatively mobile people, and when they move, they often move considerable distances. The available data indicate that migration has involved relatively large numbers of people at least since the early 1900s.

In the Philippines as a whole, two broad types of migratory movements are evident, both in the present and historically. These are rural, frontierward movements, and movements from rural to urban areas. In recent years, the latter pattern has become dominant. A third pattern has also been important for Filipinos: emigration from the country. In the past, international migrants were mainly men who went to work as agricultural laborers in the United States. At present, international migrants include both emigrants—many of whom are professionals—and those going to work as contract laborers for specified periods of time.

Migration in the Past

Much of the history of the Philippines involves movements of people from more densely settled regions to less populated areas. In the early, pre-Spanish period, most settlements were located in coastal and riverine areas. The Spanish encouraged movement into town centers or *poblacions* to bring people "under the bells" of the Catholic church, but most of the population remained rural.

In more recent times, two broad migration streams have been the movement from densely populated areas of Luzon to frontier areas on the island, and the movement from the Visayas to frontier areas on Mindanao (Concepcion and Smith, 1977:41). On Luzon, people from the Ilocos region on the northwest coast have predominated in migratory movements to frontier areas. Ilocanos migrated into the interior of Pangasinan, beginning in the early 1800s, and later both Ilocanos and Pangasinanses moved to unpopulated areas of the Central Luzon Plain, particularly Nueva Ecija (McLennan 1973). These movements are considered in greater detail below. Ilocanos also migrated to the Cagayan Valley (cf. Henry Lewis 1971), and in the early 1940s and 1950s they formed a minority of those migrating to Mindanao.[1] The majority of migrants to Mindanao came from the Visayas.

Little data is available on rural-urban migration in the early periods. Pernia argues that it was unimportant and that migration accounted for a relatively small proportion of urban growth between 1903 and 1939 (1977:47–49). Nevertheless, it is interesting to note that several novels of that period refer to provincial residents who moved to Manila, either to escape family problems at home (e.g., Bolusan 1973) or to get jobs (e.g., Laya 1941). In *Villa Magdelena*, Santos refers to areas of Manila that were dominated by people from specific provinces in the pre–World War II period (Santos 1965:10, 17).

By 1948, urban migration, especially to Manila, was increasing. Nava estimated an intercensal migration rate in the 1939–48 period of 331.3 for Manila, larger than that for any of the frontier provinces.[2]

Contemporary Migration Patterns

Long distance frontierward migration has continued to the present, with frontier movements accounting for 44 percent of all lifetime interregional migrants in 1970 (Concepcion and Smith 1977:43), while at the same time rural-urban migration has become increasingly important. According to Pernia, net migration accounted for 15.5 percent of urban growth between the 1939 and 1960 censuses, while in metropolitan Manila it accounted for 47.2 percent of growth (1977:49). By 1970, urban migration became more important than migration to frontier areas (Abad 1981:131).[3]

The 1970 census data show that every seventh Filipino alive in 1970 had transferred his residence across municipal boundaries since 1960 (Flieger, Koppin, and Lim 1976:10). These migrants may be divided into three categories—intraprovincial migrants, intraregional migrants, and interregional migrants. Fifty-one percent of all 1970 migrants had moved across regional boundaries, while 34 percent were intraprovincial migrants; only 14 percent moved out of their provinces but stayed within the region (Flieger, Koppin, and Lim 1976:10). Between 1970 and 1975, more than 6 percent of the population recorded a change of residence; of these, 38.8 percent were intraprovincial migrants while 61 percent moved between provinces (Philippines [Republic] National Census and Statistics Office 1975b:152).[4]

Further evidence of the mobility of Filipinos is provided by the 1973 National Demographic Survey. Of the total 22.5 million persons 15 years or older, 7.9 million, or 35 percent, were migrants. Of these, 82 percent had moved once between birth and 1973, 15 percent had moved twice, and 2 percent had moved three times (Pernia 1975:2).[5]

In recent years, as earlier, much movement has consisted of relatively long-distance moves (Smith 1977:128) and the major in-migration areas were the areas around Manila and Mindanao (Flieger, Koppin, and Lim

1976:20). Short-distance, intraprovincial migration also affected large numbers of people, especially in agricultural and frontier regions (Flieger, Koppin, and Lim 1976:35–37). Measurement of migration "streams" (Flieger, Koppin, and Lim 1976:38–53; Pernia 1977:91–111) provides further evidence of directionality of migration. In general, the area around Manila (Metro Manila) was the preferred destination; of twelve "significant" interregional streams (those involving at least 50,000 persons), six had the area around Manila as destination. Four of these originated on Luzon and the other two on the Visayas. Other major streams continued to flow from the Visayas to Mindanao (Flieger, Koppin, and Lim 1976:41).

By 1973, rural-urban migration had become the dominant migration pattern, accounting for 45.8 percent of all internal moves between 1970 and 1973 (Pernia 1975:2); urban-urban migration accounted for 24.8 percent of moves, while rural-rural accounted for 14.9 percent and urban-rural for 14.5 percent (Pernia 1975: table 1). Of the rural-urban moves, 29.5 percent were from rural areas to *poblacions*; 36.1 percent from rural areas to a chartered city; and 34.4 percent from rural areas to Metro Manila (Pernia 1975:3–4; table 2).

Overall, the Manila region is most preferred as a destination for migrants (Flieger, Koppin, and Lim 1976:121–22). However, urban areas other than Metro Manila also attract migrants, but tend as well to be a source for out-migration (Pernia 1977:102). Below, I will suggest that Dagupan City falls into this latter category; that is, it attracts migrants, but at the same time many others migrate out, thus giving the city a low net-migration rate.[6]

Despite the recent emphasis on statistical analyses of migration patterns, these analyses only skim the surface in revealing the dimension of migratory movements in the contemporary Philippines. They do not, for example, indicate the extent to which people may move between the intervals studied. Data on seasonal migration is completely lacking. Van den Muijzenberg's study of a Central Luzon village reveals the importance of what he labels *circo-commuting*—movements of villagers back and forth between the village and Manila (1973). Similarly, in his study of the building industry, Stretton shows that employment in the industry is based on laborers who migrate when work is available and return to the rural barrio when there are no jobs (1981:329–30). Available evidence suggests that circular movements of these sorts are increasing in importance and that statistical surveys simply do not account for the large numbers of people who are at least partially dependent on urban migration for income.

Characteristics of Migrants and
Reasons for Migrating

The statistical studies do, however, give some indication not only of where people are moving but also of who is moving and of their stated reasons for doing so. Overall, two features stand out in studies of migration differentials and decisions to migrate in the Philippines: (1) the large number of females involved in migration, and (2) the importance of family ties in the place to which the migrant goes.

As in other parts of the world, Filipino migrants tend to be young. Males between twenty and forty and females between fifteen and thirty-five predominate (Pernia 1977:114). Higher levels of education also tend to be characteristic, and migrants to Metro Manila in particular are relatively highly educated (ibid.:116, 123). In general, migrants tend to have higher socioeconomic status and to be employed in more white-collar jobs than either nonmigrants at the place of origin or natives at the place of destination (Abad 1981:133). However, Koo and Smith (1983) find that there are major differences in the labor market for male and female migrants. Female migrants are much more likely to be in informal sector, primarily low-wage occupations—including domestic service—and hence these generalizations may not apply to them.

In contrast to other countries in Southeast Asia, females are as prominent as males in the migration process in the Philippines. In fact, between 1960 and 1970 more females than males moved out of their provinces of origin (Castillo 1976:120); Pernia argues that "women have a higher propensity to migrate than men" (1977:115).[7] More than 40 percent of married females fifteen years old and over surveyed in 1973 had changed residence at least once between birth and 1973 (Castillo 1976:124).

Among women who migrated between 1965 and 1970, 57.6 percent had urban destinations, compared to 48.7 percent of the men (Eviota and Smith 1981:8). Female-dominant migration streams are found in all the cities of Luzon, including Manila, and in most Visayan and Mindanao cities (Eviota and Smith 1981:8–9). In secondary cities they are especially prominent in informal sector occupations, including domestic service; 93.8 percent of recent female migrants to secondary cities are employed in the informal sector, compared to 13.8 percent of recent male migrants and 54 percent of native female residents of these cities (Koo and Smith 1983:224–25).

Analyses of individual migrant characteristics have also attempted to examine the reasons for the decision to migrate. While availability of schooling, jobs, higher income, etc. no doubt play an important role, there is considerable evidence that ties with others, particularly family members, are also important. In one study, Planeras found that previous in-migrants from a given region influenced the choice of subsequent migrants to go to that region (1977:22). In a more detailed study, Pernia examined various factors in the decision to migrate by individuals and households. He concludes that "kinship ties at destination seem to be the decisive factor in the choice to migrate (especially for women)" (n.d.:20). Two recent studies of migration from Ilocos Norte provide further evidence on this issue. Lee (1985) examines determinants of individual migration intentions and shows that kinship linkages outside the home area constitute one important factor, while Findley's (1987) study considers the role of family and community characteristics in influencing decisions about migration. Further consideration is needed, however, not only of the household and family context at the place of origin, and of the way in which the entire family may affect the decision of particular individuals to move, but also of the continued interaction among family members after migration. In the discussion of the cases in Part 2, these issues are considered at length.

Pangasinan and Dagupan City in Philippine Migration

According to the census and other statistical evidence, Pangasinan Province is an area of net out-migration, while Dagupan City's population growth rate is about the same as that of the country as a whole. Such evidence might suggest that Pangasinan and Dagupan have little importance in the overall migration process, except as contributors of migrants to other areas. In this section, I will argue that, to the contrary, considerable in-migration is taking place, especially to Dagupan, but that because there is also out-migration, net migration figures tend to obscure in-migration's importance. In addition, most of the data on migration focuses on interprovincial and interregional movements, whereas much of the movement into Dagupan is from within Pangasinan Province. Furthermore, historical evidence indicates that, while rural-urban migration patterns represent a relatively new direction for migration, migration itself is not new in this area; in fact, much of the settlement of Pangasinan Province resulted from migration during the Spanish period, and especially in the 1800s.

Historical Background

The history of settlement of Pangasinan is part of a larger process of movement of peoples from coastal and riverine sites into the interior. Essentially, these were movements to what were then agricultural frontiers, just as later movements took place to frontier regions in Mindanao. People from the Ilocos coast were prominent in the settlement process but Pangasinanses also participated.[8] Prior to the nineteenth century, Ilocanos moved southward along the coast, into the area that is now La Union Province. In the early nineteenth century they began to move into Pangasinan, coming both overland by wagon caravans and by sea to Lingayen and up the Agno River (McLennan 1973:172–79). A 1941 novel describes the origin of a Pangasinan Ilocano family:

> In Spanish days, three Ilocano couples, carrying their small children in their arms and their worldly goods in baskets balanced on carrying poles, walked two hundred kilometers down the Ilocos coast from Vigan to the virgin lands west of the upper Agno River. They arrived at harvest time and saw that the tales of plenty were true. They helped gather rice heads for share while the bigger children shaded the smaller ones under checkered cotton blankets stretched on the stiff rice stalks. Then the couples settled down to clear land of their own. They soon wrote home in tones of prosperity. More relatives came the next year, on sailboats to Dagupan, on foot for the remaining forty kilometers across the province, to build more homes in Guisit Este, along the western bank of Balete Creek. (Laya 1941:34)

McLennan estimates that up to 1830, 500–1,000 Ilocanos a year moved southward to Pangasinan, and that this increased to 4,000–5,000 a year by the 1880s. The 1903 census recorded 58,000 Ilocanos in Pangasinan out of a total population of 398,000 (McLennan 1973:189).

At first, people moved to coastal areas and to areas along the Agno River, but by the mid 1800s, the interior was being settled. In the early stages, there were two centers of colonization: south of the Agno River, in what was then south-central Pangasinan Province and what is now northern Tarlac, and east-central Pangasinan, between the Agno River and Manaoag. Later, in the late nineteenth and early twentieth century people moved still further east, to Tayug and San Nicolas in the far eastern part of the province, and then into Nueva Ecija. In the late nineteenth century, there was a third center, in western Pangasinan and northern Zambales provinces (McLennan 1973:180–82).

In the late 1800s, the people involved in these population shifts included not only Ilocanos originating in Ilocos, but also a generation born in Tarlac and Pangasinan. In addition, it appears that Pangasinan-speaking peoples also participated, although their presence is not frequently noted. As McLennan points out, in the 1903 census, Ilocanos did not constitute more than 60 percent of the population in any part of Pangasinan Province, indicating that much of the population growth in newly settled areas of the interior must have resulted from the movement of Pangasinanses (1973:213). By 1939 however, the census data on language indicates that Ilocanos had begun to dominate, so that eastern Pangasinan was almost entirely Ilocano-speaking. As table 6 shows, the provincial population became about half Pangasinan-speaking and half Ilocano-speaking by 1948 and remains so today.

Overall, in this period of the late 1800s and early 1900s there was much moving about, especially into areas that were still agricultural frontier regions, culminating in the settlement of Nueva Ecija and the development of that province as a major rice-growing region. While

TABLE 6.   Mother Tongue as Reported in Pangasinan Province, 1948–75

Language	1948		1960		1975	
	Number	Percent	Number	Percent	Number	Percent
Pangasinan	443,923	48.2	555,481	49.4	745,839	49.1
Ilocano	440,264	47.8	527,799	47.0	707,106	46.5
Bolinao and Zambal[a]	25,028	2.7	25,343	2.3	33,638	2.2
Tagalog	4,141	0.4	8,059	0.7	18,980	1.2
Other	7,135	0.8	7,462	0.6	14,522	1.0
Total	920,491	99.9	1,124,144	100.0	1,520,085	100.0

Source: 1948 Philippines (Republic) Bureau of the Census and Statistics 1952:3:295.

1960 Philippines (Republic) Bureau of the Census and Statistics 1962–63: table 15.

1975 Philippines (Republic) National Census and Statistics Office 1975b: table 8.

[a]Languages spoken in small area of western Pangasinan

most of this movement was to rural areas, Dagupan City was at the same time growing and becoming a major commercial center. Whereas some centers in northern Pangasinan actually lost population in the mid-1800s, Dagupan's population increased from 15,042 to 20,685 during the period 1862–76 (McLennan 1973:205).

Although Dagupan's population today is predominantly Pangasinan-speaking, it, like the rural areas of the province, received Ilocano migrants. According to Basa, the first Ilocano migrants arrived in Dagupan about 1770 (1972:6). Today, there are two largely Ilocano-speaking barrios within the city; most of the residents of these areas were born in Dagupan, the children and grandchildren of Ilocano migrants.

Calmay, one of the two largely Ilocano-speaking areas, is known as "Little Vigan" in Dagupan, because so many of its residents originally came from Vigan, in Ilocos North. One of the poorer areas of the city, it is isolated from the rest of the city because the bridge which once connected it with the *poblacion* washed away in the 1930s and has never been replaced. It can be reached by boat, or by road only via a roundabout route through the town of Binmaley, and even then much of the road to the Ilocano settlement itself has washed away. Many of the residents work in the fishponds of the barrio and buy and sell fish in the city center; many of the men are "standbys" (i.e., casual, part-time laborers).

According to a barrio official, migrants from Vigan and other Ilocos towns first came to Calmay over 100 years ago; many were merchants buying rice and salt. For example, the official's grandfather came, probably in the late 1890s, and his mother, now seventy-nine, was born in Calmay, as he himself was. According to his mother, there were no Pangasinan-speakers in the settlement when she was young. The barrio official's wife was also born in Calmay; her family originated in Ilocos Sur. Among those currently in Calmay, it is in fact difficult to find any Ilocano-speakers who were not born there. One exception, a man in his early fifties, is a *sari-sari* store owner who migrated from Vigan in the early 1970s; he came to Calmay because his second cousin and his wife's sister were living there.

Calmay and Pantal, the other predominantly Ilocano area in the city, represent early centers of migration into Dagupan and were part of the larger movements of Ilocanos into Pangasinan Province. Rather than being farmers, however, these migrants worked as merchants and in fishing, two occupations that continue to predominate in those barrios.

People in Pangasinan were also involved in seasonal migration, at least by the early 1940s. In the January–February 1940 issue and in the March–April 1941 issue, the *Labor Bulletin* noted that Pangasinan farmers had gone to Baguio and Zambales to work in the mines, and others were working on public works or in rice mills; some had gone to Mindanao as settlers (*Labor Bulletin* January–February 1940:45, March–April 1941:109). On the other hand, the May–June 1941 bulletin reported that "many laborers employed in the mining companies of Baguio, Zambales, and other provinces returned to their hometowns (in Pangasinan) to plant rice" (*Labor Bulletin* May–June 1941:163).

Current Patterns of Migration to Dagupan

As with the historical evidence, statistical evidence on contemporary migration into Pangasinan and Dagupan is limited. Essentially, the available data focus on overall migration rates for the province, which compare the extent of in-migration to the amount of out-migration. This focus leads to an emphasis on out-migration as the dominant pattern and obscures the extent to which in-migration is taking place. Further, the provincial focus excludes the possibility that Dagupan may be receiving more migrants than other municipalities of the province.

Overall migration rates show that Pangasinan, like Central Luzon as a whole, is an area of net out-migration. For example, in the 1960–70 intercensal period, the provincial migration rate was −72.27 per thousand (Flieger, Koppin, and Lim 1976:29). Similarly, net lifetime migration rates (i.e., people born in one place living in another at the time of the 1970 census) show a large amount of out-migration from Pangasinan. Migrants from Pangasinan are found throughout the country; in 1970, they were living in sixty-one of the sixty-six other provinces (Flieger, Koppin, and Lim 1976:50–51).

Despite the large amount of out-migration from the province, there is also considerable in-migration. In the 1960–70 period, 43,073 persons migrated into Pangasinan, while 133,735 migrated out (Flieger, Koppin, and Lim 1976: table 29–17, p. 70). Furthermore, as table 7 indicates, many in-migrants came from specific regions of the country, and the City of Manila contributed more than 27 percent of the total.

In addition to migration between provinces and regions, much migration consists of movement within a province. In Pangasinan, between 1960 and 1970, there were 45,504 intraprovincial migrants, of whom 25,296 were female and 20,208 were male (Flieger, Koppin, and Lim

1976: table 16, p. 34). Presumably, a considerable proportion of intraprovincial migration consists of movements from rural parts of the province to urban areas, and especially to Dagupan. In general, movements from rural areas to chartered cities represent a major share of all migration in the Philippines (Pernia 1975:3–4). No statistical study specifically examines overall migration into Dagupan City. However, a study of "migration efficiency," indicates population turnover in the city more than ten times as high as its net migration (Pryor 1979:231–33). This limited evidence suggests considerable movement both in and out of Dagupan, but relatively little population growth due to migration.

Some indexes exist for estimating the extent of migration into Dagupan; these include the 1970 and 1975 census data on birthplace and previous residence, and the census data on mother tongue. Table 8 utilizes birthplace and residence information from the 1970 and 1975 censuses to indicate the percent of the population in each time period that had a different residence in the previous time period. According to this, more than 17 percent of Dagupan's population in 1970 had been born elsewhere; nearly two-thirds of these people were intraprovincial migrants, born in another municipality in Pangasinan. Smaller percentages had moved within the other time periods.

Census data on "mother tongue" provides further indication of the origins of interprovincial migrants to the city. If one assumes that those who speak Pangasinan, Ilocano, and Bolinao are native to the province,

TABLE 7.   Intercensal In-migration to Pangasinan, 1960–70

	Number	Percent
All In-migrants	43,073	100.0
Intra-regional		
(within Central Luzon)	9,066	21.0
Inter-regional	34,007	79.0
Region of Origin		
Ilocos	8,990	20.87
Southern Tagalog	5,333	12.4
City of Manila	11,816	27.4
Cagayan Valley	2,809	6.5
Bicol	1,236	2.9
Visayas	1,931	4.5
Mindanao	1,892	4.4

Source: Flieger, Koppin, and Lim 1976: table 29-17, p. 70.

TABLE 8. Migration into Dagupan City, 1970 and 1975

Previous Residence	Another Municipality in Pangasinan Province		Another Province		Total Migrants	
	Number	Percent	Number	Percent	Number	Percent
1970—Different res. at birth (base=83,582= total pop.)	9,526	11.4	5,180	6.2	14,706	17.6
1970—Different res. in 1960 (base=59,686 pop. 10 years+)	4,529	7.6	2,670	4.5	7,199	12.1
1970—Different res. in 1965 (base=71,000=pop. 5 years+)	3,284	4.6	2,330	3.3	5,614	7.9
1975—Different res. in 1970 (base=76,039, pop. 5 years+ for which 1970 res. avail.)	1,204	1.6	1,195	1.6	2,399	3.2

Source: 1970 Philippines (Republic) National Census and Statistics Office 1974: tables IV-9, IV-11, IV-13.
1975 Philippines (Republic) National Census and Statistics Office 1975b: table 16.

then there are 6,103 speakers of nonlocal languages,[9] or 6.77 percent of the city population (see table 9), corresponding quite closely to the number (6.2 percent) born in other provinces recorded in the 1970 census. As is clear from table 10, Tagalog speakers represent a sizeable proportion of this population. Tagalog speakers tend to be from the Manila area, indicating that this is a source area for many of the interprovincial migrants.[10]

Other data indicate still larger numbers of migrants to Dagupan, espe-

TABLE 9. Mother Tongue in Pangasinan Province and Dagupan City, 1975

Language	Pangasinan		Dagupan	
	Number	Percent	Number	Percent
Pangasinan, Ilocano, and Bolinao	1,486,583	97.8	83,988	93.2
Other	33,482	2.2	6,103	6.8
Not stated	20		1	
Total	1,520,085	100.0	90,092	100.0

Source: Philippines (Republic) National Census and Statistics Office 1975b: table 8.

TABLE 10. Speakers of Nonlocal Languages in Dagupan City, 1975

Language	Number	Percent
Tagalog	4,242	69.5
Pampango	503	8.2
Chinese	460	7.5
Others	898	14.7
Not stated	1	
Total	6,104	99.9

Source: Philippines (Republic) National Census and Statistics Office 1975b: table 8.

Note: Local language speakers: Pangasinan: 87.9%; Ilocano: 5.3%

cially in certain age groups and in certain areas of the city. A survey of fifteen barrios of the city, including both central city barrios and barrios on the outskirts, showed that migrants constituted 38.1 percent of all those interviewed, ranging from more than 50 percent in some sections of the city to less than 15 percent in others.[11]

Furthermore, among those city residents recording births of children in the first part of 1978, 41.5 percent of fathers and 44.1 percent of mothers recorded their own birthplace as being outside Dagupan.[12] Table 11 shows the birthplaces of the migrants in this sample, indi-

TABLE 11. Birthplace of Migrants to Dagupan City[a]

Birthplace	Males		Females		Total
	Number	Percent	Number	Percent	
Pangasinan Province (not Dagupan City)	765	62.5	853	64.4	1,618
Northern Luzon and Cagayan Valley	107	8.7	102	7.7	209
Central Luzon	118	9.6	107	8.1	225
Metro Manila	95	7.8	86	6.5	181
Southern Luzon	70	5.7	98	7.4	168
Visayas	47	3.8	64	4.8	111
Mindanao	16	1.3	12	0.9	28
Outside of Philippines	6	0.5	3	0.2	9
Total migrants	1,224	99.9	1,325	100.0	2,549

Source: Civil Register Book of Live Births, Dagupan City. Data on fathers and mothers registering births January 1978 through September 1978 and indicating mother's usual residence as Dagupan City.

[a]Total in sample: 2,952 males, 3,002 females. 41.5% of males and 44.1% of females in the sample are migrants.

cating that a substantial majority are from towns within the province; birthplaces of the rest are spread throughout the country, with most coming from Luzon. Metro Manila, Central Luzon, and Northern Luzon (including Ilocos) contribute similar percentages of migrants in this sample.

Occupations as shown by those in this sample are quite diverse and, to a large extent, parallel the occupations of those born in Dagupan, as shown in table 12.[13] There are some exceptions, however. The percentage of migrants in professional and technical occupations is larger than that of native Dagupeños, whereas a far larger proportion of Dagupan natives are farmers and fishermen. A large proportion of all males in this sample identify themselves as laborers.

Many people migrate to Dagupan as students. Among the 6,457 students registered at the University of Pangasinan in 1977–78, only 16 percent listed their home town as Dagupan. Seventy-three percent were from elsewhere in Pangasinan, 10 percent were from other provinces and 0.1 percent were from other countries.[14]

A survey of 176 migrants in Dagupan taken in April 1979 provides a broader profile of the characteristics of migrants to Dagupan.[15] Tables 13–21 provide data from this survey. Migrants living in Dagupan, like Filipino migrants in general, are relatively young, with the majority of both males and females between sixteen and thirty-five years old (table 13). More than 40 percent have lived in Dagupan for between one and five years (table 14), while 40 percent of males and 35 percent of females spent between sixteen and twenty years in their birthplaces before moving elsewhere (table 15). In other words, the largest proportion first moved as young adults. However, they did not necessarily migrate immediately to Dagupan. Only 25 percent have moved only once; that is, they migrated first to Dagupan (table 16). Another 26 percent had moved to one other place first, and then came to Dagupan, and the rest had made several moves before settling in Dagupan. Among those who have lived elsewhere, Metropolitan Manila predominates as a destination.

Work-related reasons were important as the basis for the decision to move to Dagupan (table 17). Twenty percent of males and 26 percent of females came to Dagupan to look for a job, whereas 13 percent of males and only 3 percent of females had a job there already that they were assigned to. The latter tend to be either civil service jobs or jobs for large private sector companies. On the other hand, a considerable proportion indicated that family reasons were important as the basis for their move:

TABLE 12. Occupation of a Sample of Male Residents of Dagupan City, 1978

| | Birthplace | | | | | | | |
| | Dagupan City | | Pangasinan Province | | Elsewhere | | Total Migrants | |
Occupation	Number	Percent	Number	Percent	Number	Percent	Number	Percent
Professional and technical	108	6.3	77	10.2	60	13.2	137	11.3
Clerical	9	0.5	4	0.5	5	1.1	9	0.7
Supervisory	2	0.1	4	0.5	3	0.7	7	0.6
Sales	104	6.1	56	7.4	58	12.7	114	9.4
Vendors	61	3.6	34	4.5	20	4.4	54	4.5
Laborers and other production	492	28.7	262	34.7	155	34.0	417	34.5
Services	144	8.4	64	8.5	44	9.6	108	8.9
Domestic services	18	1.1	9	1.2	3	0.7	12	1.0
Drivers	241	14.1	97	12.9	44	9.6	141	11.7
Farmers and fishermen	423	24.7	102	13.5	36	7.9	138	11.4
Other	29	1.7	13	1.7	11	2.4	24	2.0
Unemployed	80	4.7	32	4.2	17	3.7	49	4.0
Total	1,711	100.0	754	99.8	456	100.0	1,210	100.0

Source: Civil Register Book of Live Births, Dagupan City.

TABLE 13. Age of Migrants to Dagupan

Age	Males		Females		Total	
	No.	%	No.	%	No.	%
15 and under	1	1.2			1	0.6
16–35	45	54.2	59	63.4	104	59.1
36–55	31	37.3	32	34.4	63	35.8
Over 55	6	7.2	2	2.2	8	4.5
Total	83	99.9	93	100.0	176	100.0

Source: Sample survey, April 1979.

8 percent came to Dagupan because their spouses were from there, suggesting a rather small amount of marriage-based migration, and another 8 percent moved as children with adult family members. Finally, 9 percent originally came to Dagupan to study.

The majority of both males and females are married (table 18). However, a much larger percentage of males than females is married, suggesting the importance of single females in the migration process, a theme to be considered further in discussion of the cases in Part 2.

As would be expected from the census data discussed earlier, the majority of respondents in the survey were born in Pangasinan Province (table 19). However, while 57 percent of females were born in the province, only 45 percent of the males are natives of the area. Most of the rest of the migrants come from other provinces on Luzon, especially provinces in Northern and Central Luzon. There are, however, migrants in the city from all regions of the country.

Educational and occupational data from this survey (tables 20 and 21)

TABLE 14. Number of Years Migrants in Dagupan

Years	Males		Females		Total	
	No.	%	No.	%	No.	%
1 or less–5	38	45.8	39	41.9	77	43.8
6–10	13	15.7	14	15.1	27	15.3
11–15	6	7.2	16	17.2	22	12.5
16–20	9	10.8	9	9.7	18	10.2
21–25	8	9.6	8	8.6	16	9.1
Over 25	9	10.8	7	7.5	16	9.1
Total	83	99.9	93	100.0	176	100.0

Source: Sample survey, April 1979.

TABLE 15.   Number of Years Before First Move

Years in Birthplace before Moving	Males		Females		Total	
	No.	%	No.	%	No.	%
1–10	14	17.1	26	28.3	40	23.0
11–15	21	25.6	14	15.2	35	20.1
16–20	33	40.2	33	35.9	66	37.9
More than 20	14	17.1	19	20.6	33	19.0
Total	82	100.0	92	100.0	174	100.0

Source: Sample survey, April 1979.

TABLE 16.   Number of Moves

Number of Moves	Males		Females		Total	
	No.	%	No.	%	No.	%
1	20	24.4	25	27.2	45	25.9
2	19	23.2	27	29.3	46	26.4
3	13	15.9	18	19.6	31	17.8
4	10	12.2	11	12.0	21	12.1
5	7	8.5	5	5.4	12	6.9
More than 5	13	15.8	6	6.5	19	10.9
Total	82	100.0	92	100.0	174	100.0

Source: Sample survey, April 1979.

TABLE 17.   Reason for Move to Dagupan

Reason	Males		Females		Total	
	No.	%	No.	%	No.	%
Look for job	17	20.5	25	26.9	42	23.9
For own business	9	10.8	2	2.2	11	6.2
Assigned to job in Dagupan City	11	13.3	3	3.2	14	8.0
Other work-related	9	10.8	10	10.8	19	10.8
Spouse from Dagupan City	8	9.6	7	7.5	15	8.5
As child, with family	4	4.8	11	11.8	15	8.5
Other family reasons	8	9.6	16	17.2	24	13.6
To study	8	9.6	8	8.6	16	9.1
Other	9	10.8	11	11.8	20	11.4
Total	83	99.9	93	100.0	176	100.0

Source: Sample survey, April 1979.

TABLE 18.   Marital Status of Migrants

Marital Status	Males		Females		Total	
	No.	%	No.	%	No.	%
Single	22	26.5	37	39.8	59	33.5
Married	60	72.3	51	54.8	111	63.1
Widowed, divorced, separated	1	1.2	5	5.4	6	3.4
Total	83	100.0	93	100.0	176	100.0

Source: Sample survey, April 1979.

show the expected patterns. There is a rather even distribution, for both males and females, of elementary, high school, and college education. However, a higher proportion (31 percent) of females than of males (25 percent) have received college education. With regard to occupation, the largest percentages of both males and females are in sales, with 23 percent of males and 29 percent of females. Professional occupations are held by 11 percent of males and 12 percent of females. On the other hand, 11 percent of males are in transport jobs, while there are no females in such occupations. In contrast, 18 percent of females are in service occupations, while less than 10 percent of males are in such occupations. Few of the migrants engage in farm work on a regular basis, although about one-third say that they help with farming occasionally.

To return to the question posed at the beginning of this chapter—who

TABLE 19.   Birthplace of Migrants

Birthplace	Males		Females		Total	
	No.	%	No.	%	No.	%
Pangasinan Province	38	45.8	53	57.0	91	51.7
Northern and Central Luzon	21	25.3	15	16.1	36	20.5
Manila and Southern Luzon	11	13.3	8	8.6	19	10.8
Other regions	13	15.6	17	18.3	30	17.0
Total	83	100.0	93	100.0	176	100.0

Source: Sample survey, April 1979.

TABLE 20.   Education of Migrants

Education	Males No.	%	Females No.	%	Total No.	%
None	3	3.6			3	1.7
Elementary	22	26.5	30	32.3	52	29.5
High school	28	33.7	26	27.9	54	30.7
College	21	25.3	29	31.2	50	28.4
Other	9	10.8	8	8.6	17	9.7
Total	83	99.9	93	100.0	176	100.0

Source: Sample survey, April 1979.

are the migrants to Dagupan City?—we can say that large numbers come from within the province, and that there are nearly equal numbers of males and females. In other ways, migrants form a diverse category; we find migrants in a wide variety of occupational and socioeconomic strata, with varying educational backgrounds and migration histories. Many have come to Dagupan to look for work; others came first as students and stayed on to find jobs. A considerable number have moved somewhere else before coming to Dagupan; of these, some have lived first in Metro Manila. Only a few in this sample fall into the category of circular

TABLE 21.   Occupation of Migrants

Occupation	Males No.	%	Females No.	%	Total No.	%
Professional	9	11.1	11	12.0	20	11.6
Administrative	7	8.6			7	4.0
Clerical	2	2.5	13	14.1	15	8.7
Sales workers	19	23.5	27	29.3	46	26.6
Farmers and related	4	4.9			4	2.3
Transport, communication	9	11.1			9	5.2
Craftsmen and related	13	16.0	12	13.0	25	14.4
Manual laborers	7	8.6	3	3.3	10	5.8
Service	8	9.9	17	18.5	25	14.4
Housekeeper			8	8.7	8	4.6
Student	3	3.7	1	1.1	4	2.3
Total	81	99.9	92	100.0	173	99.8

Source: Sample survey, April 1979.

migrants, in the sense of going back and forth between rural jobs and urban jobs; few report doing farm work at some point during the year. However, as we shall see in Part 2, it is not only circular migrants who go back and forth to rural areas; many of those with full-time work in Dagupan move back and forth regularly and may later return to live in the rural home. These patterns, and the broader family context of migration, are discussed in Part 2.

Chapter 5

Migration, the Family, and Women's Roles

We have seen that in Central Luzon a relatively large number of individuals are involved in migration, and that a considerable proportion of these individuals are women. In the following sections, we shall be looking in detail at selected individuals and families, considering their decisions to migrate and subsequent activities and interactions. One question that arises is whether there are cultural values and aspects of Philippine social organization that affect the migration process. It is often noted, for example, that the family is an institution of prime importance in the Philippines; if this is the case, why should individuals be willing to leave their families to move to another town or city, or even overseas? Is it simply that they are *forced* by economic circumstances and have absolutely no choice in the matter? If so, then we might argue that cultural values and social organization are irrelevant. I want to argue to the contrary, that in fact institutions such as the family and values affecting behavior among family members do have a bearing on migration patterns and on the types of interaction found between migrants and others. In this chapter, I will focus on certain aspects of Philippine culture and society that seem to be key in understanding some dimensions of the migration process. I will consider, first, family organization, as the family is indeed an institution of paramount importance. I will then discuss key values which emphasize reciprocity, both among family members and in other social relationships. Third, I will consider the role of women in Filipino society, in order to provide a basis for understanding the large number of women involved in migration.

Family and Kinship Organization

In Philippine society "the basic social, economic and ritual unit" is the "family composed of the father, mother and unmarried children" (Fox 1963:346). Although other kinship ties can also be important, Fox argues that "each [nuclear] family remains a highly independent entity and the focal unit of decision-making" (1963:347). With a bilateral kinship system, there is considerable flexibility in the strength of ties to more distant relatives (Eggan 1978:54), so that some relationships may be very important and others much less so. Some anthropologists have searched for kinship units larger than the nuclear family. For example, Murray (1973) argues that there are "suprafamily" kin groups in a northern Tagalog village that he studied, and that these are formed on the basis of locality rather than descent. These groups are "structurally similar" to extended families; what is most important about them is that they are "the groups in which all important day-to-day, face-to-face interaction outside of the nuclear family takes place" (1973:33). The interaction is "in the form of constant visiting, sharing of food and other goods, and exchange of work" (1973:34). Others have argued against the existence of such suprafamilial groups (Kaut 1965).

What seems to be the case is that Filipino family and kinship allow for the development of alliances (Schlegel 1964); the most important of these are usually within the nuclear family, but alliances are also formed with other kin as well as with nonkin especially in fictive kinship relationships such as *compadrazgo*. The result in a village may be the formation of apparent "groups" as described by Murray, but in fact there is considerable flexibility in the formation and maintenance of such groups. People can and do draw on and develop important relationships beyond the nuclear family, but there is variation in which relationships are stressed and there is also variation over time.

One result of the flexibility of Filipino kinship is variation in household structure. The most common residential group is the nuclear family, but extended family households are also found. Household composition tends to vary with stages of the life cycle of family members and with the economic situation of the family (Castillo 1977:II, 394; Fegan 1979:376–87). An important result of this flexibility is continued sharing and assistance among relatives outside the residential unit; as Castillo puts it, the "household is residentially nuclear but functionally extended" (1977:II, 4l7). Yu and Liu (1980) demonstrate the extent of sharing among relatives in their study of Cebuano families, leading to what they call an "open system" of family relationships where, for example, "the status and obligations of parenthood are not vested solely in the married couple, but are shared with a wide circle of adult and elderly relatives" (1980:207). Furthermore, the "fictive kinship" institutions of godparenthood and fosterage extend the range of people potentially responsible for children; "they establish coexisting multiple equivalent bonds between adults and children without displacing the biological parent-child relationship" (1980:240).

Alliances and Reciprocity

Both within the nuclear family and in other kin and fictive kin relationships, relationships of mutual obligation and reciprocity develop and are maintained. These are informed by the core value of *utang na loob*, which has been translated as "debt of prime obligation," but the key to which is *reciprocal* obligations (Kaut 1961). The formation of alliances in which reciprocal obligations are expected is not limited to kinship relationships but rather pervades Filipino society (Schlegel 1964). However, *utang na loob* is particularly important in kinship relations. The ties and obligations within the nuclear family are strongest, with the parent-child relationship most important.

> The greatest strength of *utang na loob* is manifested in the parent-child relationship. Life is an unsolicited gift and thus the basis of a debt which cannot be repaid. In later life the child must obey and care for his parents who have given him his very existence . . . . Obligation toward the parent cannot be ignored or dissolved without extreme conflict . . . . Parents expect that their children will support them in their old age. (Kaut 1961:270)

Sibling relationships are also very important, usually forming a unit which continues after marriage (Eggan 1978:56). *Utang na loob* obligations tend to be strong here as well, so that siblings are expected to and do in fact care for one another and help each other out (Kaut 1961; Yu and Liu 1980:217). Since sharing and assistance extend to relatives outside the nuclear family, relationships of reciprocal obligations do likewise. As Hollnsteiner points out, "every Filipino . . . should be aware of his obligation to those from whom he receives favors and should repay them in an acceptable manner" (Hollnsteiner 1964:29). Thus, if a relative sends one's child to school, the sponsor creates "a lifelong obligation in the child and his family" (Hollnsteiner 1964:34). If a person does not fulfill expected obligations, then a person may be said to be *walang hiya*—

to have no shame (Hollnsteiner 1964:30–31). Together, *utang na loob* and *hiya* are "strong supports of the Filipino standards of proper behavior" (Schlegel 1964:56).

The flexibility of the Filipino kinship system which allows for the formation of alliances with relatives, combined with values that emphasize the importance of reciprocity, leads to a system of strong mutual support and assistance among relatives. One does not rely on all relatives for support or enter into *utang* relations with all. But the kinship network, extending beyond the nuclear family, provides a range of relatives who may be allies, or sources of support and assistance. In addition, the system of *compadrinazgo*, including godparenthood and ritual coparenthood (*compadrazgo*) (Hart 1977:1) can be used as the basis for further strengthening existing kin ties or for forming fictive kin relations with essentially the same sorts of mutual obligations.

How does this system affect migration and the maintenance of ties between migrants and other family members? It has several implications. First, Filipino migrants are operating in a cultural context where strong obligations to one's immediate family are expected and internalized. Hence, the son or daughter who migrates is expected to assist his or her parents or other family members, and, as we shall see, in most cases does so. Second, a range of relatives exist who may be called on for assistance, for example, in finding a job or housing. In doing this, the one receiving assistance takes on a debt of *utang*, to be reciprocated in some way at some future date. Third, residence as such is not a major determinant of the strength of relationships. As Yu and Liu have commented:

> The establishment of separate nuclear households does not necessarily sever kinship interaction, because the borderline between an individual's own nuclear family and a kinsman's family is not well defined. Relatives . . . are never considered superfluous . . . . On the contrary, they provide the underprivileged a reliable source of mutual assistance and a support network which is not diminished by time or distance. (1980:219)

This is true not only within a particular locale, but also of those who live in widely separated places. One result of the migration of some family members is that their support can be used to enable the rest of the family to continue to function as a residential and family unit. In other words, migration leads to the formation and maintenance of units that are essentially dispersed family networks (Trager 1982). Such units function to some degree as households, in that they are economically dependent on each other, but they are residentially dispersed.

Clearly, the existence of cultural values regarding reciprocity and close family relations does not mean that everyone behaves in accordance with those values. There are of course migrants in the Philippines who cut off ties with home completely. One of those described in this book later left Dagupan and, according to reports, "ran away" both from job and family obligations. Others complained of the burden of the obligations but fulfilled them nevertheless. Overall, the majority of migrants do retain strong ties with family elsewhere and a large proportion fulfill reciprocal obligations through monetary gifts. Of the 176 migrants studied in the survey described in chapter 4, only 7 were neither visiting nor sending something to relatives elsewhere. Furthermore, 88, or 50 percent, were contributing monetary remittances to family members elsewhere; as we shall see in Part 2, such remittances may make substantial contributions to family income (see Trager 1984 for further discussion of survey data on remittances; see also Ulack 1986 for another study of remittances in the Philippines).

Roles of Women

If family organization and values concerning interaction among family members affect the migration process, so, too, do particular roles and statuses within the family. In particular, the roles of women must be considered, given the current predominance of women—especially young, single women—in migration statistics. We may ask whether there are social and cultural dimensions that affect those statistical patterns. I will suggest that two issues are of particular relevance: on the one hand, the fact that women have relatively easy access to a variety of educational and economic opportunities in Filipino society; and, on the other hand, the fact that within the family, women (i.e., daughters) may be seen as most likely to fulfill familial obligations. To explore these issues, we need to consider what may appear to be contradictory elements—or to use Neher's term, the *ambiguous Filipina* (1982:154). The ambiguities, or contradictions, appear both in images and stereotypes of women in the Philippines and in reports of role behaviors. In the following discussion, I consider both the images and the roles, and then examine their relationship to data on the participation of women in migration.

As Castillo has noted, the image of the Filipina contains many contradictions:

> She is said to be exalted by history and tradition to a pedestal and yet she is low in the pecking order. There are arguments as to whether she still fashions herself as a Maria Clara 'coy, retiring and subservient' who needs to hide her intellect in order to be loved by man. On the other hand, she is supposed to have power and influence unofficially and in private. (1977:II, 481)

Some descriptions emphasize women's economic activities and control of family finances, while others point out restrictions on women's activities in a male-dominated society. Jacobson for example, argues that men and women in the Philippines are "social equals" (1974:374), with different but not unequal "spheres of interest, control and activity" (1974:349). On the other hand, Neher examines sex role images and shows that both men and women assigned men "traits usually considered appropriate for the dominant sex," while the traits assigned to women are often associated with the subordinate sex (1982:156). Furthermore, he argues that the stereotypes presented to Filipino children in school books lead to different expectations: "femaleness" is associated with "domesticity," and even where women have jobs, they are primarily depicted as homemakers, whereas "masculinity is associated with activities outside the home" (Neher 1982:167). Such stereotypes are largely supported by women's reports of their own activity: in the 1973 National Demographic Survey, married women were asked what they considered their "main activity"; 70 percent said they were mainly housekeepers, and 80 percent said their main activity takes place in the household (Castillo 1977:II, 545). Where then does the image come from of "the Filipina who combines marriage, career and children?" (Castillo 1977:II, 545).

This question can be approached by turning from stereotypes and images to actual activities of women. We find a far more complex situation than suggested either by an image of equality or an image of women as relegated to the domestic arena. Women do play important economic roles and have important areas of decision-making authority; in other areas, however, the society tends to be male dominated. Women's roles outside the home are notable in two respects. First, there is a very high level of educated women. There is no evidence of discrimination against women at any educational level, and in fact, at the college and graduate levels there are more females than males (Castillo 1977:II, 512). Second, employment opportunities are open to women, and many do work, although they may still state that their main activity is housekeeping, as we have seen. Female labor force participation is lower in rural than in urban areas, although rural women do work as farm workers and in other agricultural work. In urban areas, as we have seen in chapter 3, the major occupational categories for women are domestic service; teachers and office workers; and sales and service (Castillo 1977:II, 526–29). Women also tend to play important roles in family-owned businesses and small enterprises (Jacobson 1974:361; Alvarez and Alvarez 1972). While some employment areas tend to be male dominated, and others female dominated, it is possible for women to find employment, especially in urban areas. In fact, given that lower-level occupations such as domestic service and sales tend to be seen as "female" occupations, it may actually be easier for women than for men to find jobs in these occupations.

There are also substantial numbers of women in professional occupations—not only teachers, but also doctors, pharmacists, and others (Jacobson 1974:363). However, these women form a rather small elite, coming largely from upper-class families (Castillo 1977:II, 529); their situation is quite different from that of lower-class wage-earners and they have access to opportunities and power which the latter group do not (Szanton 1982:146).

The educational and economic opportunities open to women affect the migration patterns discussed earlier. Large numbers move into the low-level jobs in domestic service and sales, while others migrate for further education with the intention of obtaining jobs that lead to upward mobility. At the same time, middle- and upper-class women move to urban areas to work in professional occupations, including government service.

The decisions of young women to migrate are not necessarily theirs alone, however, but rather are taken within a family context. Therefore, the roles of women in the household, and expectations regarding the behavior of daughters, in particular, have an effect on the decision to migrate.

Studies of the roles of women in Philippine society have emphasized their managerial role and decision-making power in the household. The most important aspect of this is the control of the family purse and managing the household budget (e.g., Jacobson 1974:357–58); there are frequent reports of the husband handing over his earnings to his wife. Yu and Liu found that the wife has "almost absolute control" over three areas of household tasks—food preparation, family health care, and spending money (1980:170). Wives not only keep the money; they also have decision-making power over areas relating to household expenses, while they participate in joint decision making with their husbands about other expenditures, including farm-related decisions (Castillo 1977:II, 558–59; Castillo and Guerrero 1969:25–26). Hence, it is clear that women, as wives, are seen as having important managerial roles, and a capacity for taking care of areas of home management (Neher 1982:158). On the other hand, men, as husbands, are seen as the head of the family (Neher 1982:158; Castillo 1977:II, 564–69). For example, respondents interviewed in the Bicol area emphasized that "men ought to play a dominant role in decision-making within the family," that "man should be the superordinate; woman, the subordinate," and that "a man ought to be a good provider lest he fails as husband and father" (Illo 1977:54–55).

Overall, then, there are quite clear domains for males and females in the household—men as providers, and ultimate decision makers; women as managers of the purse and participators in decisions. However, these domains are those of husbands and wives, not sons or daughters. Yet it is they, especially daughters, who are migrating to cities and who are expected to fulfill obligations to their families. Here, some comments of Fox are perhaps most relevant. He agrees with others in stating that "there are no legal and few social restrictions . . . on the economic activities of women" (1963:353). On the other hand, he states, "Yet, the Filipino family and society may still be described as patricentric. The father is the head of the household . . . . Family decisions may be arrived at by consensus, the opinions of the mother and adult children being considered, but the decision will be formulated and voiced by the father" (1963:353). Hence, for a daughter in a household, decisions will be made largely by others—especially her father—though she will be consulted.

It is in this context that we need to consider the extensive participation of women as urban migrants. On the one hand, educational and economic opportunities *are* open to them, and in the jobs most likely to be obtained by migrants, there may in fact be a preference for women. Families do not discriminate between educating sons or daughters but educate those perceived as "bright" (Castillo 1977:II, 448). Again, there may actually be some preference for daughters to be educated, especially if they can move into one of those occupations (in the past, teaching; today, nursing and medical technology) in which jobs are known to be relatively easy to obtain and which many hope will lead to upward mobility. On the other hand, within the family, expectations regarding willingness to fulfill familial obligations also come into play. While both sons and daughters may migrate, and may be encouraged to do so, parents may expect daughters to be more likely to remit money and to aid in other ways. Hart has suggested that daughters "are more willing and faithful than sons in sharing their savings with the family" (1971:133). In the cases discussed in Part 2, we find one situation where a son has become a farmer while his sister works in the city, and another where both son and daughter have migrated but where their mother has much greater expectations regarding the daughter's remittances home. While both male and female migrants do remit money and otherwise aid their natal families, at least until marriage and sometimes afterwards (Trager 1984a), parents may expect daughters to be more obedient and less likely to spend money on themselves. It is daughters, for example, who sometimes choose not to marry and instead continue to live with and/or aid parents and siblings.

As Eviota and Smith (1981) have noted, large numbers of women today are migrating in the Philippines. On the surface, this may seem strange, given the still considerable emphasis on protection of women's morals and on close family relationships. However, it may be argued that, by migrating, young single women are able to help other family members in ways that would not be possible if they stayed in the rural home, where few job opportunities exist. In other words, the migration of young women and their subsequent assistance is part of a strategy that, in the long run, helps to maintain the family as a unit.

Migrants, Families, and Remittances: Case Studies

Part 2 focuses on seven migrants who were living in Dagupan City in 1978–79, describing their lives, activities, and interactions with others close to them. Chapter 6 considers three young women, all of whom were working in a store as sales clerks and all of whom were daughters of farmers in Pangasinan Province. Chapter 7 describes the lives of a husband and wife; he migrated to Dagupan from a rural barrio in Pangasinan, while she came there after her marriage, having grown up in the mountainous area of Northern Luzon. In 1978–79 they were successful cloth merchants in the Dagupan marketplace and owners of farmland in his hometown. Chapter 8 focuses on a woman working as a civil servant and the housegirl who works for her. The woman, professionally trained as a medical technologist, came to Dagupan from Tarlac, the province to the south. Her servant, the daughter of a landless family, migrated from the nearby town of San Fabian to work for her. Chapter 8 also includes information on the woman's husband, who is working in Saudia Arabia.

These seven migrants are broadly representative of a range of characteristics of migrants in Dagupan. As we have seen in Part 1, many migrants to secondary cities such as Dagupan are young, single women, daughters of farmers, working in sales. Still others are domestic servants, while those migrants from middle- and upper-class backgrounds tend to be in professional jobs, especially government civil service occupations. The couple in chapter 7 represent still another type of activity common among migrants—the ownership of a small business. As we shall see in the discussion, the seven are broadly representative in other ways as well—not only in their backgrounds, but also in the types of ties they maintain with their homes and families living elsewhere.

In another sense, however, the individuals discussed in this section represent only themselves. Each one is living his or her own life, making decisions, interacting with others in whatever family and social context they happen to be in. Each is unique. While there are patterns of activities that can be discussed, what is particularly interesting about a focus on individuals and their families is the sense it gives of the diversity and complexity in the lives of ordinary individuals. As we shall see in chapter 6, for example, despite the fact that the three women share certain broad socioeconomic characteristics, their stories are quite different. The purpose of this section is to gain an understanding of the ways in which specific migrants and their families live and interact, the decisions they make, and how they perceive their own activities.

The material in this section is, in effect, a set of case studies of migrants and their families. While each case focuses on a particular migrant, providing information on his or her life history as well as current activities, the individual is considered in his or her social context, including other family members, friends, co-workers, and so on. Therefore each case also includes relevant information on the background and activities of others, especially family members, with whom the migrant regularly interacts.

A major concern of each case is the description of interaction, especially visiting and the giving of gifts and remittances between the migrant and family members living elsewhere. Through these descriptions, we are able to view the extent to which migrants continue to move back and forth between rural and urban areas, as well as the considerable interdependence and interconnectedness between those who have migrated and those who have not. Furthermore, we are able to see how the behavior and activities of a particular individual can be structured and influenced by decisions, obligations, and demands made by others.[1]

A brief analysis follows the descriptive material in each chapter. These analyses consider the ways in which the migrants and their families are incorporated into the larger structural framework outlined in Part 1. By viewing individuals and households in the larger structural context, we can begin to understand ways in which the migration of individuals is linked to the macrostructural context in which they and their families must operate.[2]

Chapter 6

Wage Labor in the Service Sector: Three Salesgirls

Just inside the entrance to Dagupan Trading, a young woman stands behind the display of Christmas and birthday cards. She is busy taking money from customers, writing out receipts, handing the money to the cashier and the change back to the customer, and wrapping the purchase. She smiles cheerfully at each new customer, greets briefly those she knows, and then continues her work. Her green uniform accentuates her thin waist and arms. Under her makeup, her eyes look tired; she has been at work since 8:30 in the morning and will not leave until 6:30 or 7:00 in the evening.

Past her, in the middle of the store, the cashier stands on a raised platform, from which she is able to oversee the rest of the store. Along the aisle to the right stand display counters filled with religious items; figures of saints are displayed on the wall. The counters on the aisle to the left contain toys, stationery, and other gift items. Behind each display counter, two or three salesgirls, dressed like the first in a green uniform, stand ready to wait on any customer who enters.

At the back of the store, a door leads to the manager's office. The manager and his wife, and frequently, one or more of their children, move back and forth between the office, the store, and the back room, where two young men work unpacking and stocking goods. The two men also help with some of the manager's "sidelines"—laminating pictures of saints, for example, so they can be sold at a higher price.

As the largest and best-organized variety store in Dagupan, Dagupan Trading employs nine full-time salesgirls and two male assistants; part-time helpers are hired in the Christmas season. Of the salesgirls, only one is a native of Dagupan. She is older than the others, married, with a family, and has worked in the store for a number of years. The others are either migrants or commuters: four commute daily from their homes in nearby Pangasinan towns, two stay in Dagupan during the week and return home on weekends, and two return home only on holidays. The two men are also migrants. All are single and in their early twenties.

The manager and his wife run the store for a Manila-based company. They, too, are migrants to Dagupan who met when she began to work in the store. Now in their thirties, with six young children, they both work twelve-hour days in the store. Some of the salesgirls help care for the children, both during work hours and after work. The family and business merge in other ways, as well; there are frequent birthday parties and other activities in the manager's home, attended by all the employees. The major social events take place before Christmas, when for two weeks, the manager and the employees go out caroling every evening at houses in and around Dagupan, to raise money for their Christmas party. Like employees in other stores in Dagupan, those at Dagupan Trading are paid regular weekly wages. In addition, the store is covered by Philippine labor laws that prescribe specific benefits, including a monthly "emergency allowance" decreed by President Marcos (details in sections below). Unlike employees in many smaller shops, they do not receive housing or board from the employer.

This chapter examines the lives of three of the salesgirls at Dagupan Trading. All are daughters of farmers in Pangasinan. All had been working at Dagupan Trading for more than a year at the time of the study, and all are aware that they are among the best-paid salesgirls in the city. Although they complain about some aspects of their work—the long hours and the requirement to stand all day—none were actively looking for other work.

Marie

"I'm telling Marie that she shouldn't get married yet. We have too many expenses and we need her help."

Marie's mother sat in the family home in Buenlag, a barrio of Calasiao. She was describing the expenses for the family of eight children, six of whom still live at home. She explained that she felt ashamed to talk of how hard up they are, and of their dependence on Marie and her older brother, both of whom live and work in Dagupan.

"We get rice from our farm, but it is lacking" (i.e., there is not enough produced for their needs). "We have chickens and pigs; my husband sells them in the Calasiao market. He sells a pig once every six months for about ₱300. Before, I used to sew, until I began to have eye trouble. Last year, I had an operation on my right eye for cataracts; it cost ₱500 at the provincial hospital. I need to have an operation on my left eye now."

"Every day we eat five kilos of rice. I buy it at the store [a neighborhood shop]. I also buy vegetables, fish and other ingredients at the store or from people going around selling. On Saturdays, Marie brings things like meat and *bangus* [fish] from the market in Dagupan. Sometimes I borrow rice from the store and return the money later" (i.e., she buys on credit and pays later, usually after Marie brings cash on the weekends).

"That's why Marie is so thin. She is helping us out at home and also helping her sister to go to school."

Marie is a twenty-two-year-old high school graduate, the only regular employee at Dagupan Trading who has not been to college. She has worked there for more than two years, having passed the exam the store requires of applicants. She began working in Dagupan after graduating from high school. "My first job was as a saleslady at Juanitos, inside the Dagupan Supermarket. They sell buckles, buttons, and other sewing items. I found the job through my cousin, who was also selling inside the market. They paid me ₱60 a month and I stayed at their place, on Rivera Street. I worked there for two months. My second job was at Tayas Hardware; I worked there for two years. The owner of the store is my mother's godmother [sponsor at her mother's wedding]. My starting salary was ₱150 a month and I lived with the owners of the store, upstairs from the store.

"I took a vacation from Tayas and went to Manila, to my auntie's [father's sister]. I looked for a job, but after one month I didn't find one so I returned to Dagupan. But I didn't want to return to the hardware store. I saw a sign that Dagupan Trading was hiring salesladies. I applied, and started working November 4, 1976."

When she first began to work at Dagupan Trading, Marie commuted from home by jeepney. The ride takes only about half an hour, but she found it difficult to commute because the jeeps were crowded with students and people going to market. After a few months, a co-worker helped her find a room in a boarding house, one of the many places located along side streets in the *poblacion*. Located above small shops, few are identified by sign, although some of the larger ones post signs reading Boarders Accepted or Lady Boarder Only. Marie lives in one of the smaller ones. The entrance is through a dry cleaning shop; at night after the shop is closed, the owner lets boarders in through a three-foot-high opening cut in the door. To the left of the door is a narrow stairway leading to an upstairs hall. Down the hall a short distance is the door to Marie's room, where she, a co-worker, and a student live. The room is just large enough to contain a double-deck bed, a small table, and two wooden chairs. A kerosene stove is propped on the table. Marie and the student share the lower bunk of the bed; her co-worker Flor sleeps in the upper bunk. The walls of the room do not go up to the ceiling, so sounds and smells enter from the two adjoining rooms, each of which has three more young women boarders. A family rents the larger room at the front of the building. Marie and her roommates pay ₱25 a month each in rent.

Six days a week Marie follows a routine that centers on work: up early each morning, she shares cooking and cleaning with her two roommates. By 8:30, she is outside Dagupan Trading, waiting with the other employees for the manager to arrive to open the store. From 8:30 to noon she stands at her assigned station behind the counter, leaving only to run an errand for the manager. During her one-and-a-half-hour lunch break, she usually goes directly back to her room in the boarding house, eats lunch, and takes a rest. At 1:30 she is back at the store, where she returns to her position behind the counter, staying there until 6:00 in the evening. After the store closes, there is usually some more work to be done, arranging new products and making the displays attractive. By 6:30 or 7:00, she returns to her room, sometimes stopping for groceries on the way. She and her roommates again share the cooking and cleaning up, then visit with each other and other boarders or wash and iron their uniforms for the next day.

Occasionally she goes to the market with a co-worker, or stops to visit with one of her relatives who lives in Dagupan. In addition to her own brother, several of her mother's brothers and sisters live in the city. They, like her, visit regularly in the barrio; she is as likely to see them there as in Dagupan. One of her godchildren lives in Dagupan; the child's father worked with her at the hardware store. She sees the child and her parents once in a while, when she goes to the area of the city where they live.

Only during the Christmas season is there more activity. Marie works longer hours then, and the store is open on Sundays. After work, the manager and all the employees spend the evening practicing carols. Then, for about two weeks, they go out nearly every evening to sing carols at the homes of people who have invited them. In return, they are provided refreshments and a donation that helps to pay for their Christmas party. Marie enjoys this period, especially riding around to these gatherings in the manager's jeep, and the partylike atmosphere. Finally, shortly before Christmas, there is a large party at the manager's home, attended by all the employees and friends and relatives of the manager. Large quantities of food are served; the employees play party games and receive small gifts from the manager and each other.

On Saturday, Marie's routine changes: after buying groceries, she takes a jeepney to Calasiao, arriving at her parents' home in the early evening. Even during the Christmas season, when she works seven days a week, she still goes home on Sunday evenings, returning to Dagupan early Monday morning.

If it were possible, Marie would like to live in her parents' barrio instead of in Dagupan. "Dagupan is a city, like Manila. There are many people here. Life is easier in the barrio. In my barrio, there is always water and light,[1] not like here. There are vegetables and fruits in the barrio, but here, you have to pay for them and if you don't have money you can't get them. The people in the barrio know each other. In Dagupan, people don't know their neighbors. I like the barrio better."

Marie's mother and father live in an old two-story wood house belonging to her mother's parents. The downstairs is rented out to a salesman for a pharmaceutical firm, who uses it as a stock room and a place to stay when in the area. Three separate branches of the family live upstairs—Marie's parents and their children, her grandparents and the children of a widowed daughter, and her mother's sister, with her six children. The family units decided about a year ago to *akabiig so banga to* (to keep separate pots) so that they could keep track of their expenses. The rice Marie's father grows is for his family only; her grandfather's rice helps to support the children of his widowed daughter, who works in Dagupan and leaves her children in the barrio. Her mother's sister depends on money brought home by her husband, who works as a driver for a company in Dagupan. (See figs. 4 and 5.)

Of the men in the house, only Marie's father and grandfather are farmers. Her uncle and oldest brother work in Dagupan, at a furniture store. The uncle is a driver for the store, and commutes to Dagupan from the barrio every day. Her brother, like Marie, comes home on Sundays. Another brother graduated from high school several years ago, but has been unable to find a job, although sometimes he helps at the same store

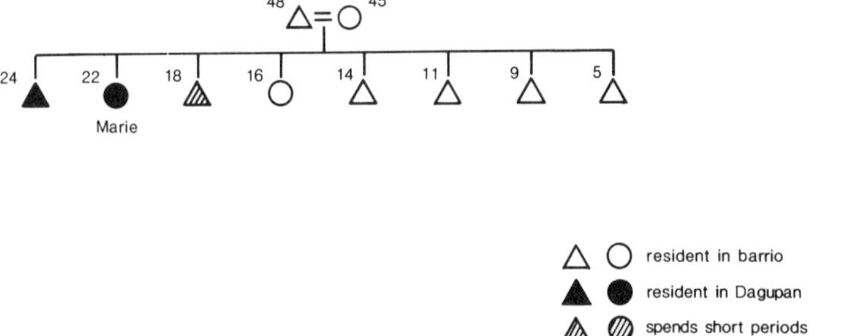

Fig 4. Marie's nuclear family; age and residence

where his uncle and brother work. Marie's younger sister will graduate from high school soon. Her mother hopes she will be able to find a job in Dagupan; she thinks it is easier for girls than for boys to find jobs.

Marie's father has been a farmer all his life. Born in Santa Barbara, the son of a farmer, he attended elementary school and then began to help out at home by selling piglets in the market. He farmed in Santa Barbara until six years after his marriage, when he and his wife moved to her parents' home in Calasiao. He then began farming on some land that was mortgaged to his wife's grandmother. The land he now farms belongs to a schoolteacher who lives in Calasiao.

He has been a lease holder on one-half hectare of land near his house for the past ten years. As a leaseholder, he pays a fixed share of the produce, regardless of the size of the harvest. His rent is twelve cavans of *palay* (unhusked rice), which equals about 528 kilos, or about 336 kilos of clean rice.[2] He pays for all farm expenses—the seed, land preparation, fertilizer, and insecticide. If he needs additional help for planting and harvesting, he hires other farmers from the barrio. He also goes out to work for other farmers in exchange for their labor. The land is not irrigated; he gets only one rice crop a year. His harvest ranges from fifty to eighty cavans of palay. But by the time of the harvest he usually has borrowed from people whom he repays with palay. So even though his last harvest was sixty cavans, and he owed the landlord only twelve, he still had only nine cavans for his own use. Nine cavans (396 kilos) lasts the family for two to three months; after that, they must buy rice.

In addition, every week Marie's father buys piglets at houses in the barrio and takes them to the Calasiao market to sell. He makes between

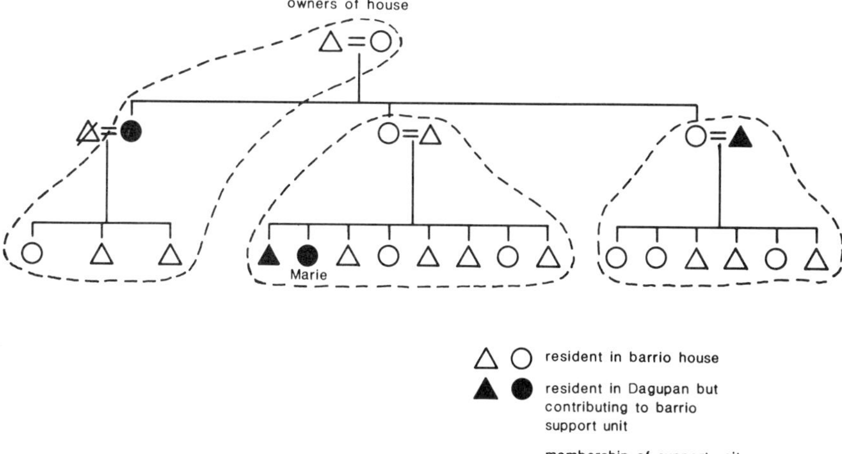

Fig. 5. Marie's extended family; support units and extended family members resident in barrio house

₱5 and ₱10 each week doing this. Sometimes he also accompanies another man who sells dogs and makes a few pesos doing this. He and his wife raise their own chickens and pigs, which they sell to help pay for school tuition for the children in high school. They get about ₱300 whenever they do this, once or twice a year. In the past, Marie's mother sometimes sewed clothes for people, but in recent years she has had cataracts on her eyes and has been unable to see well enough to sew.

When Marie is at home in the barrio on Sundays, she attends mass, helps to clean house and cook for the family, and visits with family and neighbors. During the harvest she is especially busy; her mother and brothers help in the fields, while she does the cooking at home. About once a month she and her sister go to Santa Barbara to see her father's parents. Sometimes some of the younger girls who are neighbors in Calasiao come to her for advice; "They ask me for advice about their boyfriends. Sometimes they ask me to lend them money too. If I can, I give them maybe five pesos."

Marie's parents would prefer her to stay in the barrio all the time. She, too, thinks of Beunlag as "home" but dislikes commuting. She thinks that someday she'll return to a barrio to live, if not her own, then her husband's after she marries. "I want my children to grow up in the barrio, so that they'll know the work there." But, on the other hand, she also says that she expects her children to have "white-collar jobs."

Income and Expenses of Marie and Her Family

With her monthly income of about ₱300 (see table 22), Marie is able to meet her regular expenses and provide support to her parents and siblings. She estimates that she spends about ₱30 a week for food for herself and ₱25 a month in rent. She also pays for her transportation home each week and for supplies, such as cooking fuel. She does not get any food from home. In addition, she regularly remits money home, between ₱20 and ₱50 a week, and buys groceries to take home with her. She also pays her sister's fare for transportation to school. Overall, she estimates that her monthly expenses range between ₱240 and ₱360, amounting on average to just about her total income, and perhaps more at times (see table 23). Nevertheless, she says that she is able to save some money, amounting to about ₱20 a month.

At Christmas, Marie and the other Dagupan Trading employees received special bonuses. She got ₱700 in all, from a combination of payments for sick leave, vacation allowance, and salary bonus. Like her salary, this money was quickly spent. She bought gifts for her parents, sisters and brothers, cousins, and several godchildren. To each close relative she gave money as well as a shirt or dress. Each cousin received ₱1, and the four godchildren got clothing. Only her youngest brother, who is five, received a toy (see table 24). In contrast, Marie received very few gifts, one from her brother who works in Dagupan, one from her roommate, and one from her employers.

TABLE 22.   Marie's Monthly Income

Income	Pesos
Salary[a] (₱60/week)	240
Emergency allowance[b]	90
Subtotal	330
Deductions (social security, withholding)	25
Total	305

Note: Based on interviews with Marie.

[a]In May 1979, at the end of the research period, her salary went up to ₱72/week.

[b]Emergency allowance was decreed by President Marcos for certain categories of workers.

TABLE 23.   Marie's Monthly Expenses

Expenses	Amount
Regular in Dagupan	
Rent	₱25
Food (₱30/week)	120
Transportation to barrio (est. ₱1.50/week)	6
Incidental expenses (gifts, clothes, toiletries)	variable
Cooking fuel (₱.90 every 3 weeks)	1
Subtotal	₱152
Regular in Barrio	
Money to parents ₱20–50/week	₱80–200
Money to sister for transport to school (₱5/week)	20
Subtotal	₱100–220
Total estimated regular expenses	₱252–370

Note: Based on interviews with Marie.

TABLE 24.   Marie's Christmas Gifts

Recipient	Item and Value		Money	Total Cost
Father	T-shirt	₱25	₱20	₱45
Mother	cloth	22	50	72
Brother			20	20
Brother	T-shirt	20		20
Sister	sandals	25	5	30
Brother	T-shirt	6.50	5	11.50
Sister	cloth	18		18
Brother	T-shirt	5		
	pants	12	2	19
Brother	T-shirt	5		
	pants	12	5	
	toy gun	9.30		31.30
Cousins (10)			1 peso each	10
Godchildren	dress	16		
	dress	17		
	T-shirt and			
	pants	10		
	dress	12		55
Co-worker[a]	figurine	20		20
Total				₱351.80

Note: Based on interviews with Marie.

[a]For gift exchange at store Christmas party.

In addition, at Christmas her parents needed ₱350 to repair the stairs on the family home in the barrio. She gave them the money, so that, combined with Christmas gifts, she in fact spent her entire ₱700 bonus. However, in order to have some money to spend on herself, for clothing and to put a small amount into a savings account, she borrowed ₱100 from a co-worker, which she repaid during January and February.

Marie helps to pay other unusual expenses during the year as well. Her sister's high school tuition amounts to ₱244 a year, and Marie and her brother usually help to pay it. When her mother needed an eye operation, Marie provided the ₱500 that was necessary.

The money that Marie regularly remits is essential to the family income. In a sample week (see table 25), Marie contributed ₱30, plus some meat, while her brother gave ₱20. Her father, on the other hand, made ₱8 selling piglets and won ₱5 in a cockfight.

According to her family's report, their expenses totaled ₱161.75, of which ₱27.60 was given on credit by the local store. In another week, they reported expenses totaling ₱88, and income of ₱65, of which ₱50 was given by Marie. It is clear that she regularly provides more than half the reported family income. What is not clear is how they get the rest of the money necessary to pay their expenses.[3]

Overall, Marie's mother estimates that the family expenses total about ₱600–800 a month, simply for necessities. This includes, in addition to food, the cost of cooking fuel, electricity, clothing, school fees, and transportation. Water is free in their barrio. For special occasions, such as Christmas and the barrio fiesta, they spend additional amounts (₱50–100), mainly for food. Marie's father has a variety of farming expenses, for seed, fertilizer, and so on (see table 26). Following the rice harvest, the family does not have to buy rice for two or three months; after that, as we have seen, they spend a considerable portion of their income on rice.

Other than rice, their only income comes from their occasional sales of pigs and chickens, from Marie's father's buying and selling at the market and his occasional winnings at cockfights, and from the remittances sent by Marie and her brother.

Flor

"Life in the barrio is very hard. We are poor in the barrio" (Flor, comments during visit to her home, November 26, 1978).

TABLE 25. Sample Weekly Income and Expenses of Marie's Parents and Household, April, 1979

	Monday	Tuesday	Wednesday	Thursday	Friday	Saturday	Sunday
Income	*Source: Amt.* Father ₱8 (profit from buying and selling piglets in market)						*Source: Amt.* Marie ₱30 Brother 20 Father 5 (won in cockfight)
In kind							Marie 1/2 k meat
Expenses (in pesos)	5 k rice 12.25 1/2 k meat 8.00	5 k rice 12.25 Fish 3.50 Veg. 2.00	2 k rice 4.90 Fish 9.50 Soap 3.00	3 k rice 7.35 1/2 k. meat 8.00 Veg. 4.50	2 k rice 4.90 Fish 9.00 Soap 4.00	5 k rice 12.25 Fish 4.00 Veg. 2.00	5 k rice 12.25 Fish 9.00 Other 1.50 ingredients
On credit from store in barrio	Soap Cooking ingredients Kerosene 5.00		3 k rice 7.35	2 k rice 4.90	3 k rice 7.35 Veg. 3.00		
Total income	₱63 + 1/2 k meat						
Total expenses	₱134.15						
Total credit	₱27.60						

Note: Based on self-report of income and expenses, recorded daily.

"[If I could live anywhere I would] live in the barrio. My own. Because it is a quiet place. We will not buy our foods. We will not be hungry. You can wear ordinary dresses. You can save money, instead of riding you can walk . . . . In Dagupan you have to buy vegetables, but not in the barrio. You cannot sleep here. There is always fire in Dagupan" (Flor, March 9, 1979, interview).

Q: "Where do you think you will be living in five years?"
A: "Of course, the barrio. When I get married to someone from the barrio, I will live in the barrio. . ."
Q: "What will you do in the barrio?"
A: "I will raise vegetables."
Q: "What kind of work will your husband do?"
A: "Just so he can support me."
Q: "Where will he work?"
A: "In an office. He will work in Dagupan and commute."

TABLE 26.   Rice Production of Marie's Father[a], 1978 Harvest

Expenses	Cost
Seed	₱45
Tractor rental	₱200
2 bags fertilizer at ₱53 each	₱106
Insecticide	₱12
Labor	
Planting: 12 people for 2 days ₱6 each day	₱144
Harvest: 12 people for 2 days ₱6 each day	₱144
Thresher	5 cavans *palay* for 100 cavans threshed
Rent for land	12 cavans a year
Rice Produced	
	60 cavans
To landlord	−12
	48
Owed to others	−39
For own consumption	9 cavans = 396 k *palay* = 252 k cleaned rice

Note: Based on interview with Marie's father.

[a]Although he stated amounts in pesos, he pays for some of these costs with rice or *palay*. He also exchanges labor with other farmers.

Q: "You want to live in the barrio, but your husband will work in
    the city?"
A: "Yes, of course."

(Flor, interview, March 9, 1979)

Twenty-two years old, outgoing and attractive, Flor is always meticu-
lously groomed—her hair curled, her fingernails polished, her face
powdered. Voted "most charming girl" at a recent barrio event, she has
several boyfriends and suitors whom she sees occasionally and who cor-
respond with her. Like Marie, she is assigned to a station just inside the
entrance to Dagupan Trading, where she can greet all who enter the
store. Like Marie and the other employees at Dagupan Trading, she
adheres to an exhausting schedule. Up every morning between 5:00 and
6:00 A.M., so that she can use the bathroom before the other boarders are
awake, she cooks and eats breakfast, dresses in her store uniform, and
walks to the store, arriving before 8:30. She usually has a few minutes
before the manager arrives, to visit with the other salesgirls and compare
notes on the customers. At noon, she returns to the boarding house for
lunch, sometimes doing errands on the way, and rests for a few minutes
before returning to work. The workday ends around 6:30 or 7:00 P.M.

Although she has little time for social activities in Dagupan, she regularly sees her co-workers and fellow boarders, going shopping with
them, attending parties given by the store manager, occasionally visiting
other friends in town together. Sometimes she sees friends but has no
time to visit: "At noon I saw my barrio mates who are studying at
University of Pangasinan so for five minutes we converse . . . and then I
like to invite them but we're so tired 'cause we are busy [in the store]."
Flor's only relative in Dagupan is an uncle; she sees him about once a
week when he stops by the store. Sometimes she reads newspapers and
comic books and romances, but she rarely attends movies. "I last went to
a movie more than a year ago. I'm afraid to go alone, and even if I have a
companion I don't have time."

Flor has been living and working in Dagupan for about two-and-
a-half years. She attended high school at the barrio school in Mangatarem, the nearest one to her house. After graduating, she went to a
small Catholic college in Lingayen, where she took a two-year secretarial
course. While there, she lived in a boarding house. After that, she returned to her parents' house in Aguilar, south of Dagupan, and helped

her parents, cooking, cleaning house, washing clothes. Her uncle in Dagupan, who is a friend of the manager of Dagupan Trading, heard that there were job openings there. He went to the barrio to tell Flor; she applied and got the job.

Flor found a place to live in Dagupan through friends: she moved in with others from Aguilar who were already living in the boarding house over the dry cleaner's shop. They have since left, and now she shares her room with Marie and a student. Her roommates are among her closest companions, sharing cooking and cleaning, borrowing money from one another, visiting and gossiping when they have spare time. She also sees co-workers frequently, especially Delia, whom she describes as her best friend, the person to whom she talks about confidential and personal matters.

But Flor's network extends far beyond those she sees daily in Dagupan. Nearly every weekend she goes home to Calsib, her barrio in the town of Aguilar. There she visits with family and friends, discussing local news and gossip. If for some reason she can't go home, her father or one of her sisters comes to Dagupan to see her, and to take her uniform home to be washed. Her boyfriend, also from Calsib and working in Manila, sometimes comes to see her at home. Other friends, from nearby barrios and even from other towns, visit to invite her to a wedding or a barrio fiesta. As a member of the Young Lovers Club in Calsib, she meets with other young people from the barrio (many of whom are also working elsewhere) to organize the yearly barrio fiesta. Occasionally she goes to Binmaley, her mother's hometown, to see friends and relatives; one of her three godchildren is from Binmaley, and the other two are from Aguilar.

Flor's own record of activities shows the pattern of events in her life— routine work broken by interaction with friends, co-workers, and relatives (see table 27).

Family Life and Work in the Barrio

Every Saturday evening after work, Flor takes the bus to Aguilar. The bus goes south along the Lingayen-Manila highway, a newly cemented road. Beyond the river and fishponds of Lingayen, the land is bright green with newly planted seed rice. Some of the recently harvested rice is spread along the highway to dry; the bus cuts in and out of its lane to avoid driving over the rice. To the west, the Zambales Mountains are turning blue with the setting sun. At the town of Aguilar, the old church of yellow stone stands prominently on the corner. Soon, Aguilar has disappeared and the land is green again on both sides of the road. A few miles further on, the bus stops at a cement waiting shed next to a dirt side road. If it is not too late, tricycles are waiting to take passengers into the barrio. Flor, carrying a plastic bag with a few overnight clothes and her uniform to wash, gets into a tricycle which takes her several kilometers down the dirt road, past a number of small bamboo houses. If there are no tricycles, Flor's father walks out to the main road to meet her, carrying a pair of rubber sandals so she won't ruin her good shoes.

Flor's parents' house is in an area with several substantial wood houses, surrounded by banana and papaya trees. Their two-story wood house has glass windows in the front, capiz shell windows on the side. On the ground floor, an open area provides space for pounding and storing rice; an enclosed area contains the kitchen, with clay stoves and a clay water jar, and an eating area with a long table. The three rooms upstairs include a *sala* (living room) and two bedrooms. There is little furniture in the *sala* except for a large cabinet displaying dishes, kitchen utensils, and many packages of soap and toothpaste. Electrical wiring was installed, in expectation of the arrival of electricity in the barrio later that year. In back of the house, coconut trees provide a supply of young coconuts for snacks; *aba* (taro) and other vegetables provide the family vegetable supply. Nearby, Flor's father has about one hectare of riceland that he owns; across the road are the fields on which he is a tenant. Next door is a smaller house, belonging to Flor's brother, also a farmer. Her married sister lives in a nearby barrio.

Flor's father inherited his land from his father. He was born in the barrio, but began farming only after he married. When he was about fourteen or fifteen years old, he went to Naga, in the southern Philippines, and worked as a houseboy for a cousin there. After he returned to Aguilar, he became a *calesa* (horse-drawn carriage) driver and remained one until his horse died about eight years later. After World War II, he got married and began to farm. Now fifty-six years old, he heads a household that includes Flor's mother, who was born in Binmaley and lived there until her marriage; Flor's two younger sisters, both still in high school, and a four-year-old granddaughter. The granddaughter is the child of a daughter who died when she was twenty-five years old; the child's father lives in another province and visits occasionally. A married son lives next door with his wife and four children; a married daughter

TABLE 27.   Flor's Activities and Interaction, January, 1979

Date	Place	Activities
Monday, January 1	barrio	I woke up early because it's New Year; we're very happy together with my family, and some of my relatives and friends are here. At 11:30 my father did the cooking and we ate together.
Tuesday, January 2	barrio, Dagupan	I came from my barrio at 6:00 A.M. and waited at the waiting shed for the minibus to Dagupan. At 7:30 I got to my boarding house and rested. I brought from home one ganta of rice, bananas, and three fish that my parents bought in the market. Then I went to work.
Wednesday, January 3	Dagupan	After getting up and having breakfast, I went to work together with Marie. At noon, I returned to my boarding house and rested. After work I went with a co-worker to the grocery store, and bought face cream for ₱14.95. She accompanied me back to my boarding house.
Thursday, January 4	Dagupan	After work my co-worker invited me to downtown where she had her haircut. I also had a manicure for ₱2.50.
Friday, January 5	Dagupan	In the morning I cleaned our room. At noon I ate alone because Marie went to the market. I returned to the boarding house immediately after work. Before sleeping I conversed with my board mates.
Saturday, January 6	Dagupan, Binmaley	After work, I went with Delia to Binmaley, to stay with her sister and attend the wedding of a friend.
Sunday, January 7	Binmaley, barrio	Delia and I and her cousins cooked, cleaned, and ate, then I changed my clothes and went home to Aguilar. I arrived at 12:30, we ate at once, conversed with my parents and took a rest. In the afternoon, we conversed again, I cultivated my plants, and the friends of my oldest sister visited us from San Carlos to invite us to a wedding January 13 and 14.
Monday, January 8	barrio, Dagupan	At 4:00 I woke up already so that I can prepare my things to be brought to Dagupan. At 7:30 I got to Dagupan and took a rest. I brought bananas, fish, rice, and mangos from home. After work, I returned to the boarding house, ate, and slept.
Tuesday, January 9	Dagupan	After work, Marie and I went to the market, where we bought fish, mango, vetsin, and salt. We returned to the boarding house at 7:00 and ate, then I washed my uniform.
Wednesday, January 10	Dagupan	At lunch, I ate with Marie and my other roommates.
Thursday, January 11	Dagupan	I woke up very early to take a bath and cook and eat. After work all the Dagupan Trading employees went to Atche Mary's [employer's] house because it was her birthday. I returned home with Marie, Delia, and others; we enjoyed walking because it was cool.
Friday, January 12	Dagupan	After work Marie and I went to the *sari-sari* store and bought meatloaf for ₱2.40; then I cooked and we ate.

TABLE 27—*Continued*

Date	Place	Activities
Saturday, January 13	Dagupan	Marie did the cooking this morning so I woke up at 7:45 and went to work at 8:05. At noon, Marie and I ate and I curled my hair. After work, my sister and my cousin arrived from Aguilar and invited me to go to my auntie and uncle's at Perez Blvd. They gave us calendars. Then we returned to our boarding house and my sister ate with us. My sister stayed overnight.
Sunday, January 14	Dagupan, barrio	My sister and I woke up early because we wanted to buy sandals. I bought sandals for her for ₱35 for her high school prom. Then we went home at 9:00 and my parents are proud about the sandals and my sister is very happy. At noontime we converse with my parents and sisters and I'm very happy because it's Sunday, we don't have work. In the evening my mother cooked and we ate together. After preparing my things to return to Dagupan we visited the house of our neighbor who died last Sunday. We went home at 9:00 in order to sleep, because I will return to Dagupan tomorrow.

Note: Based on diaries kept by Flor, from late November 1978 to late January 1979. I have edited the English and omitted repetitions of routine events, such as preparing for work.

lives in another barrio with her husband and four children. Both son and son-in-law are farmers, but only the son-in-law helps on Flor's father's farm (see fig. 6).

Calsib, Flor's barrio, is situated in a productive rice-growing region. Located in a flat plain between the Agno River and the foothills of the Zambales Mountains, the area receives sufficient runoff water for irrigation, making possible two or three rice crops a year. Like many other farmers in the area, Flor's father is both a smallholder and a tenant farmer. He owns one hectare of land behind his house, on which he produces about forty to fifty cavans on the first crop and somewhat less on the second. A short distance away lies another one and one-third hectare belonging to a landlord from Lingayen. He has farmed that land since 1965 and is able to produce between seventy and ninety cavans of palay on the first crop, fifty to sixty on the second, depending on the weather and other seasonal factors.

Through a complex set of relationships involving not only Flor's father and the landlord but also hired labor and other landsharing arrangements, he is able to produce enough rice to provide most of the family's needs as well as to sell some. The arrangements are relatively simple on his own land. He pays for fertilizer and insecticide (if he has the

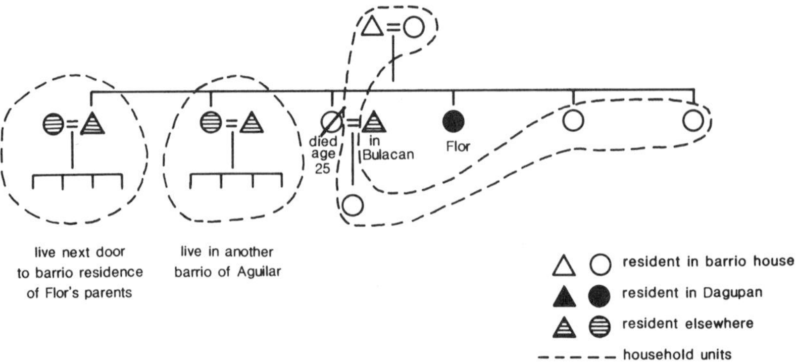

Fig 6. Flor's extended family; residence

money to use them) and hires some people from the barrio to help with the planting. All the rice produced belongs to him and he uses it mainly for the family's consumption. On the rented land, he has a fifty-fifty sharing relationship with the landlord, whom he met through a *compare* (god-relative). The landlord pays for fertilizer and insecticide, and receives 50 percent of the crop. Flor's father hires labor to help with planting and harvesting. But because the only regular family help he has is that of his son-in-law, he also has a *kakaluma* arrangement with a number of landless people from another barrio. This means that these men are each responsible for planting and harvesting a small portion of the land on which he is a tenant. They then receive a portion of the rice produced; out of ten cavans, such a person will receive two, while Flor's father divides the remaining eight between himself and the landlord. For example, in one season he had fifteen people working as *kakaluma*. He himself produced only thirteen cavans, while the total harvest of the others was sixty cavans, after each subtracted their share of two cavans for each ten produced. Therefore, he had a total of seventy-three cavans to divide with the landlord, ending up with his share of one half. The result of these arrangements is that Flor's father does the actual farming only on the land he owns and on a small portion of the land on which he is a tenant; he acts as an intermediary between the landlord and those who actively work the land on the rest of his land. He receives less rice but doesn't have to hire as much labor.

Flor's father uses the rice he produces on his own land for the family's consumption, while selling much of his share from his tenanted land. He sells it one cavan at a time, as the need arises, to pay for regular household expenses as well as special expenses such as school fees and medicine. He was able to spend ₱350 to install electric wiring. Nevertheless, in August and September the family usually has to buy rice. In some respects, the household is relatively self-sufficient. They produce their own vegetables and fruits, and sometimes Flor's mother sells bananas and coconuts at the market in Mangatarem. They sometimes obtain fish on their ricefields; more often, they must buy meat or fish in Mangatarem or from people going around the barrio selling. They have a pig and chickens that they use for their own consumption; and when they have piglets they sell them when they are one and one-half months old. In addition, Flor's mother buys and sells *bagaong*, a sauce made from shrimp. She buys a large can in Lingayen about once a month and sells it in smaller quantity to neighbors.

Income and Expenses of Flor and Her Family

When Flor visits her parents on weekends, she gets food to bring back to Dagupan for the following week. She gets about one *ganta* (2.3 kilos) of rice a week, whatever fruits and vegetables are in season, and sometimes some meat or fish. As a result, she spends relatively little money on food in Dagupan. At the same time, Flor brings ₱30 to her parents each week, which they use for whatever expenses they have, including paying off food purchases made earlier in the week. On special occasions, Flor also brings extra money and gifts to family members at home.

Flor's salary is the same as Marie's—₱305 a month, after deductions. Her regular expenses include rent; some basic food items, such as meat, fish, vegetables, and ingredients such as *vetsin* (monosodium glutamate); cooking oil and kerosene; toiletries such as shampoo and soap; fare to and from the barrio and sometimes within Dagupan, and various incidentals such as biscuits and soft drinks (see table 28).

Because her total expenses are slightly less than her salary, she is able to buy small gifts for family members and others. One week she spent ₱5 on candies for relatives at home; another week she contributed ₱3 for a birthday cake for her employer; on still another occasion she bought a pair of sandals for ₱35 for her younger sister. Like Marie, much of Flor's gift giving occurred at Christmas, when she received her bonus from Dagupan Trading. Of the ₱720 she received, she spent ₱382 on Christmas gifts, mainly for close relatives and godchildren (see table 29).

TABLE 28.   Flor's Regular Expenses

Expenses	Average weekly	Monthly
In Dagupan		
Food and cooking expenses	₱10.50	₱42
Biscuits, soft drinks, etc.	7	28
Toiletries	6	24
Transport	4.50	18
Rent		25
Subtotal		137
In Barrio		
To parents	30	120
To younger sisters (sometimes)	2	8
Subtotal		₱128
Total		₱265

Note: Expenses are based on records kept over a six-week period. There is considerable variation from week to week, e.g., expenditures on toiletries ranged from nothing to ₱17.

The only gifts she received were from her employers, a boyfriend, and a fellow employee, the last as part of a gift exchange among employees organized by the store. Of the money remaining from her bonus, she spent ₱160 on a dresser for herself, to use at her family's home in Agui-

TABLE 29.   Flor's Christmas Gifts

To	Item and Value		Money	Total Cost
Mother	cloth for dress	₱18.50	₱60	₱78.50
Father	cloth	22	20	42
Sister	watch	80		80
Sister	sandals	15	10	25
Sister	wallet	5.85	5	10.85
Brother	cloth	15	5	20
Sister-in-law	wallet	5.85	5	10.85
Brother's children (4)			2 each	8
Sister's children (4)			2 each	8
Niece living at barrio house	dress			8.50
Godchildren (3)	towel	10 each		30
	dress	8 each		24
			5 each	15
Co-workers (4)	handkerchief	2.85 each		11.40
Parents of Delia[a]	towel	10		10
Total				₱382.10

Note: Based on interviews with Flor.
[a]Flor visited Delia's home at Christmas.

lar; she also bought some clothing for herself. After Christmas she said that she had only ₱8 left.

Flor's family's income derives primarily from their riceland and secondarily from buying and selling activities in which they occasionally engage. Her contribution of ₱30 a week is an important source of cash, especially during the months when their rice has been consumed (see table 30). On the land owned by Flor's father, he must pay his own expenses. One result of this is that he doesn't always use fertilizer and

TABLE 30. Flor's Family; Estimated Income, 1978–79

Source	Production	Use
Land		

Owned by Flor's father
  (2 crops rice)
	(1) 40–45 cavans palay
	(2) 27 cavans palay
	Total about 70 cavans
	  palay
		For consumption
		
		Will provide rice for family. Will need to buy rice Aug. & Sept. only

Vegetables and fruits		For own consumption

Tenanted land (2 crops
  rice)
	(1) 65 cavans (is usually more, 85–90 cavans)
	  − 50% to landlord
	  = 32.5 cavans palay
	(2) 55 cavans
	  − 50% to landlord
	  = 27.5 cavans palay
	
	Total about 60 cavans
	  = 2640 kilos palay if sells at ₱1.15/kilo
	  = ₱3,036 possible income
		Sells when necessary at ₱1.15/kilo

	Amount
Selling	
1. piglets: sell 10 at ₱150 each	₱1,500
2. bananas: sell once a month, Mangaterem market make about ₱3 a day	36
3. *bagaong:* buy a can at Lingayen and sell to neighbors during month	?
Contribution from Flor ₱30/week	
× 52	₱1,560
Total cash income	est. ₱6,132

Note: Based on interviews with Flor's parents.

thus is unable to produce as much as on the tenanted land. In 1978 and 1979, for example, he did not use fertilizer on the first crop but did on the second, spending ₱195 for three bags of fertilizer. His other expenses include insecticide and hiring labor to help with planting. On the land where he is tenant, the landowner buys the fertilizer and insecticide, but Flor's father hires any labor that is necessary. He plants "variety" (improved) rice both on his own land and on the tenanted land. Flor's father says that he has always had a fifty-fifty sharing relationship with his landlord: "The people who own the land are very good, so we have to divide it in half. I prefer sharing to leasing because the owner pays the expenses. But of course I prefer to own my own land." In addition to the expenses associated with planting rice, there are expenses for harvesting and milling. When Flor's father hires people to help with planting and harvesting he pays ₱3.50 a day for about three days work to between six and twelve people. But because of his *kakaluma* arrangement with the landless workers, he does not have to hire as much labor as he would otherwise. After the rice is harvested, he stores it under his house until it

TABLE 31.   Flor's Family; Regular Expenses in the Barrio

Expenses	Monthly	Yearly
1. Household[a]	₱168	
Meat ₱14/week		
Chicken ₱9/month		
Bagnus (fish ₱14/week)		
Vegetables ₱5/week		
(Rice in Aug. & Sept. only)		
Cooking ingredients ₱5.50/week	22	
Soap ₱3.50/week	14	
Electricity	5.50	
2. Feed for pig	60	
3. School		
Fare for 2 daughters ₱10/week	40	
Tuition for 2 daughters		200
Uniforms for 2 daughters		200
4. Clothing		250
	₱309.50/month × 12 = est. ₱3,700/year	650/year
Total		est. ₱4,350/year

Note: Based on information provided in interview with Flor's mother.

[a]Some is given to Flor.

is needed. Then he takes it to the rice mill, where he pays ₱6 per cavan for milling. Because of the considerable variation in his expenses, depending on whether or not he uses fertilizer and insecticide and how much labor he hires, it is difficult to estimate Flor's father's overall farming expenses.

While Flor's father keeps track of his farming expenses, her mother handles the household expenses, which include food, clothing, and school fees; feed for the pig is also considered part of regular household expenses. Since they do not have to buy rice during most of the year, they can buy more meat and fish (see table 31). Like Marie's mother, Flor's mother can borrow from a small neighborhood store when necessary; in fact, she can even borrow money there to use to buy something elsewhere. She repays what she borrows after Flor comes home with her salary.

With the contribution of income from their rice land and from Flor's regular contributions, her family does not need to turn to her for unusual or emergency expenses. For example, in 1978 they were able to pay ₱350 to install wiring for electricity in their house. During the same year they spent ₱300 for the baptism of their granddaughter and another ₱350 for other unusual expenses, such as medical fees and the Christmas and fiesta celebrations (see table 32).

Flor's parents refer to their rice land as their only source of income, but

TABLE 32.   Flor's Family; Special Expenses

Expenses	Amount
Prior to 1978	
For special occasions including weddings of 1 son and 2 daughters (amount unstated)	
For funeral of daughter	₱1,500
1978	
Baptism of granddaughter	300
Christmas	150
Fiesta	150
Medical	50
Installation of wiring	350
First Half of 1979	
Daughter's high school graduation	50
Medical	60

Note: Information provided in interview with Flor's mother.

then add that Flor is "helping." Her contribution is in fact very important but not absolutely essential to the maintenance of the barrio household.

Delia

"At home, I am called Daling but here at work in Dagupan they call me Delia. I've been living in Dagupan for almost ten years now; I'm ready to go back to Anda. My mother wants me to come back by June. She wants me to teach there. At the barrio fiesta last week, the principal of the high school in the next barrio spoke to me and said there might be a job as a home economics teacher there. I still have to take the board exam for teaching first. If I go back, I'll be able to make more money there. If you're not buying rice and are single, you can make money. Also, I get bored in the city."[4]

Born in Anda, an island in the Lingayen Gulf, in 1953, Delia has been living in Dagupan since 1971, first as a student and then since 1975 as an employee at Dagupan Trading. She attended a private Methodist high school in Anda, and after graduation, went to Manila, where she lived with a cousin of her mother. She planned to stay in Manila and wanted to work there, but her relative would not allow her to go to someone else's house to work; instead she paid Delia ₱30 a month for her to help out at her own house. After seven months, Delia says, she "felt bored in Manila," so she left and returned to Anda. At the beginning of the next semester, she came to Dagupan to enroll as a student at the University of Pangasinan. She remained a student until April, 1975, when she received a B.S. degree in Home Economics. She then returned to Anda, staying there for six months while looking for a job. Eventually, she was hired as a census worker, but at about the same time a friend from her boarding house in Dagupan told her about the job at Dagupan Trading. She began work there in November, 1975.

During all the time that she has lived in Dagupan, Delia has stayed at a boarding house run by her sister's mother-in-law. She had been visiting there since she was in elementary school, and when she first moved in, one of her older sisters was also living there. All the boarders are either from Anda or from San Carlos; they include Delia's younger sister, two of her cousins, and a friend from Anda, as well as a boy from San Carlos who works at Dagupan Trading and his sister, brother, and cousin. With the exception of Delia and the other employee at Dagupan Trading, all are students. The house is located a short walk from the University of Pangasinan, on marshy land that must be crossed on narrow boards during the rainy season. Large and comfortable, with sizable rooms shared by two boarders, the house contains many modern appliances obtained through the landlady's son-in-law who is in the United States Navy. Delia shares cooking with her sister, cousin, and the landlady; she and the other boarders can use both the kitchen and the sitting room. All the boarders except Delia pay ₱25 a month in rent; the landlady likes to have Delia there "as a companion" especially when the students are away on vacation, and does not charge her anything.

Like Marie and Flor, Delia follows a regular routine during the work week. She gets up early in the morning, cooks and eats breakfast, takes a jeepney or walks to Dagupan Trading, and begins work by 8:30. Somewhat less outgoing and more serious than Marie and Flor, her work station is located further inside the store, where she is responsible for selling religious articles and for helping to arrange them on the counters and on the walls behind her. At lunchtime, she usually goes back to her boarding house, visiting with fellow boarders or with neighbors, and then returning to work. Although the store closes at 5:30, Delia and the others usually work until 6:30 or 7:00, arranging new displays, checking receipts, and so on. After work, she sometimes accompanies a co-worker to the market. More frequently, she returns immediately to her boarding house, eats dinner, and then relaxes—reading magazines, chatting with other boarders, visiting the home of a neighbor to watch television. The boarders are a close-knit group and spend much of their spare time together. One of the boys has a guitar that he plays while the others sing. On three evenings in November, Delia recorded the following:

> November 25, 1978: "Saw my best friend outside Dagupan Trading. Have chat for a few minutes and then went home with my cousins Lisa and Jesus. Upon arriving home, I ate with my eldest sister [visiting from Anda] and after eating I manicured my nails with my roommates. I went to sleep late."
>
> November 26: "After cooking, I went to the neighbor's house with my landlady, my sister, and my fellow boarders. We watched Superstar show on their television for almost two hours. Then went back home at about 8:00, so I ate my supper late. After eating, we chat a little with my landlady, then I slept."

November 27: "I rode going home. Upon arriving I rest a little, then ate. After eating, we enjoyed singing with my fellow boarders for almost an hour, then I sleep."

Delia regularly sees other friends in Dagupan as well. Her co-worker Flor is one of her closest friends, and she feels she can confide in her. Several distant relatives and a number of friends from Anda live in the city; she usually sees them by chance, on the street or when they shop at Dagupan Trading.

In addition, she has friends and relatives in other towns, whom she visits and who visit her. They include her married sister and her father's cousin in Binmaley, a former co-worker in Lingayen, and most important, her family in Anda. On weekends and sometimes during the week she may visit Binmaley, staying overnight with her older sister or returning the same day. Sometimes there is a special occasion, such as a cousin's wedding or the barrio fiesta, and then a few co-workers like Flor or Marie accompany her. More often, she just goes to see her sister and nephews. During the month of January, for example, she visited Binmaley five times, and friends from there visited her in Dagupan once. When she goes, she usually brings bread to her sister's family; since her brother-in-law is a fisherman she sometimes returns with fish he has caught.

One of her co-workers lives near the beach in Lingayen; Delia and others sometimes visit her on Sunday afternoons, especially in the hot months between February and May. She has visited Flor's home in Aguilar once or twice, and the homes of several other co-workers as well.

Family and friends often come to Dagupan to see Delia. Her mother visits about once a month, after stopping in Binmaley to visit her sister. On Saturdays, Delia's oldest sister travels from Anda to Lingayen early in the morning to attend classes at a college there. Afterwards, she comes to Dagupan to visit Delia and the others in the boarding house, staying the night and returning to Anda the following day. Cousins and friends also visit; Delia receives visitors from Anda two or three times a month. Some of these visitors come just for the day and return to Anda immediately; they say that they don't like to sleep overnight in Dagupan because it's too hot.

On the other hand, Delia's visits to Anda are relatively rare, and mainly for special occasions. Because of the distance and the time it takes to get there, Delia does not go home every week like Flor and Marie do.

Instead, between October, 1978, and March, 1979, she visited five times—for All Saints' Day, at Christmas, at New Year's Day, in late January for a baptism at which she was a *ninang* (godparent), and for the barrio fiesta in early March. On each occasion, she stayed at least one night and saw a number of different relatives and friends, not just her own immediate family.

The Barrio

Delia's family lives on Anda, an island off the northwest coast of Pangasinan. Her family's home is in a barrio about four kilometers from the *poblacion*, located on top of a small hill so that it catches the breeze. To get there from Dagupan, one travels for two hours by minibus to the narrowest spot between the mainland and the island. From there, a landing barge operated by the Philippine Navy carries vehicles (maximum, three at a time) and people to the other side. If the landing barge breaks down, as it frequently does, motor boats take passengers across. Once on the other side, the minibus continues on the dirt roads around the island, stopping at Delia's barrio. If the bus is not running, or if someone from the barrio wants to go only as far as the *poblacion*, the only transportation is by *calesa* (horse–drawn cart) or on foot. To reach other barrios on the island, one walks on dirt roads and trails. The usual round-trip fare from Dagupan to Anda is ₱10. But once, when the landing barge was broken, Delia and a friend had to pay ₱28.50 to rent a motor boat, and then she still had to walk eight kilometers at night from the place where the boat left her.

Although fishing is a major occupation on Anda, the water is not visible from Delia's family home. All that can be seen is dry, brownish-green land, with some trees in the distance. Most people living there are both farmers and fishermen, and many own their own land; but the land is dry and not irrigated, and produces only one rice crop a year.

Delia's parents live in a house belonging to her older sister and her husband; the land belongs to her parents. Her brother-in-law had the house in Dagupan and moved it to Anda after his marriage. A wooden house, it rests on stilts high off the ground. Underneath is a storage area for rice and a place for chickens to roost. The front stairs lead to an open veranda, where Delia's ninety-two-year-old grandfather likes to sit to watch people go by on the road. Inside, the sitting room is long and narrow; two chairs and a bookcase comprise the furniture. The walls are decorated with a current calendar, a painting of Christ, and several paintings of Filipino scenes. A battery-operated record player and a radio sit on a shelf. The two bedrooms are located off the sitting room; one is large enough for a single bed and a large case for storing clothes. The other only has a bed. The walls are decorated with school awards belonging to Delia's sister's children. Beyond the sitting room, the dining area contains a wooden table and bench. The kitchen, with space for two wood fires and a wooden counter where a jug of water is stored, leads to the back door of the house. Outside the back door, an open porch is used for preparing food and washing up. Some yards behind the house is a water-sealed toilet and a shed for pigs. To obtain water, the family goes across a field to a well, about five minutes' walk from the house. In the dry season, the well often dries up, and they must go to a nearby barrio to get water.

When Delia goes home, she is usually still wearing her city clothes—either her Dagupan Trading uniform or a blouse and well-tailored slacks and high-heeled shoes. As soon as she reaches her house (or earlier if she has to walk) she takes off her shoes and rolls up her slacks to the knees. Later, she changes into old slacks or shorts and a T-shirt. She immediately begins to help with chores around the house: carrying water from the well, washing dishes, preparing and cooking food.

At home, Delia speaks a different language from that which she speaks most frequently in Dagupan. On Anda, most people speak Bolinao, a language spoken only in Anda and in the town of Bolinao. This is the major language used by her parents and other relatives at home, although they also speak Ilocano. In contrast, in Dagupan, Delia mainly speaks Pangasinan, with some Ilocano, Tagalog, and English. At her boarding house, however, Bolinao is frequently used as well. Delia is used to switching from one language to another and sees nothing strange or difficult about the situation.

Since Delia visits home only occasionally, she spends most of her time when there seeing friends and relatives. Since most of her visits are made for special occasions, there are many parties and much eating.

"At New Years, I went home to Anda on December 31. I arrived about 3:00 P.M. and had lunch. Then I went with my sister and cousins to the Asbury [school] Children's Project Prom and saw plenty of friends so we stayed longer. Had a snack in the house of the co-teacher of my sister. In the evening, we attended a benefit dance with my sister, cousins, nieces, and friends. We stayed there until 11:00 P.M. and upon arriving home it was already midnight so we celebrated the New Year at once by setting off firecrackers.

"The next day I woke up late. Around 9:00 A.M. I went with my sister, nieces, and nephews to gather *buri* leaves—it is my mother's business. Along our way we met some friends so we chatted with them a little and then went home for lunch. I rested for about two hours and then around 3:00 we went to Lisa [cousin's] house and made cakes. We saw some friends again and then went home around 5:00 to prepare our supper. After supper we got a party together again at Lisa's house, we stayed there about an hour and then went home and visited with the family."

Several weeks later, Delia again went home, for the baptism of the child of a close friend. The child's father is one of the bus drivers on the Dagupan-Anda route.

"My friends asked me to be a *ninang*. There were three pairs of godparents; we are all friends. Before I left Dagupan I bought a dress for the child for ten pesos in cash and made a five-peso donation to the chapel. I left work early on Friday but arrived in Anda late because the landing barge was broken. On Saturday morning I went with my cousin to the barrio where the baptism was. It took place at 10:00 A.M. Then there was picture taking in the church afterwards. Then we went to my *compare* and *comare's* [the parents of the child] house for lunch. After lunch, my cousin and I and some friends went home. Then I went to my cousin Jesus' house to give his letter to his mother and father. After about two hours, I went to get vegetables with my sisters, cousins, nieces, and nephews. In the evening, the family talked together until we slept. Very early the next morning, I took the bus to Dagupan. When I got to Dagupan, I saw my cousin Jesus and went with him back to the bus station so he could send something to his family."

In March, the barrio fiesta again provided an occasion for a visit home. On Friday evening, after eating, Delia went with several cousins and other relatives to the barrio auditorium—an open cement platform across from the school—to attend a dance. Delia's sister was one of those in charge of the event. Delia stayed until about midnight; some of her cousins stayed even later. The next morning she went to the vegetable plot near her parents' old house to pick vegetables, many of which she brought back to Dagupan. Late in the morning, the children at the elementary school presented a performance of exercises and dances; Delia met friends there and visited with them on the way home. At home, her father had butchered and was cooking a goat; he and other male relatives spent the afternoon drinking *nipa* wine and eating the food he cooked.

Delia's sister from Binmaley and her husband and children arrived in the afternoon. Her brother-in-law also came for the weekend, so by Saturday night, the entire family was at home. On Saturday evening Delia visited relatives in another part of the barrio. Her father's brother and her grandmother live in a large bamboo house near that of her mother's brother. "If I visit one I must visit the other, or they will get mad." The weekend was to culminate with another dance on Saturday night and the coronation of the barrio queen but there had been a fight and a stabbing late on Friday night, so Delia did not attend Saturday's dance.

When Delia cannot get home, she sends messages and requests through the bus drivers; for example, if she needs rice, she writes a letter to her parents and the bus driver delivers it for her. Her parents send rice and vegetables back to her this way. The drivers do not charge for this service: "They are our friends, and they are also from Anda."

The Family

Of the four daughters in Delia's family, only her oldest sister lives in Anda. She is a schoolteacher at the barrio elementary school. She and her six children share the house with her parents and grandfather. In the past, her parents lived in their own house, about a ten-minute walk away, but the house needed to be repaired, so the two households decided to combine and share expenses and caring for the children. The second-oldest daughter lives in Binmaley where her husband is a fisherman, while the youngest attends the University of Pangasinan in Dagupan, and lives in the boarding house with Delia (see fig. 7).

Delia's grandfather is ninety-two years old; formerly a farmer, he now spends most of his days in the house. He weaves baskets that are sold in the Anda market. "I was born in Spanish times. There was a Spanish priest in Anda from Manaoag, and my mother was from Vigan [in Ilocos North]. But I was born on Anda. Most of the people here then were strangers; there weren't many people here. There was no market here then; we went to Alaminos for the market. To go to Manila was like going to the U.S. now; I have never been to Manila. My parents were tenants, on land owned by a man from Bolinao. But I bought land, I had about ten hectares which I divided among my sons and daughter when they settled down."

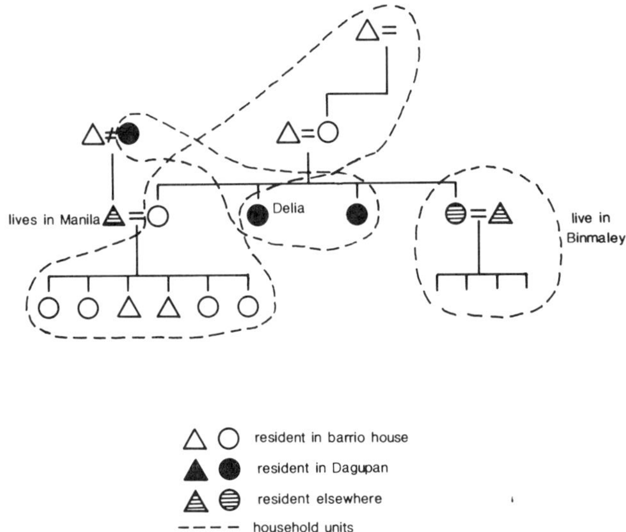

Fig. 7. Delia; kinship and residence of family members

Delia's mother is his daughter. Now in her fifties, she was born on Anda, in the same barrio where she now lives. She had about one year of schooling, during which she learned to read and write. She buys and sells *buri* leaves and sticks for brooms. *Buri* (a reed-like grass) is grown by people on Anda. Delia's mother buys the leaves, then dries them at her house, and sells them by the hundred at the Lingayen and Anda markets. The leaves are cut to uniform size and are then used for weaving mats. When their vegetables are in season on the farm, she also takes some of them to sell in the market.

Delia's father was born in the same barrio as her mother. Born in 1920, he attended school in Anda for five years. "If you wanted to go to high school you had to go to Lingayen. Only a few could afford it. It was hard to get money before, not like now. Transportation was hard. There was no money for clothes or shoes. In the rainy season it was very hard to get around. When I was young, there were no roads and no *calesas* (horse-drawn carts). You walked everywhere. There was no market. If you wanted to go to a market, you had to go to Alaminos. The only way to get there was by sailboat.

"The first time I went to Dagupan was when I was eight years old. I went with my uncle, by sailboat. The trip took two days."

For most of his life, Delia's father has been both a farmer and a fisherman. "My father taught me about farming; I was the oldest son, so I helped him. I started fishing with my uncle, when I was fifteen years old. There were plenty of fish then." When he was eighteen, he began to go to Zambales to work in the mines. "After the farming season was over, I went to Zambales. Then when the rice was ready I came back to harvest it, then went back to the mines until the next planting. I earned seventy-five centavos a day." He did this for three or four years, until just before the start of World War II. At that time, he was called for training in the armed forces, and went on active duty. He spent six months in prison after the Japanese came into power, and then was released and allowed to return to Anda, where he spent the rest of the war years. He got married during this time. After the liberation, he was called into active duty again, and spent three years in the army in Manila.

When he finally returned to Anda in 1949, he began farming and fishing again. "I was planting rice in the daytime and fishing at night. I went out fishing every night with a companion. We sent the fish to Alaminos; someone there bought it. We could catch five hundred to six hundred fish in one night, and they were paying twenty-five centavos per fish. So I could let my children study in college.

"When my oldest daughter was in college, I was fishing and also farming. I had five or six hectares and I was producing more rice than I am now. I had five or six cows and two or three *carabao* [water buffalo]. Now I have three cows and one *carabao*. I stoppped fishing about ten years ago because my eyesight got bad. I sold some land to help pay for my children's college expenses. Now I am farming more than one hectare of rice. In the last harvest I produced thirty cavans of milled rice. Sometimes I plant 'variety' rice and sometimes I plant local rice. I am working alone, but I hire four or five people for planting and the harvest. I pay them with rice. Sometimes I exchange labor with other farmers. I'm also planting beans, squash, and okra, on about one-half hectare. It's hard to plant because there's no water. We have some hens, pigs, and goats. And we sell the fruit from the four mango trees that grow near our old house."

Delia's oldest sister was born in 1945. She attended elementary and high school in Anda and then went to Dagupan to attend the University of Pangasinan. She boarded at the home of her future mother-in-law. After her second year in college, she stopped attending, got married, and had two children. Then she went back to school, and got a degree in education. She got a teaching job on Anda, in another barrio. By that time, her third child had been born. The barrio was too far from her parents' home to commute daily. Instead, "my husband and I boarded near the school, and we went to my parents' house on weekends. Our two older children stayed with my parents, and my husband took care of the boy during the day."

Later, she got a job at the barrio school in her parents' barrio and she and her husband and children moved there. Her husband, who has not finished high school, tried his hand at farming: he planted rice and vegetables, and they had pigs and chickens. But, he grew up in Dagupan and had never farmed before. "Farming is hard work and he's not used to it," his wife says. "He has weak lungs; it was hard for him to carry water. He was only growing enough rice for about six months of our needs." Therefore, in 1976 he found work in Manila, assembling fans at a Hitachi factory. A brother-in-law working at the same factory helped him find the job, and he lives with his sister and brother-in-law. He gets to Anda about once a month; "at busy times of year, we work Saturdays and Sundays. It's hard to get a pass to get time off." His wife explains that it was very difficult when he began to work in Manila. "He was doing all the work at home, so we missed him very much. He didn't like being away. In the first six months he talked about coming back to Anda. He missed the children. But now he can help with our expenses; he buys all the clothes for the children. Sometimes I go to Manila to see him but I don't like it there. The longest I've stayed there is one week; it was very hot. It was difficult for me to adjust to his working in Manila."

Income and Expenses of Delia and Her Family

In the city, Delia supports not only herself but also her younger sister who is studying at the University of Pangasinan. Sometimes she complains about not having money for herself, but she comments that "if your parents have put you through school, then it's more or less an obligation to help out others in the family, especially since I don't have a family of my own yet."

Delia's regular expenses in Dagupan include buying food for herself, her sister, and her cousin (who also lives at the boarding house), transport costs to and from work, and other incidental expenses. She also pays her sister's rent, tuition, and other school expenses. At the same time, she receives rice from home on a regular basis, and occasionally fruit and vegetables as well. Sometimes her sister and brother-in-law in Binmaley give her fish. Overall, Delia averages about ₱30 a week on regular expenses, but frequently her weekly salary is not enough to cover all her other expenses. As a result, she often borrows ₱10 or ₱20 from her landlady or from one of her co-workers and then returns the money one or two weeks later. Table 33 shows Delia's average regular expenses over a twelve-week period in late 1978 and early 1979. Table 34 indicates some of her additional expenses during the same time period.

As table 34 indicates, Delia contributes in various ways to the family at home, although not on a regular basis. Whenever she goes home, she takes groceries with her. At Christmas, she brought about ₱40 worth of canned and packaged goods, and did the same at New Year's. In addition to a variety of Christmas gifts to family members (see table 35), she gave ₱100 to her mother so she could buy piglets. She had planned to save that money, but gave it to her mother when she indicated that she wanted to buy piglets. She did, however, have money left to spend on herself at Christmas, buying a watch and some clothes. Like Marie and Flor, she received few gifts in return.

Overall, the sources of income for the family in Anda are diverse. They include: the rice produced by Delia's father, all of which is used for their own consumption; the vegetables and fruits they raise, some of which they consume and some of which they sell; the *buri* leaves Delia's mother sells; the small amount from her grandfather's sale of baskets; her sister's salary from teaching; and her brother-in-law's salary. However, although her parents and her sister's family have combined their households, the brother-in-law's wages are used only for the expenses of his wife and children and not for the household as a whole. His monthly contribution of less than ₱200 goes for clothing and school expenses of

TABLE 33. Delia's Regular Expenses over a Twelve-Week Period, 1978–79

	Total 12 Weeks	Low Week	High Week	Average Per Week
Food	₱246	₱6.25	₱34.25	₱20[a]
Transport	102	4.50	14.30	8.40[b]
Toiletries	24	0	5	2

Note: Based on daily records kept by Delia.

[a]This includes goods such as bread brought to her sister's family in Binmaley; it does not include food brought to Anda (see table 13).

[b]This includes transport within Dagupan—mainly jeepney fares to and from work—and transport to her sister's in Binmaley, but not fares to Anda.

TABLE 34. Delia's Other Expenses

Expenses	Amount
Payments for sister	
Tuition, University of Pangasinan	₱300/semester[a]
Rent	25/month
Books	18 during 12 weeks
Allowance	5–10 every few weeks
Clothing when needed	13 during 12 weeks
Other personal expenses during 12-week period	
Medicine and doctor	37
Clothing	85
New uniform	18
Gifts during 12-week period	
Wedding	5
Birthday	3.50
Wedding	17.50
To godchildren at baptism	15
To parents and for travel to Anda during 12-week period	
To mother for piglets	100
Groceries brought to Anda	40+
Transport to Anda	48
To mother	10

Note: Based on daily records for a twelve-week period and on interviews with Delia.

[a]Tuition paid in ₱50 installments.

TABLE 35. Delia's Christmas Gifts

To	Item and Value		Money	Total Cost
Father	T-shirt	₱10		₱10
Mother	slippers	8	₱100[a]	108
Sister	pants	60		66.50
	underwear	6.50		
Grandfather	T-shirt	10	5	15
Sister in Binmaley and her family			30	30
Nieces, nephews in Anda			30	30
Cousin	blouse	15		15
Cousin			10	10
Godchild			5	5
Co-worker (exchange gift)	T-shirt	16		16
Friend	handkerchiefs	10.50		10.50
Total				₱316

Note: Based on interviews with Delia.

[a]Used to buy piglets.

the children. Her salary, on the other hand, helps support her parents and grandfather as well as her children.

Delia's father's rice production lasts the family for about eight months of the year; from May to September they must buy rice. Delia's sister describes that period as a "crisis time" and says that sometimes she must take out a loan then. Although Delia's sister's gross salary is ₱574 a month, she actually receives only about ₱340, since she has deductions for insurance and for previous loans. Her mother averages about ₱40 a week from her sales, and occasionally they sell goats, pigs, or chickens.

Delia's sister estimates that the family in Anda spends about ₱90 a week on its regular expenses—food, toiletries, etc. Her children's school expenses are relatively low; the oldest receives free tuition and only has to pay a ₱20 fee, while the other child in high school pays ₱105 tuition. The elementary school children occasionally have to make contributions, amounting to about ₱20 per year per child.

During four weeks in March and April 1979, Delia's sister kept records of the family's income and expenses. Their weekly expenses ranged from ₱90 to ₱115, and went for items such as food, medicine, school allowances, rice milling, and occasional purchase of clothing. During the same period, their income came from her salary and sales of vegetables, mangoes, and hens. When necessary, she bought groceries on credit at a local store and paid this back after receiving her salary (see table 36). As

TABLE 36.   Delia's Family; Income and Expenses During a Four-Week Period, 1979

Income			Expenses		
Source		Amount	Regular[a]	Other[b]	Credit
Week 1	Sale of vegetables	₱50	₱79	₱30	
	Sale of hens	23			
		Total 73	Total 109		
Week 2	No income recorded		44.60	46	
			Total 90.60		
Week 3	Sale of mangoes	50	60.80	55	Groceries (worth ₱20)
			Total 115.80		
Week 4	Sister's salary	340	55.30	37	
			Total 92.30		
	Total Income	₱463	Total Expenses ₱407.30		

Note: Based on records kept by Delia's sister.
[a]Regular expenses include food, toiletries, school fare and allowance.
[b]Other expenses include clothing, uniforms, rice milling.

table 36 indicates, the family's total income in this particular time period was slightly more than their total expenses. At other times of the year, when there are no vegetables or mangoes to be sold, it may well be less.

Discussion

Within the overall context of Dagupan City's labor force, the three young women discussed in this chapter are working in jobs that are relatively well-paid, in a company covered by government regulations. As we have seen, there is essentially no industry in Dagupan. Therefore service sector jobs comprise most of the employment in the city. Flor, Marie, and Delia are working in the service sector, but unlike many others in that sector, they are paid regular wages and receive a variety of government-mandated benefits. In a relative sense, then, they may be seen as being part of a wage-labor formal sector "elite" in the city. On the other hand, they work long hours, are expected to work additional hours when necessary, and are expected to participate in nonwork activities organized by the store's manager (birthday parties, Christmas caroling, etc.). These are characteristics more generally associated with informal sector employment than with formal sector jobs.

As is typical of workers in third world cities, all three women have relied on their personal ties and networks in finding employment. In Flor's case, in fact, one gets no sense of a "job search" but rather of happenstance and a degree of luck; her uncle learned of the job through his friend, the store manager, and she got it. Personal ties seem to have been less important for Marie in finding her Dagupan Trading job, but they were essential for her initial entrance into employment in Dagupan. Similarly, all three have used personal connections to find places to live in Dagupan. As would be expected, co-workers, relatives, and fellow townspeople played major roles in this search. However, only Delia lives in what might appear to be a small ethnic enclave, surrounded by others who are mostly from the same town as she and who speak the same first language. Even in her case, she is certainly not restricted to interaction with others from Anda, and language poses no particular barrier. In fact, several of the residents of the boarding house who are not from Anda are now able to speak some Bolinao.[5]

The reliance on personal networks for finding jobs and places to live is only one aspect of the broad importance of personal ties for all three women. Within the city, each has a set of people with whom they interact regularly and whom they may rely on when necessary. These include co-workers, including the store manager and his wife; fellow boarders, as well as landladies, in the places they live in; relatives living in Dagupan; and other friends, both from their hometowns and from other places. Although they have relatively little spare time, what time they do have is mainly spent visiting with others.

Beyond their urban ties, all three have extensive contact with family and relatives at home. Although they differ in the extent to which they visit their home barrios, all see relatives on a regular basis. Whereas both Marie and Flor go home every weekend, Delia goes home only for special occasions. On the other hand, Delia receives many more visits from both immediate family and more distant relatives than do either Marie or Flor. Furthermore, she visits her older sister and her family in Binmaley nearly as often as Flor and Marie visit their parents.

It is clear, then, that all three are tied into extensive personal networks, involving others both in the city and elsewhere, which have helped to determine, and continue to play a part in, the activities in which Marie, Flor, and Delia are involved. There are some important distinctions to be made among them, however, in terms of their relationships with family members at home, and particularly in terms of the extent to which the family in the barrio is dependent on the daughter working in the city.

Marie's family is dependent on her for basic subsistence; her monetary contribution, together with that of her brother, pays for food for the rest of the family. In contrast, Flor's income does not appear to be essential to her family, although they do use it to pay for some of the food they buy. Income from the rice they produce provides most of the money needed, both for necessities and for other expenses. Flor's income, in other words, enables the family to live at a somewhat better level than they might otherwise be doing, and they are less subject to the seasonal vagaries of the rice harvest. Delia's contribution is different still: she is helping the family to continue to invest in the education of their daughters, by paying the college tuition of her younger sister. In addition, she has directly contributed to productive investment on the farm, by buying piglets for her mother.

The different contributions made by the three women rest in large degree on the different situations of the families. All of the fathers are rice farmers. However, Marie's father has little land and produces a single small crop each year, whereas Flor's father farms on irrigated rice land where he can produce two sizable crops each year. As a share tenant, he

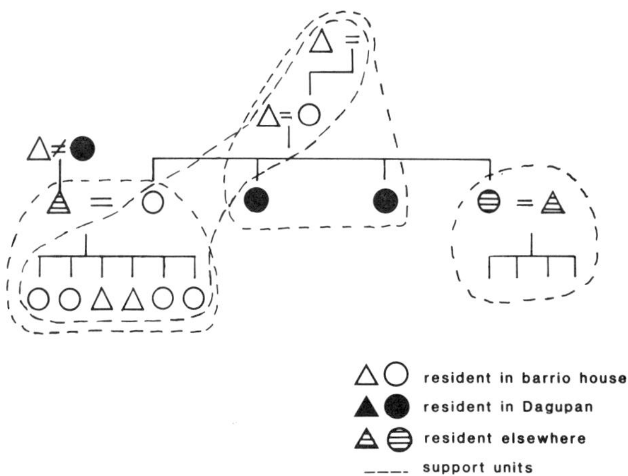

Fig. 8. Delia's family; support networks

does not pay for productive inputs on the land he tenants; as an owner of some land, he has a crop that may be used completely for his family's consumption. Delia's father, likewise, owns his own land and produces enough rice for most of the consumption needs of his family. One result is that both Delia's and Flor's fathers are able to send rice and other produce to their daughters in Dagupan, whereas Marie's father is not.

Delia's family's situation is the most complex of the three considered here. It is not a case of a simple nuclear family with one member working in the city. Rather, they have formed an extended family unit with a variety of income sources. Delia's family has, in effect, three residences with shared maintenance among them: Delia and her sister in Dagupan; her parents, grandfather, sister and children in Anda; and her brother-in-law in Manila (see fig. 8). Her father provides rice for the Dagupan and Anda households; the brother-in-law pays his own expenses in Manila and also helps to provide for his wife and children in Anda; Delia's sister's salary in Anda pays expenses both for her parents and grandfather and for her children; and Delia provides for her sister in Dagupan while contributing occasionally to the Anda household.

It becomes impossible to understand such mutual support and maintenance simply by examining economic ties between the sets. Rather, the economic support is embedded in the network of personal and emotional ties that link the family members. The same is true of Flor's and Marie's support for their families, although in their cases one sees less complex arrangements. In fact, Marie's family has recently moved from greater to less complexity, switching from sharing food and maintenance within the extended family that lives together to a "separation of the pots" into three separate household units.

In examining the family units as wholes, we become aware of the diversity of income sources that help to maintain rural households. Again, Delia's family is most complex, with members in all economic sectors. In the rural area, her father farms, her mother engages in buying and selling, and her grandfather weaves baskets—all typical occupations for rural households. At the same time, her older sister is a schoolteacher, one of the few rural professionals (and one of the few professional activities possible in rural areas). Delia works in the urban service sector; her brother-in-law is an industrial worker in Manila. In addition, her sister and brother-in-law in Binmaley, while forming a separate unit from the others, depend on fishing for their livelihood.

In the cases of Flor and Marie, there are several different sources of income as well. Both fathers are farmers; both mothers engage in buying and selling although Marie's mother does relatively little. In the past she contributed income as a seamstress. Marie's brother works in a store in Dagupan, as she does. Flor's brother, on the other hand, is a rice farmer like her father, as is her brother-in-law.

In addition to diversity of income sources at one time, we find flexibility in families and individuals and changes in their activities and arrangements over time. This is particularly evident in Delia's case. She herself first worked in Manila and then tried to find a job on Anda before going to work in Dagupan. Her brother-in-law tried to farm, and only when that proved unsuccessful did he find a job in Manila. The current household arrangement reflects flexibility as well: when the son-in-law went to Manila, the parents moved into their daughter's house and formed a single income- and expense-sharing unit. The present arrangement should not be seen as permanent; if Delia moves back to Anda and is able to help her parents rebuild their old house, they are likely to move back there.

Flexibility is also apparent in Marie's case, particularly in examining her work history. She started off in a poorly paid job, moved into a somewhat better one after only two months, then went to Manila to look for a job, and finally returned to Dagupan and got her present job. When housing was no longer available through her employers, she tried living at home and commuting, but gave that up when it became too difficult.

In discussing the activities of these individuals and families it is easy to give undue emphasis to a contrast between the "urban" members of the family and the "rural" family members. In fact, the women considered here do not make this kind of strong distinction between themselves and others in the family. Granted, they spend most of their time living and working in the city, and despite their own goals for the future, are probably going to continue to do so for some time to come. They are in many respects well adapted to life in the city, enjoying some of the amenities possible there, such as hairdressers, shopping, and so on. Like many urban residents, they express ambivalent feelings about the city, complaining about heat and noise and perhaps romanticizing the peace of the barrio, but at the same time they recognize that they cannot find adequate work elsewhere (except perhaps for Delia who is trained as a teacher). At the same time, there is no doubt that their strongest ties remain with family in the barrio and that they continue to view the barrio as "home." Marie makes this most clear when she says that "Buenlag is my home . . ."

Flor, too, seems to see her time in Dagupan as a sojourn, an interlude before marriage and settling in the barrio like her parents. Even now, the only organization she belongs to is one in the barrio and many of her friends are from her hometown.

As urban migrants, Marie, Flor, and Delia move easily between city and barrio, both literally and figuratively. That is, as we have seen in great detail, they move back and forth on a regular basis. But more than this, they function in both places equally well. When they are at home, they do not parade about as "urban girls" but rather participate in necessary activities—cooking on a wood fire, drawing water, helping with other tasks, and interacting in appropriate ways, such as visiting the family of a relative who has died or speaking the Bolinao language on Anda. But when they are in Dagupan, they appear like hundreds of other urban workers—dressed in their store uniforms, with makeup and coiffed hair, waiting on customers and again, behaving appropriately for the context and setting. They are not "peasants" who have somehow landed in the city and are confused by it. Rather, they have learned how to use the urban environment—finding jobs, housing and, in general, participating fully in the urban economy. From a cultural perspective, in other words, it is not possible to describe Marie, Flor, or Delia as "rural" or "urban" in dominant orientations. They, like many others, are flexible and adaptive enough to move equally well in both settings and to know how to shift from one to the other.

Chapter 7

Annie and Roberto Santos: Cloth Vendors

The main marketplace in Dagupan, known as the Supermarket, is a low, enclosed area taking up an entire block facing the main street of the city. Inside are hundreds of stalls and shops selling all kinds of goods—foods such as fish, meat, rice, vegetables, and groceries; dry goods such as hardware, shoes, clothing, cloth, and so on. Most of the cloth shops are located in the southeast corner of the market, not far from the side streets where many of the tailoring and dressmaking shops are located. Each of these stalls appears to be much like the others—an open display of a variety of clothing materials, some of which is laid out on a table and the rest of which is hung from wires above the table. Each stall has wooden sides, and large wooden doors that can be put up at night to enclose the shop. Narrow passageways, covered with cement or wood flooring, provide access to the shops.

One of these passageways leads to the shop of Annie and Roberto Santos. Although at first glance their shop looks much like all the others, closer inspection reveals that they have a larger stock and better display than many of the other sellers. Further, they do not have just one or two stalls like other sellers, but instead they are using nine stalls, eight of which are along one passageway, four on each side, and the other a few aisles away. At one stall, they sell only denim materials, at another, cotton and voile for dresses, while still another has mainly corduroys and material for slacks. According to Annie and Roberto, they have the largest cloth shop within the marketplace with stock worth ₱200,000–300,000. However, their shop is still much smaller than cloth stores outside the market, most of which are owned by Filipino Chinese.

Every morning except Sunday, Annie Santos comes to the market before 8:00 A.M.; on Sunday she first attends mass at the cathedral, where she is one of the women who collect contributions. By the time she arrives at the market, the girls who work for her as salesgirls are already putting the cloth out for the day. The cloth has been brought to the market by three boys who work as *cargadors* (carters) for Mrs. Santos. Their job is to load the cloth on pushcarts and push it the four or five muddy and rutted blocks from the Santoses' house to the marketplace. Although her market stall can be closed and locked for the night, she brings home nearly her entire stock of cloth every night. Like most of the dry goods sellers in the market, she has a constant fear of fire. There have been several fires in the commercial center of the city and many rumors that someone is planning to set fire to the marketplace. According to Mrs. Santos, she can insure only ₱5,000 worth of her cloth, nowhere near the total value that she owns. Therefore, every evening Mrs. Santos and her assistants spend more than an hour folding all the cloth and wrapping it in large pieces of plastic, which the cargadors load onto their carts and take to the house, where it is stored overnight; in the morning the process is reversed.

At the market, Mrs. Santos and several salesgirls arrange the cloth to show it to its best advantage. Some especially attractive pieces are hung from the ceiling beams to catch the eye of potential customers. Each of the stalls consists of a long wooden table and a rear wall; the cloth is piled on the table and against the wall. A few feet at the end of one center table are left empty. Here Mrs. Santos will sit throughout most of the day, with her back against the wall and her feet stretched out in front of her. A petite woman with short wavy hair, she oversees her salesgirls and tends to customers herself. Under the low tin roof of the marketplace, she complains of the heat and lack of ventilation in midday, and of the mosquitos and odor emanating from the drainage ditches that run next to the cement floor that forms a passageway between stalls. But she rarely leaves her spot, arguing that if she is not there an important *suki* (regular customer) might come along, and not seeing her, go on to another shop.

The salesgirls spread themselves out among the remaining stalls, calling out "*Saliwen yo?*" ("what would you like to buy?") to passersby. One salesgirl is in charge of the stall around the corner; she sells already cut pieces of the less expensive types of cloth. Each time she makes a sale, she comes to Mrs. Santos's stall to give her the money or to get change.

Usually, Roberto Santos comes to the shop later in the morning and sits at the other end from his wife, conversing and joking with other men who sell in the market, especially the man who owns a small lunch counter at the end of the aisle. Like the salesgirls, he calls out informal greetings to passersby, especially to those whom he knows, encouraging them to stop and visit and possibly, to buy. On many days, he leaves the running of the shop entirely to his wife, while he goes out to the barrio, where he supervises the farming of land that he and his wife have purchased. He and his wife have invested some of their earnings from their cloth business in land in his home barrio, believing that "if your money is invested in a bank, you get small earning. But if your money is invested in land, you earn if you are successful." Relatives, including brothers and cousins, are tenants and hired workers on the land. From the farm, the Santos couple gets most of the rice they consume, as well as some income—how much is difficult to say—from other crops that they plant.

On other days, visitors come from the barrio and Roberto stays at home to entertain them. Mrs. Santos explains that it is better if her husband does the entertaining at home, because she knows more people in the market, and makes more sales than her husband. One day, just before Christmas, a woman walked by Mrs. Santos's shop. After recognizing and greeting each other, they realized that it had been about seven years since they had last seen each other; the woman explained that she and her husband had just returned to Dagupan from Manila to set up a branch of her father's business. Within a few minutes, the woman had bought ₱280 worth of cloth. According to Mrs. Santos, if she had not been in the shop, that woman would not have bought there but would have gone elsewhere.

Annie and Roberto Santos both came to Dagupan about twenty years ago; Roberto came first, as a young man looking for work, while Annie arrived there from her home in the mountain area of Northern Luzon when she married Roberto. They have separate stories, as well as intertwined ones.[1] This chapter relates their separate biographies, and then considers their joint efforts as cloth merchants in Dagupan and as owners of land in Roberto's hometown. Their social networks are complex, and include many people both in the city and in their hometowns. Analysis of these networks helps to demonstrate how individuals who appear to be fully committed to urban residence and institutions can at the same time form and maintain important links with their rural homes. Migrants such as the Santos couple, who have long been residents in Dagupan, help to illustrate long-term strategies that may be followed, and how these may change in the course of a lifetime.

Annie Santos: Early Years

"I was born in Tuplac, a barrio of Kiangan in the Ifugao area of Mountain Province. I don't know exactly the month and the year, but I think it was 1936. My parents were farmers in Tuplac. During World War II my parents entered me into the dormitory of the Belgian sisters[2] so that they would take care of us. I stayed there from grade one through high school. I used to go home to my parents' house on weekends to get food because we provided our own food. When I was in high school sometimes I worked in the big groceries in town to earn money. I wanted to earn money so that I could help my parents in paying my tuition and to buy anything that I want. That's the way I learned how to become a business.

"I was the youngest in the family. We were six, four boys and two girls. My elder brother, José, went to school, but my sisters were lazy. You know, the custom of our people, they are courting already by the age of fifteen. They don't care for going to school. Since I was the youngest, I tried my best to finish high school.

"During my high school days, I used to participate in programs, like singing. I was a member of the choir. Sometimes I was chosen as a declaimer.[3] We were all assigned to go to barrios, to our own barrios, to baptize those unbaptized children and teach people how to pray. We were catechists.

"After my graduation in 1956 my parents became sick. They could hardly support me. So I was very, very lonely. I came to Baguio[4] to stay with my brother who was working in the mines. I stayed with them a little while, but they also had children to support. So my auntie (the cousin of my father) in Baguio called me and said, 'You had better come and help me in the market.' She had a woodcarvings shop in the market, so I went there as a salesgirl. I worked for her for three years. I lived with her. She paid me sixty pesos a month in the beginning and then when I knew how to sell and how to explain the woodcarvings, she gave me a raise. It was a big business; many tourists were coming there. I met many people, many friends, and some of them were admirers of mine.

"When I was in Baguio, I met my husband. We were penpals. One day I received a letter addressed to Miss Annie, but no family name. I was the only Annie in that stall, so I read the letter. He said that he had dreamed of me, around three-thirty one morning. And then he went to a fortune teller, who said that he should go and see this woman because she is your future wife. According to him, he learned my name and address from the dream. And the fortune teller told him 'you just write, write this girl.'

"When he wrote me, I answered. His second letter came. Of course I was very curious. I said, 'Why don't you come here in Baguio and we will see each other?' Then he sent his father to see me. Then his older sister and some other relatives came to see me. Then one time, Roberto and his father came to see me personally. I did not know him, of course. He was looking at me. I said to my [future] father-in-law, 'where is your son?' 'Oh, he did not come.' But, in fact he was looking at me.

"Then I realized that he was the one. He was Roberto. He was a good looking man. We went to his brother's house in Naguillian. We went to talk to each other there, about my decision. After that, we decided. We went right away to get a marriage license. We went to the health center for the license and then we went to the priest to set the marriage date.

"Then, when Roberto and his father left Baguio, I went to my brothers' house, and I told them I am going to get married.

"'To whom? Why did you not bring him here? Who is that person?'

"I said, 'He is from Pangasinan, the family of Santos.' And then they scolded me. They said, 'Suppose someday something happens to you? Are you going to blame us? You decided alone. You did not inform us.'

"I told them that if something happens to me, I won't blame anybody. I will blame my own self. Because I was the one who decided by myself. That's what I told my brothers. That's why even if I have problems, I can't tell anything to them.

"I didn't tell them before because I know they don't like Pangasinan people. They wanted me to marry in my own place, so in case something happens to me, at least I have many relatives. But here in Pangasinan, I am all alone. I do not have any cousins, or brothers, or anything. I do not have any uncles here.

"But I didn't care about that. All I wanted was to run away from my place. I wanted to marry in another place.

"So we set our marriage date, on April 29, 1960. We got married in the cathedral in Baguio City. After the wedding we went to a restaurant for breakfast. Then we came to Dagupan and had a reception in a hotel, and then there was another reception in the barrio.[5] My brothers came to the wedding, but my father was already dead and my mother was too old.

"I have only been home to Kiangan once since my marriage. In 1962 I went for the funeral of my mother. And then in 1977 I went to Lamut [a nearby town] to attend the wedding of my niece. But I did not go to Kiangan then. I'm too busy. And I no longer have parents. I am not going to see anyone. Some of my brothers are in Baguio, some in Lamut, so now I am lazy to go there.[6]

"When I came to Dagupan, I could hardly speak in Pangasinan. So sometimes I spoke in Tagalog, sometimes in English. People laughed at me because I spoke English; they asked if there was a lost American in the market. But then I came to learn Pangasinan, and I learned how to sell in the market."

Roberto Santos: Work and Movement

"I, Roberto Santos, was born October 3, 1938. We are eight children in the family. I am number five. But I was different from all my brothers. They were always scolding me. When I was five or six years old, I was already pasturing our cows and *carabaos*. I also cooked and cleaned the house. Most days when I was a small boy, I received whippings. If I was late ten or thirty minutes, my parents scolded me again. They whipped me again.

"My father was a foreman in the Agno River Flood Control and he was also farming. Up until I was about fourteen years old I went to school and helped with the cows and *carabaos*. After that, I went to the town, to Urbiztondo, to look for a job. I went to work for my uncle, loading and unloading at his *bodega* [warehouse]. I lived with my uncle and he paid me 45 pesos a month. All my salary was given to my parents.

"After almost two years, I moved again. I decided to look for a better job. Sometimes, when I was working for my uncle, I went with him to Dagupan City. I was always looking for a shop that wanted to hire a helper. I saw a sign one day and returned the following day to apply. That's how I got work here in Dagupan City as a battery charger. I told my uncle that I had found another job, in Dagupan City.

"When I came to Dagupan, I was an apprentice. I got no pay but received free room and board. After six months, I knew everything. I was the one responsible for fixing dead batteries. And they gave me one peso a day. I did not give any money to my parents, because I was living here in the city and one peso is not much. After about one year, I changed jobs again, and went to work for Yellow Taxi in Dagupan. They offered me sixty pesos a month, but with no room and board. Again I was charging batteries.

"I was sleeping in the market. One old man was very kind. He was the one who cared for me. He had a small restaurant in the market and he told me to sleep inside it. Every morning when I went to my job, he prepared my meal. And every afternoon when I arrived back, he prepared my meal.

"Later, I applied for a job in Manila. My grandfather (a cousin of my grandfather on my mother's side) was in Manila working as a driver for a sand and gravel company. He helped me find a job in the same company. I stayed with my grandfather for almost a year. I was loading and unloading sand and gravel. It was very hard work. I made one peso per trip [trip to get a load of sand and gravel] and sometimes we made four trips in a day. I didn't like life in Manila. It was very hard. The job there is very hard. It was like being a prisoner. If you cannot work a day, you have no money. Manila is expensive. I have not even a single centavo saved in Manila. If you have the capital in Manila you can start even a small business and you can earn much money. I had no money, no capital, so I returned to my town [Bayambang, near Urbiztondo] and applied to be a conductor on jeepneys going from the barrio to the town. I worked there only about ten months and then came back to Dagupan. I returned again to Yellow Taxi.

"Then my sister [an older sister who already lived in Dagupan with her husband] noticed that I am here in Dagupan. She came to me, talked to me. She said I had better live with her and learn to sell goods. She was selling cloth in Dagupan. I knew that the advice of my sister is good. I came to live with her. And then I sold goods, I sold in the market. I gave the sales [money] to her. That is the time I learned the business.

"I stayed with my sister and I was selling cloth from town to town, in Lingayen, Mangatarem, San Carlos, Bayambang, Manaoag. Every market day I went to sell cloth. I started in 1957 and then in 1960 I got married. My three brothers were selling also.[7] We were what are called *bargaineros* [bargain sellers]. I had lots of customers; until now some are with me.

"You know, before, the dry goods were very cheap. Sometimes we bought cloth for three pesos a kilo. And later six pesos to twelve pesos per kilo. My sister bought the cloth in Manila, in Divisoria. Every week they purchased goods in Manila and they distributed them to me. I could sell sometimes fifty pesos, a hundred pesos, twenty pesos of cloth in a day. They counted my sales every day. Sometimes I got fifty centavos from them. Sometimes I had only twenty-five centavos in my pocket. I gave the rest, all the rest to them.

"I started my own business after I got married. I got married in 1960. I met my wife in Baguio City, through my uncle there. We borrowed three hundred pesos from my sister for the start of our business. I went to Manila with the three hundred pesos and I purchased seven hundred pesos worth of cloth. So I have a balance [credit] of four hundred pesos.

Little by little my balance with my *suki* [regular supplier] grew bigger. After a month I returned the 300 pesos to my sister.

"In 1967, I went to Viet Nam. There was lots of money there. I went on a tourist visa and then converted to a working visa. My best friend was already there and he was the one who prepared me for a job. But when I arrived there, I did not know anything; I had to find a job. I stayed in Saigon for almost two weeks and then I met the personnel manager in the PX; he was from Pangasinan, from Mangatarem. He hired me to work in the PX in Cam Ranh Bay. I was store supervisor but I was doing the work, loading and unloading the trucks and doing other jobs. I stayed there almost a year but I did not finish my contract because it was very hot and I was becoming thinner and thinner. I was earning one hundred fifty to two hundred dollars every week, but I could not save much money because I went out with my friends. I only sent home around five hundred or seven hundred dollars.

"When I returned here, I applied for a job at Clark Air Force Base, but they didn't accept me. But I didn't apply anywhere else—I prefer to manage my business. But now I am applying in Guam; my uncle is there; if he can find a job for me he will write me and I will go there. I want to go there to seek a better job. My wife can run my business here. She can manage already. For me, I have nothing to do at home here in Dagupan City. I am there in the barrio to plant, but my brothers can do that and my wife can manage."

Annie and Roberto: Life in the City

The Santos's house, located a few blocks behind the marketplace on a rutted dirt road, is a two-story wooden building. Visitors to the house in the evening find the downstairs sitting room piled high with the sacks of cloth brought home from the market, leaving little room for entertaining. Upstairs, a few benches on the landing are used for sitting to talk with visitors. Annie and Roberto's bedroom is nearly filled by the large double bed. A smaller bedroom is used by their two adopted daughters, while their salesgirls sleep in a room at the back of the house. A small room at the front of the house on the ground floor is set aside for Roberto's mother, who tends a small *sari-sari* shop from the front window. The young men who work as *cargadors* for the Santoses also use this room during their spare time.

When the Santoses first married, they lived across the street from their present house. Three years later, they rented the upstairs room of the present house, which then belonged to a *comadre* of Annie's; a few years later, they bought the house for ₱1,500. Since then, they have expanded the upstairs and put in a cement floor downstairs. More repairs are needed, but because the Santoses do not own the land on which it is located, they are unwilling to invest more money in the house.

Roberto's parents moved in with them in 1965; when his father had an accident, the parents moved back to the barrio but Annie and Roberto continued to support them, sending rice and other goods, and finally finding a faith healer who, according to Annie, was able to cure him. His mother and father later returned to Dagupan. When the father became ill in 1978, Annie and Roberto paid his hospital expenses in Manila, and when he died they paid his funeral expenses. Now Roberto's mother, dressed in her mourning clothes, oversees events in and near the house from her front room window.

Roberto and Annie's biggest disappointment is that they have no biological children. Instead, they have adopted two daughters, but they worry that adopted children will not behave as they should, and that they might not have anyone to care for them when they are old. The two adopted daughters are both nieces of the Santoses: the elder is the daughter of Roberto's brother, who continues to live in the barrio with his wife and other children. She was nine months old when adopted, but she continues to visit her parents in the barrio occasionally. The younger one was five years old when she was adopted; she is the daughter of Annie's brother, whose wife died when the child was three.

In addition to Roberto and Annie, their daughters, and his mother, nine other people were living in their house on a regular basis in 1978–79 (see fig. 9). A niece who visited for several months told Annie that the house is "like a restaurant" because there were so many people living there. Everyone living at the house also worked at the shop. Two sisters, Rita and Lisa, are the daughters of one of Roberto's brothers; their father died a number of years ago and their mother lives in Roberto's home barrio. Rita has stayed with Annie and Roberto since she was twelve years old; now eighteen, she is responsible for taking cloth to markets in neighboring towns. Every day, she goes by bus to Lingayen or Malasiqui or Calasiao to sell, returning to Dagupan in the evening. She earns ₱110 a month. Her sister, who is sixteen, attends high school, but helps to arrange cloth in the shop early in the morning and returns to sell in the afternoon. Another niece, also sixteen, whose father still lives in the

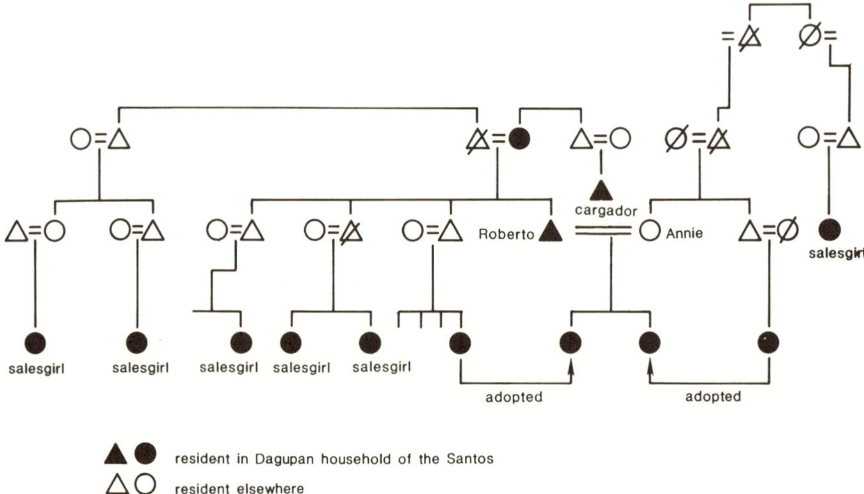

Fig. 9. Santos household; relationship between members
(nonrelatives—2 cargadors)

barrio, works in the market every day, as does the daughter of a cousin;
both have been working for about four years. Another cousin helps with
the cooking in the house, and helps in the shop when needed. Annie's
second cousin, a nineteen-year-old high school graduate, arrived from
Kiangan and was put to work in the market, although she spoke no
Pangasinan. She had already worked as a housegirl in Manila for one and
one-half years. All of the salesgirls earned ₱60 a month as well as room
and board at the house.

Only one of the *cargadors* is a relative, a cousin related to Roberto
through his mother. But all three live in the house and can get food there,
in addition to their regular wages of ₱70 a month.

When one of the salesgirls talked of going to Manila, where she
thought she could get a better job and earn more money, Annie got
angry: "Here, they get their room and food for free and we give them
₱60 a month for their expenses. In another job they will have to find a
place to live and buy their own food. I have treated them like daughters,
and now they talk of going off for another job." When another, who had
lived with them since she was twelve, was found seeing a boyfriend
secretly, she was sent back to her parents in the barrio until she promised
to change her behavior.

When these two girls left, temporarily, as it turned out, Roberto and Annie hung a sign near their shop advertising for salesgirls, and Annie complained of the difficulty of training new girls. A few days later, two new girls arrived in Dagupan, not as a result of the sign, but as a result of a trip Roberto made to see an aunt in a barrio near his own. The aunt sent two girls to be tried out. At about the same time, Annie's niece—a sister of Annie's adopted daughter—arrived for a visit with a cousin. Annie asked her to stay, and within a few weeks, she, too, was at work in the shop. Like the other salesgirls, she moved into the Santos's house.

Roberto and Annie began their business in 1960, with the ₱300 borrowed from his sister. At first, he traveled around from town to town selling at the markets, just as he had done for his sister, and she sold in open spaces in the Dagupan market, which were available for forty centavos a day. Then they "borrowed" (i.e., paid the rent on) a stall belonging to his sister's *comadre*, and later, by 1961, were able to buy that stall, paying ₱500 for the rights to it.[8]

Roberto and Annie speak in general about the early years of their business, suggesting that it was "luck" and help from God that enabled them to succeed. But, that was certainly not all there was to it. Early on, Annie was introduced to the wife of a Chinese merchant in Dagupan and accompanied her to Manila to buy cloth. With an introduction to suppliers, she was able to obtain a considerable amount of credit; "even if you didn't have money, you issued a postdated check and you could get plenty of cloth." According to Roberto, at that time it was relatively easy to make a profit on cloth. "If you have sales of around fifty pesos, you have already ten pesos [profit]. But now, if you sell twenty pesos, you get only two pesos gain." When they had a profit, they used it to buy more cloth, so that they would have a complete stock to satisfy their customers.

Annie's ability at judging customers is perhaps the most important explanation of their success, although she would probably not claim that. As Roberto puts it, "she learned the character of Dagupenos" very well. She says, "If I see a person—I can psychologize a customer—if the person is a good buyer, then you adjust yourself. If a person is a hard buyer, then I tell stories. I ask their name, where they are from, about their children—I ask questions, and they ask me—I tell the truth that I am from Mountain Province. Many people think that I am a Tagalog woman, but I'm proud of where I come from. So I've come to know many people from all around Pangasinan.

"Even if the gain is only fifty or twenty centavos I will give it to them, so that they'll come back. I'll remove fifty centavos from the total, especially if they buy a lot. Even though I didn't learn commerce, I get customers. I tell them to come again. If I'm not here, they look for me. If they need something that I don't have, I will order it from my *suki* [regular supplier].

"If a customer is *suplada* [aristocrat]—you can see, feel, it in her actions. If she is a good buyer then you give a cheaper price. Also I have many *comadres*. In dealing with people you must be patient. Even if they continue to bargain, even after the cloth is wrapped, you can't get angry, you have to be nice, not quarrel. Even if you have headaches, you are forced to smile."

By 1966, they were able to obtain another stall in the market, purchasing the rights for ₱600. A third one was acquired in a different location directly from the city; hence no payment was required for it. Much later, in 1977, they paid ₱6,000 for the rights to two more stalls near their first ones, and in early 1979 began to use and pay the rent on four more adjoining stalls belonging to someone else.

When Roberto and Annie started their business, his sister was already a successful seller in Dagupan with several stalls in the market. But, at about the same time Roberto and Annie were developing their business, his sister's declined. Unable to cover a number of postdated checks, she asked Roberto and Annie to borrow money in their name and then lend it to her to use. Afraid that she would not repay them, they refused. Shortly thereafter, she went deeper into debt. Her husband, a bank employee, was transferred to Mindanao, so she left her business in Dagupan and later started a new one in Mindanao. But Annie believes that Roberto's sister has been angry with them for their refusal to lend money, and jealous of their success ever since. In seeking the cause and cure for a number of illnesses over the years, she has been told by faith healers that these are illnesses caused by someone who is jealous. The bad feelings caused by their success, and to a large extent their replacement of his sister in the market (even using some of the same stalls she had once owned) have continued to the present. When Roberto's father died, his sister did not offer to help pay funeral expenses, saying "Anyway, you are rich."

At the start, the Santoses went to Manila to buy their cloth, primarily from one supplier. One day in 1971, their money was stolen from the market when Roberto was about to go to Manila. Annie was very upset;

while she sat in her shop, trying to figure out what to do, a woman who supplies cloth from Manila came along and offered to give her cloth to get their business started again. They have continued to buy from this supplier. She gets cloth from the factory and distributes it to a number of sellers in Dagupan. She brings new types of cloth with her on her weekly trips. All transactions with her are on a credit basis; she provides the cloth, they pay her for it the following week. But if sales are poor, she allows them to delay payment.

There are many days when the Santoses and their salesgirls sit in the market and have few or no customers. Especially in the slow months of July, August, and September, when many are short of money, few people are buying cloth. But around Christmas, and then in the months leading to Holy Week (Easter), it seems that everyone is buying. Everyone wants a new dress for Easter. At Christmas, many give gifts of cloth. Young women working in Dagupan buy cloth to take home to their parents in the barrio. Employers give their workers gifts of cloth; one day before Christmas a woman bought ₱280 worth of cloth just for gifts for her employees. Another day, a school teacher from Ilocos bought about ₱1,000 worth, to give to people from the barrio who visit at Christmas. As a result of these large purchases by regular customers, and of smaller quantities purchased by others, the Santoses can easily make sales of ₱2,000 or more per day in the days before Christmas.

The Santoses keep no records of their sales. Annie says that she did at first, but stopped when the business got bigger. She handles the money, and estimates her gain on the basis of the lowest amount she can get for a type of cloth. She might, for example, sell cloth for ₱5 more than she paid for it, but will estimate ₱3 gain. In this way she accounts for her expenses like stall rental. A bookkeeper is hired to keep her records for tax purposes.

Annie does keep records of those who buy on credit; she sells on credit only to her *suki* (regular customers).[9] Over the years, she has developed a set of regular customers, some of whom buy in large quantities. A few buy quantities of cloth from her in order to resell to others. Two women sell to employees at the University of Pangasinan; another sells at other institutions where there are salaried employees, such as banks and hospitals. In all three cases, the *suki* obtains cloth worth as much as ₱1,500, sells it, and pays Annie after the employees receive their salaries, every two weeks or at the end of the month.

She met one of these *suki* through the Cursillista organization;[10] according to Annie, this was "number one in getting customers," in the late 1960s. At Cursillo meetings, "We would all introduce ourselves. I would say that I am Mrs. Santos; I have a store located in the market. I met people from all over Pangasinan, and they would bring others."

Some of the regular customers—the *suki*—have become more than *suki*, they have become friends, and some are tied into formal *compadrazgo* (godparent) relationships. One woman from Mangaldan continues to buy from her: "We met because when she was buying, I entertained her very well, so she came back. I got acquainted with her. If she was finished buying, she sat down, we talked with each other, told stories." The woman asked Annie to be a godparent for her daughter; the child is now in high school and the mother continues to come to the market once every month or two. Another couple used to come from Aguilar to shop; they met in the market and later Annie was the sponsor (godmother) at their son's baptism. In another case of a godparent relationship that began in the early 1960s, the child's mother continues to buy from Annie; in fact, "She doesn't buy from others, just from me."

Some of Annie's *comadres* and Roberto's *compadres* are linked to the business not as customers but as creditors. A complex, and strained, relationship exists between them and the owner of the four stalls that they are now "borrowing." The relationship began when Roberto's sister still had stalls in the market. When she lost her business, her stalls were acquired by her brother-in-law, Mr. Mabini . These stalls are located next to those now owned by the Santoses. In addition, Mr. Mabini lives on the same street as they. So, for some time Mr. Mabini and his family were neighbors both in the market and at home. When Mr. Mabini's daughter was born, Roberto was asked to be her godfather. Meanwhile, Annie got to know Mr. Mabini's niece when she was studying in Dagupan and would visit her uncle. When the niece got married in 1971, Annie was her sponsor. Up to about 1977, there was a relatively simple relationship—neighbors in the market and at home, a *compadre* relationship between Roberto and Mr. Mabini, a *comadre* relationship between Annie and Mr. Mabini's sister-in-law (the mother of the bride). Meanwhile, Roberto's sister, married to Mabini's brother, had moved to Mindanao.

Mr. Mabini occasionally borrowed money from the Santoses, as good neighbors in the market might do. But in 1977, he began borrowing money on a regular basis: he now sells T-shirts at markets around Pangasinan, and every week he borrows ₱1,500–2,000. He uses this to buy

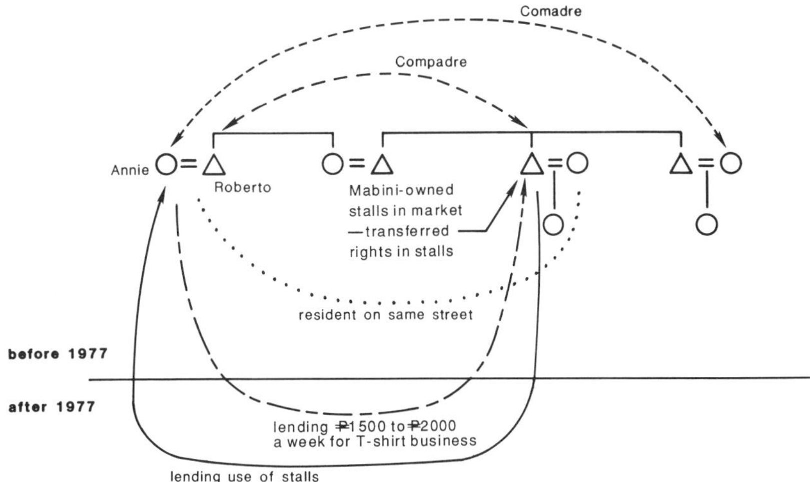

Fig. 10. The Santoses; business and compadre relationships with neighbors

the shirts, then pays back the money the following week after making sales (although not always on time). Then he borrows more a few days later to start the cycle again. He owes money to a number of other people and is paying off the loans with the money made from T-shirt sales. In late 1978, Mr. Mabini began letting the Santoses use his stalls in the market (the same stalls originally owned by Roberto's sister). He still owns the rights, but they pay the rent to the city, and now they are considering buying the rights from him (see fig. 10).

According to Annie, Mr. Mabini goes around telling stories about Roberto and herself, but says she continues to help despite the unpleasant things that are said because "I pity the animals."

Although from day to day and week to week, Annie Santos spends most of her time in the marketplace, from early morning to late after-noon, seeing many of the people she knows, her life is not totally cir-cumscribed by the business. She is active in church organizations, includ-ing the Four Day Club, associated with the Cursillistas, and the most prestigious, the Daughters of Isabela, which admitted her as a member in 1970. On a typical Sunday, she attends mass and helps to collect contri-butions with other members of the Daughters of Isabela. Sometimes the group serves breakfast after mass and she helps with that. Later in the morning, she may go to the market. On one Sunday in mid-November, she served breakfast and then went to the market, staying there until 6:00 P.M. When she returned home, she was tired and wanted to rest; but she was invited to a baptismal party at a neighbor's. She went: "I had to go, because if you don't go to these things people will think you don't have good P.R."[11]

Roberto spends less time in the market. He takes more responsibility for entertaining visitors, especially those who come from the barrio. And he often spends one or two days a week in Bayambang, overseeing his farm activities there. He, too, belongs to a church organization—the Knights of Columbus—but has fewer regular activities associated with it. Both Roberto and Annie perceive themselves as being firmly tied to the city: "Anything you need, you can find it in Dagupan," he states simply. She is more specific: "If you are a merchant, then of course, you want to live in the city." Nevertheless, they have maintained and in fact strengthened their ties to the barrio, especially in recent years.

Ties to the Barrios

A large dike runs between the towns of Urbiztondo and Bayambang. On one side of the dike, the river floods the fields every year during the rainy season—sometimes the water rises six to seven feet high. Farmers must wait until the floods have receded to plant their rice. Dirt tracks meander out from the dike to clusters of houses, small *sitios*—some of which are officially in Bayambang and others of which are in Urbiztondo. Roberto Santos's "barrio" is one of these clusters of houses, at the end of a track between corn and peanut fields. Seven or eight wooden houses on stilts lie close together; at the end of the road one cement house belongs to a cousin. Everyone living in the *sitio* is related; Roberto's brothers and sisters-in-law are there, as are his cousins. His "family house"—his birthplace—is an old wooden house, decorated with old photos of family members, some old diplomas, and a statue of the Virgin Mary. A one-room house next door is occupied by Roberto's sister-in-law, a widow whose husband was shot in 1970.

Roberto and others in the area grow only one rice crop a year, after the floods recede. (Sometimes it floods again and then the crop is lost.) There is no irrigation for later crops of rice, so instead corn is grown as a second crop. Some people also grow peanuts, some onions, and others, such as Roberto, are growing watermelon for the seeds.

The Santoses first bought land in 1970; Roberto explains they decided to buy land because "my wife can already tackle our business here in Dagupan, so I have to spread some knowledge also, to have a little income again in the barrio." They bought between four and five hectares that had previously belonged to Roberto's sister. His sister and brother-in-law had mortgaged it, and when they left for Mindanao, stopped making payments. Through a friend at the bank, Roberto heard that the mortgage was to be foreclosed. They took over the mortgage, paying it off at ₱300 a month over three years. In late 1978 Roberto obtained two more hectares that had belonged to his father. Again, he took over the mortgage at the bank, although he had already been using the land for several years.

In addition to the land which they own, they are mortgaging plots of land for three cousins, totaling about five hectares. In other words, rather than going to the bank, the owners have borrowed money from Roberto, and in return, he gets a share of the harvest. In each case, Roberto has lent between ₱1,200 and ₱1,600 to the landowner; in return he gets one-third of the harvest each time rice or corn is harvested. Roberto views mortgaging the land as a good investment: "You have a share of every product of the land you mortgage. If your money is saved in a bank, you cannot earn as much as from shares in the barrio. I prefer to mortgage, even a little amount. I can earn more money than to deposit money in the bank."

Roberto uses both tenants and hired workers on his land. He has nine tenants, including his two brothers who live in the barrio and several cousins. When he grows rice, he pays for the fertilizer, insecticide, and other inputs, and gets 50 percent of the harvest. And on his newest crop, watermelon, the tenants are receiving only one-third because, Roberto says "I spent lots of money" (to plant the crop).

In one rice harvest, Roberto receives a total of between forty and fifty cavans of rice. This provides most of the rice necessary for the household in Dagupan, as they consume about one cavan a week. When they harvest corn, they sell it and use the cash to buy rice. He also has coconut trees; his widowed sister-in-law collects and sells the nuts, and pays him forty centavos for each.

Roberto has been trying to find another crop to provide him with a cash income. He has tried peanuts and recently has been growing watermelon. He was told that he could get a good profit from the sale of watermelon seeds to a Japanese buyer located in Tarlac province. Hence in late 1978, after his rice was harvested, he planted watermelon, spending a total of about ₱3,000 for seeds, plowing, insecticide, fertilizer, and labor. Most of his tenants agreed to try watermelon; those that didn't planted *camote* (cassava). On two hectares where he has no tenants, Roberto paid hired workers ₱4 a day to plant and weed. Altogether ten hectares were planted to watermelon.

In December, when he was first planting, Roberto expected to be paid ₱12–14 a kilo for his watermelon seed. By April, he realized that he probably would not make a profit. He was getting only ₱7 a kilo and after selling most of his crop had received only ₱1,500. Since all the money invested in watermelons came from their cloth sales, both Roberto and Annie were worried about their loss. But both were also optimistic; he thought they should try something else—perhaps onions—next time. She feels that it's good to have an investment in something other than cloth. "It is dangerous if all your money is in the store. If all the money is in the business, than all the money for expenses comes from that source, for clothing, for education, etc. This is how others have gone down. We have another source of income; there is at least some saving. It helps in expenses. It's a big help, especially if there's a good harvest. Of course if there's a typhoon, then there's no income and you lose."

Roberto travels back and forth to the barrio frequently, sometimes staying several days at a time. During the planting and harvest seasons, he goes every few days, to supervise tenants and hired workers, to bring more seed or insecticide, and just to see how things are going. Sometimes he brings gifts with him, a bottle of whiskey, for example, during the harvest. Special occasions—a funeral, wedding, death anniversary—bring him there. When his own father died he and Annie spent ₱10,000 for a large funeral in the barrio. He enjoys playing the role of landlord and emphasizes that he wants to "help" the people in the barrio. At Christmas, he gave gifts of cloth to his brothers and sisters-in-law, and brought a stock of cloth to be distributed by his sister-in-law to other workers on his farm. More importantly, he lends money to tenants.

Conversely, relatives make use of their ties with Roberto and Annie when they need something in Dagupan. They visit frequently, stopping by and expecting at least minimal entertainment—beer, snacks, a meal if possible. As Annie says "When we have visitors, unexpected visitors, we have to feed them breakfast and then again at noon. Even if our food is already cooked, we have to buy again, cook again. It's very expensive."

Special occasions bring large numbers of people from the barrio to Dagupan. When Roberto's niece graduated from a local college, the Santoses spent over ₱100 entertaining fifteen guests. A week later, during Holy Week, they provided lunch, dinner, drinks, and a piece of cloth to thirty-one relatives who came to the house to say prayers. The Santoses spent over ₱800 on this entertainment and gifts.

When problems arise, relatives come to Roberto and Annie for assistance. A second cousin, a student in a local college, was accused of stealing. She came to Annie, who went with her to see the City Fiscal, a *cursillista* like herself. The following day, the girl's parents arrived from the barrio, went again to see the Fiscal to request dismissal of the case, and stayed for breakfast and lunch with the Santoses. A relative needing cloth for a gift will find Annie in the market and "borrow" a piece, i.e., obtain it on credit.

Annie, too, receives visitors from her home town, although she herself has not been there since her mother's death in 1962. She sees no reason to go; only one brother has returned there, after working for twenty-four years in the mines near Baguio. But she keeps well informed on events there, and even offers advice in a land dispute between her nephew and a more distant relative. Visits from her relatives tend to last longer than those from Roberto's. One niece came from a remote mountain town in Bontoc Province where she lives with her husband; she stayed three months, left once briefly to go see her husband and returned for another month. On her return home she took ₱300 worth of cloth that she planned to use for sewing graduation uniforms that she would then sell. During the time she was in Dagupan, several other relatives of Annie arrived for shorter stays, including three other nieces and cousins, two of whom stayed on to work in the shop. Annie's brother from Baguio came for a short visit, as did the father-in-law of one of her nieces.

Income and Expenses in the City and the Barrio

Annie and Roberto do not keep records in their shop, in the farm, or in the household. Money flows from the cloth business to the farm; household expenses are paid for out of cash available in the shop. Similarly, cloth from the shop is used for gifts. Nevertheless, they are in general aware of what they earn and what they spend, and can often provide quite detailed accounting.

In the city, their major expenses are in the business and the household. Money earned from the cloth business is used to invest in the farm, and theoretically, money from the farm is to be put back into the cloth shop, but there is no evidence that this has occurred. Personal ties span both the city and the barrio and form the basis of certain expenses, giftgiving and contributions in particular.

During an ordinary week, without visitors to the house, Annie spends ₱300 to ₱400 on food and other household necessities. If they have visitors from the barrio they spend more; as noted above, they spent over ₱800 on Holy Week entertainment. They pay only ₱30 a month to rent the lot on which their house is located, and because they get rice from their farm they need to buy rice during only part of the year. As a result, most of their household expenses consist of food—mainly meat, fruit,

TABLE 37.   Santos Household; Daily and Weekly Expenses and Income, Sample Week, March, 1979

Expenses	Household	Business		Loans	
Monday	₱35	Hired jeep to remove clothes during fire ₱30		To cloth seller To T-shirt seller	₱500 1,500
Tuesday	125				
Wednesday	50				
Thursday					
Friday					
Saturday	Entertained visitors from barrio 100				
Total	310	30			₱2,000

Income	Cloth Sales	Profit	Loans Repaid
Monday	₱1,700		
Tuesday	1,000		
Wednesday	900		
Thursday	720		
Friday	2,600		
Saturday	2,000		₱500 1,500
Sunday	1,200		
Total	₱10,120	Estimated ₱2,024 (20%)	

Paid to supplier: ₱8,000

Note: Based on interviews with Mrs. Santos.

and vegetables—snacks for themselves and visitors, and items such as cigarettes, soft drinks, and beer. Their daughters are in elementary school and pay no tuition; they are given a few pesos each day for snacks and jeepney fares (see table 37).

Annie estimates that their weekly cloth sales run between ₱8,000 and ₱10,000, on average, but may go much lower and may also go higher. She estimates her profit, after paying her supplier for the cloth and after business expenses, as 20 percent of sales, or ₱1,600–2,000 per week. For example, during a week in late March, 1979, a peak selling-period because it was shortly before Holy Week, Annie had sales totaling ₱10,120; she paid ₱8,000 to her supplier at the end of the week (see table 37). During other weeks, business expenses are higher, with salaries to be paid, stall rentals, and so on. Overall, salaries, stall rental, and other regular costs amount to nearly ₱800 a month (see table 38). In addition, the Santoses have purchased new stalls and regularly lend money and/or cloth to other sellers.

Money and goods flow from the Santoses to others, particularly to relatives in the barrio, in a variety of ways. First, because nearly all of their employees are relatives, the salaries they pay indirectly contribute to the support of those in the barrio. Second, at Christmas time and at

TABLE 38.   Santoses' Business Expenses

Expenses	Amount
Monthly salaries	
Salesgirls	₱100
	75
4 at ₱60	240 (plus room and board)
Cargadors	
3 at ₱70	210
Stall rental	
₱14/month/stall × 9	126
Electricity for stalls	33
	₱784
Purchase of new stalls, 1978	₱6,000 for 2 stalls
Money lending	About ₱2,000/week to cloth and T-shirt seller
Cloth on credit to other sellers	Total of about ₱2,000 every 2–3 weeks

Note: Based on interviews with Mrs. Santos.

other times they give gifts directly to relatives and others. At Christmas, in addition to giving gifts to workers in the shop and to immediate family members, Roberto brought a pile of cloth to the barrio and distributed twenty to twenty-five pieces to the people working on the farm, and to other relatives there such as his sister-in-law. These are for the most part the same people who come to Dagupan for special occasions, such as the Holy Week celebration, when pieces of cloth were again distributed to all who attended.

The most important way in which Roberto and Annie contribute to those in the barrio is through their farming activities. Table 39 shows various investments they have made and the shares they and others receive from them. It is not at all clear that they are in fact profiting from

TABLE 39.   Santoses' Investments and Income in Barrio[a]

	Investment	Payment and Shares to Others	Income
Purchase of land	(a) ₱12,000 for 4–5 ha, 1970		
	(b) ₱3,000 for 2 ha, 1978		
Mortgaging land	(a) ₱1,300		33.3% of harvest
	(b) ₱1,200		
	(c) ₱1,200		
	(d) ₱1,650		
	(e) ₱1,500		
Rice	Est. ₱2,000 total on planting, 1978	Tenants receive 50% of harvest	50% of harvest = 12 sacks of milled rice, 1978
Watermelon	Est. ₱3,000 total for seed, tractor rental, labor, fertilizer, insecticide 1978–79	Labor (relatives), ₱4/day for planting, weeding; tenants receive 1/3 share	Sold 240 kilos at ₱7/kilo = ₱1,680
Corn	Planted 4 ha, had seeds, ₱180 for fertilizer	Tenants receive 50% of harvest	50% of harvest
Cows	6		
Coconut trees		Sister-in-law sells coconuts at ₱1.50 each	₱.40 each coconut ₱30–50 over 3 months

Note: Based on interviews with the Santoses. In the past the Santoses planted peanuts; in the future they planned to plant onions.

[a]Amounts based on statements and estimates of Roberto; some seem likely to be overestimates.

their purchases of land in the barrio. On the other hand, they have provided both employment and some income to relatives in the barrio. Yet those relatives receive small shares of the total produce. Finally, Roberto expresses interest in trying out new crops—watermelon one year, onions the next—but his tenants do not always want to follow his ideas. They may prefer the somewhat more assured income from rice.

Discussion

In many ways, the Santoses are firmly tied to life in the city. "If you are a merchant, then of course, you want to live in the city," she says. He simply states that "anything you need, you can find it in Dagupan." Annie has not even been to her husband's home barrio in recent years. Observed in the urban context alone, they seem to be fully "urban"— belonging to prestigious organizations, owning a small business, etc. Yet Roberto has reestablished a strong link to his barrio by buying farm land. Why he has done this is not entirely clear. He talks idealistically of "helping the folk" in the barrio, but pure motives such as this are unlikely. It is clearly an investment, from which both he and his wife expect to profit. But it is not simply an investment in the sense of an urban man buying land and letting someone else run it. Rather, Roberto has himself become heavily involved in the day-to-day operations on his farmland, and in the support of his relatives there.

Roberto and Annie have made effective use of their personal networks in the process of becoming successful merchants and landowners. Like most migrants, when he arrived in the city, Roberto drew on existing relationships—his sister, relatives in Manila, and so on—to find jobs. Eventually, he and his wife obtained the starting capital for their business from his sister. In developing that business, they—and especially Annie—have used a complex set of ties established in the city. Annie has formed friendships, customer relationships, and *comadre* ties with people she has met through church and business. Few of her *suki* are simply regular customers; likewise, few personal relationships are simply personal. Rather, personal, church, and business relationships are intertwined. In hiring help for the shop, personal networks again dominate. And, again, employees are not simply employees; they are also relatives and members of the Santos's household.

In the use of personal ties to establish their business and succeed in the city, the Santoses are not atypical; this is a common thread in descriptions of the development of small businesses in third world cities. This is true as well of the ways in which others can now use them: relatives from the barrio see the Santoses as successful urban residents who can provide assistance with problems, lend money, and most importantly, provide jobs. Annie and Roberto are aiding in the migration of younger relatives to the city.

But Annie and Roberto's interactions with relatives and others are not only based on their urban residence and business. Had they not bought land in Roberto's hometown, their ties to the barrio would revolve around their assistance to barrio relatives and perhaps occasional visits home, probably for the fiesta or other special occasions. The decision to buy land, and to be actively involved in farming it, has made their ties more complex. Money earned in their urban business has been spent on land and on agricultural inputs—seed, fertilizer, insecticide. In a sense, he has made large-scale "remittances" not only through these investments but also through the employment of labor and the giving of gifts and money lending to relatives there. He is trying out new crops and clearly sees farming as an investment, although it is questionable whether he is in fact having any real success.

At the same time, these complex linkages between the Santoses and their rural homes and relatives must be seen in the larger perspective of the situation in the lowland Philippines. From this perspective, Roberto may be seen as a rather traditional type of landlord, engaged in developing and maintaining a set of patron-client ties with tenants and employees. Like other landlords, he lends money, helps out with problems, and helps to obtain jobs for their children. In return, he expects to receive his share of the produce and profits from the land. The tenants on the land—his brothers and cousins—are in the same situation as thousands of other share-tenants in the Philippines. One way for them to deal with that situation is to encourage the urban migration of their children, some of whom have become the Santos's employees.

In Annie's case, the distance and lack of direct contact might suggest that she is cut off from her home barrio. But in actuality, both information and people flow between the two places. She is knowledgeable about events there. More importantly, relatives from there, like Roberto's relatives, see her as an important urban link and as one way to enable their own migration and employment. Thus, despite cultural and linguistic differences that are larger than any found within the province, her cousins and nieces have been able to come live and work with her. She

herself provides a model for others of one who has successfully over-
come the problems of being called a "lost American" because of her
inability to speak the local language. While Annie does not make direct
contributions to her home or relatives there, she does so indirectly, for
example, by giving cloth to her cousin to sell there.

Chapter 8

From the Barrio to International Migration: A Housegirl and Her Employer

This chapter examines the cases of two interconnected family groups—one, that of a young girl working as a domestic servant; the other, that of her employer, a government employee whose husband works in Saudi Arabia. The girl's family and her employer's husband's family have been linked for several generations, with members of one working for members of the other. Their ties resemble the patron–client ties typically found in landlord–tenant relations, but neither family is directly engaged in farming.

Both the housegirl and her employer are migrants to Dagupan. The case of the employer describes the situation of a middle-level civil servant who maintains ties with both her own and her husband's family, who reside in a variety of places on Luzon. Beyond that, it indicates the widening horizons of those for whom overseas migration is a possibility, and the ways in which strategies involving overseas migration are developed. The housegirl, on the other hand, leads a much more circumscribed life; much of what she does is determined by who she works for and the already-existing connections between the two families.

Mrs. Andrea Ferrer: Civil Servant and Wife of Overseas Migrant

The church in San Fabian was filled with people, mainly women and babies. It was the weekend of the town fiesta, and a mass baptism was taking place, for all children born in the past year who had not yet been baptized. Women from the barrios, dressed in their best clothes, sat with their babies waiting for the previous group to be finished and for their names to be called. As the others left the church, the new group took its place in a large circle in the front of the church. Each baby was held by its *ninang* (godmother) and was surrounded by its mother and the other sponsors.

Mrs. Andrea Ferrer arrived at the church with the wife of her husband's cousin, for whose child she had agreed to be a godparent, or sponsor. She went immediately into a room at the right where each child was being registered and where the godparents were paying the ten peso fee per sponsor. She greeted the clerk, a *compadre*, whose child she had sponsored for his confirmation a few years ago; the clerk said he would pay the baptism fee for her. By this time the other sponsors for the child had arrived: two on the mother's side—a cousin and a coteacher—and two on the father's side—Mrs. Ferrer and her brother-in-law. While they waited their turn to join the group in front of the church, Mrs. Ferrer pointed with pride to an elaborately dressed statue of the Virgin Mary near the altar, and told the other *ninang* that she had donated that to the church in 1973.

The baptism ceremony took fifteen or twenty minutes; babies cried and shook plastic rattles that their mothers and sponsors had purchased outside the church. Afterward, the Ferrer group was joined by Andrea's brother-in-law, Father Ferrer, a priest in a nearby town. Outside, Andrea bought a plastic cross for the baby from a vendor in the churchyard, and then all proceeded to the house of the child's parents for lunch. Andrea joined the women and children upstairs in the *sala* (living room); the men, including the child's father, who did not attend the baptism, sat outside around a big table where *lechon* (roast pig) and goat were served.

Mrs. Ferrer's four-year-old daughter Nina played with Lisa, her babysitter, and the other children. Soon after lunch, Andrea said goodby to her husband's relatives and returned to Dagupan with Lisa and Nina. She would return the following day to greet her sister-in-law who had just arrived from the United States. But she had decided not to join her parents-in-law at their dinner for friends and relatives in town for the fiesta.

Because her husband is away working in Saudi Arabia, Mrs. Ferrer is expected to fulfill his obligations in San Fabian, such as being the sponsor at the baptism of his cousin's child and giving a donation for the town fiesta. She does not fulfill all the obligations her parents-in-law think she should, however; they view her as "proud" in refusing to live with them while her husband is away and in refusing invitations such as the one to have dinner with them and their friends during the fiesta.

Mrs. Ferrer is involved in a complex network of relationships, including not only her husband and his relatives, but also her own relatives, and friends and co-workers in Dagupan. She not only fulfills expected obligations in these relationships, but also draws on them in various ways to improve her own situation and most importantly, that of her adopted daughter, Nina. The biographies and family background of Mrs. Ferrer and her husband help to provide a context for viewing their present activities and strategies.

Mrs. Ferrer

Mrs. Andrea Ferrer, known as Atche Andrea or Mrs. Ferrer to her neighbors, is thirty-seven years old. Small and fair, she presents a contrast with her adopted daughter who is dark, and at four years old, bigger than the six-year-olds in the neighborhood. Atche Andrea was born in Camiling, Tarlac, the province south of Pangasinan. Her family is Ilocano-speaking; her father's father migrated to Camiling from Ilocos Norte, and became a rice merchant. Both her grandmothers were Ilocanas born in Camiling, while her mother's father was from Lingayen, the capital of Pangasinan. Atche Andrea's father was a mining engineer who died in a mine accident when she was about nine years old. Her mother, who is a high school teacher in Camiling, sent Andrea to a technical high school in Manila because she was interested in engineering. An aunt accompanied her to Manila; they rented an apartment near the school and the aunt cooked for her.

After high school, Andrea took premed courses in college and then entered medical school. After two years, she had to leave school for a year to help care for her brother, who had been attacked by someone with a *bolo* (a long knife or machete) and had suffered a nervous breakdown. When she was able to return to school, she studied medical technology as the family no longer had enough money to support her in medical school.

After college, Andrea got a job teaching physics and math at a secondary school in Camiling. She also applied for a job as a medical technologist at the Regional Health Laboratory in Dagupan, and got the job about a year later. Her uncle, a doctor, was working at the regional health office and helped her get the job. She moved to Dagupan, lived briefly in a boarding house, and then married Tony Ferrer, whom she had met in college.

Atche Andrea has one sister, who lives and works in Manila as a sales manager for a restaurant. Her brother continues to be unable to work and lives with aunts and uncles in Camiling. Andrea, her sister, and her

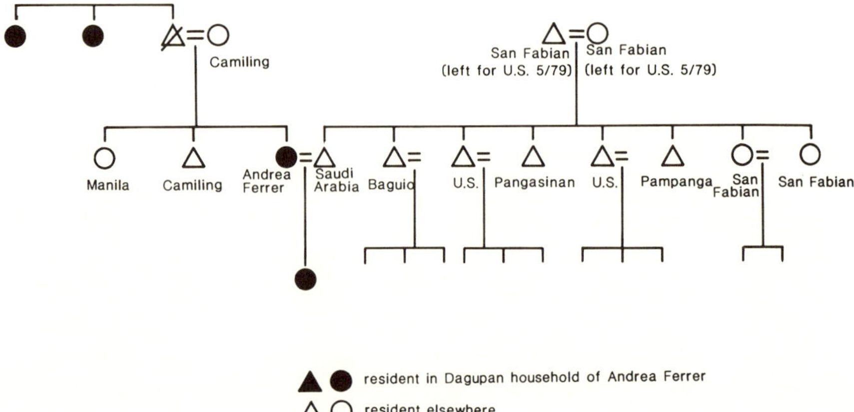

Fig. 11. Andrea Ferrer; residence of family members and in-laws

mother help to support him. (See fig. 11 for the residence of Andrea's own relatives and those of her husband.)

Tony Ferrer

Tony Ferrer was born in San Fabian, the son of a locally prominent family. After graduating from a Manila university with an engineering degree, he worked for a textile firm for two years, and then, after his marriage, returned to Pangasinan to work at the provincial engineers office. He stayed there less than a year, and then obtained a job in Guam as a civilian employee for the U.S. Navy. He worked there four and one-half years, coming home every fifteen months for a month's vacation. In 1974, his contract ended and all Filipinos were told by the Philippine government to return home.

On his return to the Philippines, Tony Ferrer established a small shell-craft business with some other people and began exporting handicrafts to the United States. But they received a bad check, lost a lot of money, and were unable to continue the business. Tony then found a job with a construction firm in Manila; he lived on the job site during the week and came home to Dagupan on weekends. After about two years on that job, he learned from a friend about jobs with a construction firm in Saudi Arabia, and decided to apply, as he could make much more money working there. He left for Saudi Arabia in late 1977, with the intention of working there for about five years, to make enough money "to live in the style we like," as his wife puts it.

Tony is not the only member of the Ferrer family living outside the Philippines. Two of his older brothers live in the United States. One was in the U.S. Navy and is now retired; the other is a doctor who was able to immigrate because he married a woman who was already living in the United States. Tony's parents went on an extended visit to the United States in late 1979, with the intention of making it possible for their youngest daughter, a medical technologist, to immigrate there.

Tony's father worked for many years as a civil servant in local government offices. He started out as a toll collector and market fee collector, then moved on to clerk positions, and then into a variety of positions in the treasurer's offices of several local and provincial governments. When he retired he was the Provincial Chief Cashier. He and his wife have always lived in San Fabian, and have had a house in the *poblacion* most of that time. During World War II, they moved to a barrio where he had a farm, and he cultivated his farm for almost three years while the town was occupied by the Japanese. Later, when several of their eight children were studying in Manila simultaneously, he mortgaged the farm to obtain cash. After his retirement, he used his retirement pay to redeem his farm; he now has five tenants on the five hectares of land he owns, and grows rice, tobacco, and vegetables, from which he receives a share.

The Ferrer house has been rebuilt three times. It was destroyed twice during World War II (burned by the Japanese, shelled by the Americans). The present house is a modified ranch style, with a large airy living room, open bookshelves and a modern kitchen. The front portion of the house contrasts with the dark, cement work-area at the rear, where the laundrywoman (the mother of Andrea's housegirl, Lisa) spends her days washing and ironing with a hot-coal iron. Lisa's mother and father live in a small house in the yard of the Ferrer house.

According to Andrea, her father-in-law likes to tell people that he is the only one in town who has a son who is a doctor and a son who is a priest. While in general he is proud of the success of his children, he is less happy about the decisions Tony and Andrea have made. He approves of Tony going to Saudi Arabia to work, but thinks that Andrea should live in San Fabian while her husband is away, and that Tony and Andrea should build a house there rather than in Dagupan as they have planned.

Andrea and Tony: Household Organization

When Andrea and Tony first married, they did live for a time with his parents. Then they rented a room in Dagupan, but when Tony went to Guam, she went back to live with his parents, and stayed there for the entire four and one-half years that he was away. After he returned, they rented their present apartment in Dagupan. Located in a two-story building one block from the city center and plaza, behind a funeral parlor and a tricycle repair shop, the apartment has a small *sala* and kitchen downstairs, and two bedrooms upstairs. Andrea lives there with her daughter, two elderly aunts, who share the cooking, and two housegirls, one of whom is Andrea's cousin and the other of whom, Lisa, is the daughter of her in-laws' *lavendera* (laundrywoman). In addition, a cousin and nephew of Andrea's who were both working for an agricultural supply company stayed at the apartment some of the time. They worked as salesmen, and used the apartment as a home base for their sales trips around northern Luzon. When one of them got sick and was in the hospital, his parents came to stay with Andrea in order to be able to visit him.

Tony and Andrea adopted their daughter, Nina, when she was nine months old. They carried out the arrangements through a government agency, but adopted the child of relatives of a close friend. Atche Andrea feels that "it is very difficult to be childless" in the Philippines. Her husband wanted a child very much, but his parents did not approve of their decision to adopt Nina. Now, many of Andrea's decisions are made in regard to Nina's future; although Nina is only four, she is already attending an American-style nursery school, was to start music lessons soon, and Tony and Andrea have purchased an insurance policy to assure her education should anything happen to them.

Social Networks in the City and Beyond

"My sister is the senorita type; she likes to have her maids, and not have to do too much for herself" (Andrea Ferrer's sister, March 23, 1979).

"People think I am a snob because I just stay in the house. I don't like to gossip, people repeat things and they bear grudges for a long time. It is very difficult to get along with neighbors; people get jealous of each other" (Andrea Ferrer, February 1, 1979).

"People think I am rich. They come to me almost every day asking to borrow money" (Andrea Ferrer, March 16, 1979).

These three statements suggest various aspects of Andrea Ferrer's relationships with others. To a large extent, her life does focus primarily on her household and her work. But she does not in fact just "stay in the house"; she knows many people in Dagupan, including both those who are essentially social equals and those who perceive her as a source of aid. Through her own family and that of her husband, her networks extend beyond Dagupan to Camiling, San Fabian, and Manila.

On most days Andrea Ferrer simply goes to work and comes home. The people she sees most often are her co-workers, several of whom are neighbors and one or two of whom have become friends. In particular, she is friendly with one co-worker whose husband works in Saudi Arabia with Andrea's husband; she calls her on the telephone if she wants to talk with her. At home, she primarily sees her daughter, her maids, and her aunts who live with her and help care for the house. Of the two maids, she favors Lisa: "She is loyal, she doesn't gossip. Her family has worked for my husband's family for a long time and they are close, like part of the family."

Andrea's closest friend lives at the funeral parlor next door; her friend's husband, like Andrea's, is from San Fabian. They visit daily, and when her friend became involved in a new buying and selling enterprise, Andrea decided to join with her to develop a new "sideline" for herself. Andrea obtained embroidered goods from a cousin in Manila on consignment, and her friend was to sell the goods to her customers to whom she also sells other goods. The friend received a commission on the sales; Andrea got the rest of the profit.

Both Andrea and her friend are actively involved in a woman's church organization, the Legion of Mary. The organization meets every Saturday; in addition, members are supposed to spend time each week in some sort of social or "apostolic" work, such as counseling people, visiting hospitals to pray, and once a year, visiting prisoners in Lingayen or Dagupan and organizing a program for them. Like other such church organizations, this group organizes block rosary groups: statues of saints circulate from house to house, with each member keeping it in her house for one to two weeks at a time, during which time she prays the rosary every evening. At the end of the period, the members of the block rosary group come to the house to take it to the next place and are served food by the person whose house the statue is leaving.

Contrary to her own statement that she does not get to know neighbors, Atche Andrea is in fact quite prominent in the neighborhood. Her close neighbors, including neighborhood children, know her and visit her occasionally. In addition, she is the treasurer of the organization that sponsors the yearly fiesta for the street, for which they collect a lot of money from residents. Neighbors are also prominent among those who have asked Atche Andrea to be a godparent for a child's baptism or confirmation, thereby establishing a *compadrazgo* relationship with her. Among those with whom she has established such a relationship are three neighbors, including a relative of her landlady. Three others were neighbors when she lived in San Fabian, and the other three are her husband's relatives, including two of his brothers.

Following her husband's departure for Saudi Arabia, Andrea became part of a new network—the group from Dagupan whose husbands all work for the same company. Since the owner of the company is from Dagupan, many of the men who have been hired are from the city or neighboring towns. A group of about thirty women maintain contact with each other; husbands send mail and packages with others returning home for visits. When one man was home for a visit in a nearby town, ten women hired a jeepney to take goods to him to be carried to their husbands; each of them paid a share for his overweight luggage costs.

Finally, because Atche Andrea is seen as relatively well off, especially now that her husband is working overseas, many come to her for help, especially to borrow money. One neighbor asked to borrow ₱1,000; she refused to lend the money. But when neighbors approach her for smaller sums (₱50–100) she usually lends it. Co-workers at her office also borrow from her; on two occasions she lent ₱500 for several months. Relatives, as well, approach her for money. When her parents-in-law were planning to travel to the United States, her father-in-law asked to borrow ₱1,200 to help pay for travel expenses and visas; she agreed to lend it, saying she would rather lend sums like that to him than to others.

Atche Andrea visits friends and relatives outside the city occasionally; more frequently, they come to see her. She sometimes goes to see her sister in Manila, but finds that she doesn't have much time because of her work, which sometimes calls for teaching and speaking engagements as well as the regular laboratory work. She goes to Camiling even less frequently to see her mother. But when a cousin died suddenly, she went there three times in a two-week period; "His wife is too shocked to make decisions so I'm helping her in attending to the details, especially the legal matters."

Her mother and sister visit Dagupan a few times a year; at other times, they keep in touch by telephone. Other relatives visit more often: aunts from Camiling, another aunt living in Baguio, cousins from Camiling, relatives of her husband from San Fabian and Manila. Some stop once or twice a month, when passing through Dagupan or when they are there on business.

As shall be seen below, Andrea Ferrer's ties to Camiling and even to San Fabian are considerably more complex and intense than the relative lack of visiting would suggest.

Work, Sidelines, Remittances, and Investments

"I'm very disappointed. My husband isn't coming home on his vacation. He was offered a promotion but he only gets the promotion if he doesn't take a vacation. He'll be one of two Filipinos working at a Saudi Arabia customs office and he'll make more than $1,200 monthly. Now he makes $700 a month. I wrote him that he loves money more than his family."

Although she was unhappy when her husband did not come home for his vacation, Andrea supported his decision to remain in Saudi Arabia, to accumulate the money they desire both for immediate expenses and long-term goals. When he was last working in the Philippines, he made ₱1,000 a month, but had to spend part of it for room and board in Manila, transportation back to Dagupan, and so on. According to Andrea, that was not enough to enable them to live as they would like to: "We want to live in a comfortable way; we like to have nice things."

Andrea estimates her basic expenses to be about ₱1,800 a month, including rent, payment to the maids, food, gas, and electricity. In a four-week period in which she kept records of her expenses, she spent over ₱1,100 for food, and another ₱200 on her fare to work and snacks for herself, and other household expenses (see table 40). Other more or less regular expenses amounted to about ₱210.

Andrea's salary—typical of that of a middle-level civil servant—is ₱602 a month, before deductions for retirement and insurance; she earns an additional ₱100–200 each month for lecturing and teaching. Clearly, her salary alone, or even in combination with that of her husband when he was working in Manila, could not sustain their present lifestyle (see table 41).

In contrast, in Saudi Arabia, Tony Ferrer was earning $1,200 (U.S.) a month after about a year there. According to Philippine law, overseas contract workers must remit 70 percent of their salary to family members at home. The money comes through the banks and is converted at the official exchange rate from U.S. dollars to pesos. In 1978 before his promotion, Atche Andrea was receiving about ₱3,500 a month in remittances. After his promotion she received about ₱5,000 a month (see table 41). Like others in similar jobs, her husband also earns overtime pay, and as he has little to spend money on there (his room and board are free and there is little recreation for Filipino men in Saudi Arabia), he frequently sends additional money home. This comes through friends and co-workers who are home on visits; they bring 100-dollar bills which Atche

TABLE 40.   Andrea Ferrer's Expenses During a Four-Week Period, March–April, 1979

Expenses	Total over 4 Weeks	Average per Week
Regular Expenses		
Food	₱1,127.50	₱282
Fare and snacks for herself and other		
household members	197.50	49
Other household expenses	98.00	24.50
Subtotal	1,423	₱355.50
Other Expenses		
Dressmaker	40	
Church donations	13	
Medicine	31	
Flowers for funeral	14	
Gift for baptism	14	
Subtotal	112	
Payments for Houses		
For proposed house in Dagupan		
Surveyor and title	1,150	
For family house in Camiling		
Architect's plans and cement	3,000	
Subtotal	4,150	
Remittances		
To husband	4 cans of food	
To Camiling	100	
To brother	100	
Help for funeral of cousin	400	
Subtotal	600	
Loans		
To maid	15	
To neighbor	200	
Subtotal	215	
Total expenses and payments	₱6,500	

Note: Based on records kept by Andrea Ferrer.

Andrea exchanges at the going black-market rate (varying from 8.5 to 10 pesos on the dollar).

Andrea Ferrer does not depend exclusively on her husband's remittances, however. Rather, like many other salaried workers, she engages in a number of "sidelines," including buying and selling goods, lending money, and mortgaging land. For buying and selling she uses small sums of money from her own salary; for other sidelines she uses some of the money remitted by her husband. In her buying and selling activities, Andrea obtains goods from friends and relatives and then resells them, either on commission or for a straight profit. One friend sells diamond jewelry; on occasion, Andrea sells jewelry for her on 10 percent commission. For example, when relatives were going to the United States they brought ₱6,000 worth of jewelry; Andrea made ₱600 on the transaction. In another case, a co-worker had obtained some wooden serving dishes made in Baguio. Andrea bought one for ₱100 and then gave it to a friend who lives near Clark Air Force Base and who buys and sells PX goods. The friend was to sell the dish, and split the profit with Andrea. Andrea started up another buy-and-sell sideline when a cousin based in Manila began to obtain embroidered goods made in Bulacan. She started with ₱1,000 worth of goods and then handed them over to her close friend and neighbor who engages in buying and selling on a full-time basis. The friend does the actual selling; Andrea tells her the price she wants, and the friend keeps any money made by selling above that price. For a four week period for which she kept records, she made ₱420 on such transactions (see table 41).

In a number of other, more profitable transactions, Atche Andrea

TABLE 41.   Andrea Ferrer's Income During a Four-Week Period, March–April, 1979

Partial salary	₱270
Other from job (honorarium, per diem, etc.)	475
Sidelines (selling embroidered material)	420
Pawn gold necklace	50
Remittances from husband	
March	3,500
April	5,000
Total	₱9,715

Note: Based on records kept by Andrea Ferrer.

essentially acts as a banker, making loans and paying others to collect for her. The transactions involved are often complex:

> I am providing money for fertilizer to some farmers in Alaminos; in return I get a bag of rice for each bag of fertilizer. The man I know there is the father-in-law of my cousin in Manila. He has five hectares of land; I provide fertilizer for him and for some of his neighbors, but he makes all the arrangements with the others. Each bag of fertilizer costs between ₱70 and ₱85. For the first rice crop this year [1978], I gave money for twenty sacks of fertilizer. In return, after the harvest I got twenty cavans of rice. For the second rice crop, I provided twenty-five bags, and another twenty-five bags for the third. I am selling the rice to neighbors and to some people in Calmay [one of the island barrios of Dagupan]. The buyers pay on a monthly basis; I sell one cavan of rice [about sixty kilos] for ₱130. From this, I get ₱120 and ₱10 goes to the woman from Calmay who collects the money. She is the niece of my landlady, and she and her husband are jobless and have four children. So she distributes the rice and collects the money for me.

The woman on Calmay also introduced Andrea to some fish vendors there. "I am lending money to six of them. Every month I lend a maximum of ₱100 to each, and then renew the loan each month. They pay me ₱10 on each ₱100 borrowed." She comments, "I really don't make much money on these loans. I also want to help these people. But I was worried that the transactions might be usury, so I spoke with the priest about it before I began."

In the time since her husband began to work in Saudi Arabia, Andrea Ferrer has made a number of major purchases for the household. The living area of her apartment is filled with furniture—a *sala* set consisting of two adjoining couches covered in red and a matching table with footstools, a television, a new stove, and a second-hand sewing machine. Altogether, she spent more than ₱7,000 on these items. By the time her husband returns from overseas, he and Andrea plan to have a house of their own. With money sent by Tony, Andrea purchased a house lot in a new subdivision on the outskirts of Dagupan; she paid ₱10,000 down on a ₱19,000 lot. She began to look over house plans, but deferred selecting one until Tony returned to help in the decision. Andrea and Tony are also planning for their daughter's future; they purchased an educational insurance policy for her when she was one year old; they pay ₱600 a year so that she will get ₱10,000 when she is eighteen, or sooner, if something happens to Tony.

In addition to such purchases and investments, Andrea has used money sent back by her husband in a number of other ways. She has begun mortgaging land for others, something she also did when Tony was in Guam. Her husband's cousin needed money to pay a bank mortgage, to avoid having the mortgage foreclosed. Andrea provided ₱2,500 and in return she receives the owner's share of the produce. The land produces both rice and tobacco; on the rice crop, she got fifty cavans of *palay* (unhusked rice) in 1978 and she expected to receive about ₱500 for the tobacco. This represents a 50 percent share of the total crop.

Probably the most important investment was the purchase of rice land in Andrea's hometown of Camiling. "Three months after my husband left, I bought one hectare of rice land from my cousin, for ₱10,000. It produces two rice crops a year and is irrigated. There is a tenant on it. I provide the fertilizer and insecticide and receive a 30 percent share of the produce. My aunts in Camiling help to watch the land for me. In the first harvest this year I got twenty-four cavans of palay, making more than twelve cavans of rice, but the land had been hurt by the flood [from a typhoon] and the rice was very dark. I sell some of the rice, but we mainly eat it. At least now I don't have to buy rice any more.

"Some of my friends whose husbands are overseas have invested in fishponds and have gotten a return on their investment in six months. But I'm afraid to do this because I don't know fishponds and I don't know anyone to oversee them for me. I might be cheated."

In addition, Andrea and Tony have invested in two companies; they bought stock in an oil exploration firm and in an agricultural supply company that had been formed by friends and relatives of Tony in San Fabian. Andrea plans to purchase more stock in the future, and is also considering buying more land in Camiling and possibly providing money for mortgages on others' land.

At the same time that Andrea is spending and investing the money remitted by her husband, she is also involved in remittances and gift giving of her own. Many of these are gifts which exist as part of her social obligations. At the time of the fiesta in San Fabian, she contributed ₱100 when the mayor of the town (a friend of her husband) called on her. When she acted as a godparent there, she gave a total of ₱65. Each year at Christmas, she gives gifts to a variety of people—godchildren, in-laws and other relatives of her husband, and some of her own relatives. For the most part, she gives clothing or small amounts of money, although she also gave rice to her landlady and to the person who helped her husband get his job in Saudi Arabia.

Andrea's only regular remittance is to her brother in Camiling; both she and her sister send ₱50 a month to help support him. But in the four weeks when she kept records, she gave another ₱100 to family in Camiling and also helped with funeral expenses for a relative (see table 40). In addition, she and her sister were helping to pay for the rebuilding of the family home in Camiling. In that same four-week period, she spent ₱3,000 for an architect and for cement for the house in Camiling. The old Spanish-style house had been torn down and a new house was being built, which was to have four bedrooms and be large enough for family visits. Andrea doesn't ever expect to live in Camiling: "Camiling is a town, not a city, it's somewhat backward. I like it here [in Dagupan] better. But it is a family house and I will take my vacations there."

Even though she is spending large sums of money both on a house in Camiling and on plans for her own house in Dagupan, her ultimate goal is to live in neither place, but to emigrate to the United States. She and Tony dream of eventually joining other members of his family there. In preparation for that possibility, she is sending their daughter to an American-style nursery school. Even though she feels that she is criticized for spending too much money, and that she has incurred the jealousy of her husband's relatives as a result, she feels that she should buy things and invest the money while she has it, especially for Nina's sake, as she is her only child.

Lisa: The Life of a Domestic Servant

"I would like to live in this house. It's very large to look at. The people living here are rich. There are many plants. There's coconut. Maybe their father is overseas and their mother is employed in a government office. Maybe they have three children, maybe they are studying, like nurse and med–tech, doctor. They have complete appliances, like TV, stereo. They have two maids."

"I don't want this house; it is a dark place. It's a barrio. The people are poor like me and maybe their mother is a laundrywoman and they have many children." (These are Lisa's responses to photos of different types of houses. Lisa was asked to describe the people living in thirteen houses shown in photos and to say where she would like to live.)[1]

In these comments about two houses pictured in photographs she was shown, Lisa Cruz, a thirteen-year-old housegirl, clearly distinguished between the style of living of someone like herself and her family and that of someone like her employer, Andrea Ferrer, who works in a government office and whose husband is overseas. But as a domestic servant, Lisa in fact lives in the household of her employer—a "rich" person—not with her own parents, and to some extent is able to share in the lifestyle of the former. In moving to Dagupan to work for Mrs. Ferrer, Lisa has radically changed the type of household in which she lives, yet remains tied in many ways to her own family who depend on her for much of their livelihood.

Work and Life in Dagupan

Born in San Fabian, Lisa grew up and went to school there. When she was in the fifth grade, she began to come to Dagupan every weekend to clean house for Mrs. Ferrer and to babysit for Nina. She also cleaned house for Mrs. Ferrer's parents-in-law in San Fabian. The following year, she came to live with Mrs. Ferrer and completed primary school in Dagupan. She then stopped attending school and began to work full time for Mrs. Ferrer.

As a housemaid, her life and activities primarily revolve around her household duties, as the following quotes from a journal she kept indicate:[2]

Monday, February 5

In the morning I washed the milk bottle. We went to our neighbor's house with Nina to greet Kuya John a happy birthday. Then I stayed at home and took care of Nina. After lunch, I washed all the dishes. I went to the market and bought some fishes, vegetables, shrimps, and others. I bathed Nina and prepared milk for her and let her sleep. I stayed at home and took care of her. Also watched TV show. After dinner, I washed all the dishes. Took care of Nina. Watched TV show. Prepared milk for her and let her sleep. Threw all the garbage and brought water upstairs.

My father came to see me. He brought a skirt from my sister

Helen. I gave him ₱5.00 Mrs. Ferrer advanced me ₱20.00, a deduction from my salary.

Tuesday, February 6

I cleaned the house, wiped the jalousies and took care of Nina. I went out together with Nina, visited the birds of Roger [pet birds belonging to a small boy living nearby]. I went to the market and bought some eggs, vegetables, and fish. After lunch, I washed all the dishes. I bathed Nina, prepared milk, and let her sleep. I took care of her again in the afternoon and strolled at the plaza. As usual, after dinner, I washed all the dishes. Threw all the garbage and after that brought two pitchers of water upstairs.

Wednesday, February 7

I cleaned the house. Went to the market and bought milk, fish, laundry soap, vegetables, meat, eggs, and other things. Took care of Nina. I prepared milk for Nina after lunch and then let her sleep. We strolled at the plaza. I watched the TV show. After dinner I washed the dishes. Prepared milk for Nina and threw the garbage. Watch the TV show.

Thursday, February 8

In the morning I wiped the jalousies. Swept the yard. I went to the store. Bought something to eat for her [Nina] *merienda* [snack]. We played ball game and I took care of her. Later, I took care of her lunch and gave her a sponge bath. I let her sleep. We went to the house of Atche Gloria to see the birds of Roger. In the evening I prepared the food for her and then prepared the milk. I washed the milk bottle. Threw the garbage and watched the TV show.

Friday, February 9

I wiped the jalousies and cleaned the house upstairs. We went to the store and bought something to eat for Nina. We strolled around and also went to Teachers Memorial. After lunch I took care of Nina. I let her sleep, then gave her a sponge bath. Then we strolled at the plaza. We rent bicycle at the plaza with Nina and Nanang Auring. We went to the market for window shopping. After dinner I washed the dishes. I prepared food for Nina and threw the garbage. I watched TV show.

Saturday, February 10

I went to the market and bought fish, tomatoes, calamansi fruit, slippers for Nina and Mrs. Ferrer. I gave Nina a bath and fixed everything to be ready [to leave] for Manila. We left here at 10 A.M. We stopped in Santa Barbara because the bus had trouble, then we returned here in Dagupan. We transferred to another bus. We arrived in Manila at 4 P.M. and rested for a while. (Lisa accompanied Mrs. Ferrer and Nina to visit Mrs. Ferrer's sister in Manila; it was her second visit there.)

Lisa's routine remains much the same from day to day. It is a life circumscribed by her employment and by the few people she meets in the neighborhood where she lives. Primarily responsible for the care of Nina, she spends most of the day with her, occasionally going to the market or the plaza. Living in Mrs. Ferrer's apartment just off the main road and only half a block from the plaza, she rarely goes far. It takes ten or fifteen minutes to walk to the market, less to go to the plaza. She visits with neighbors in the apartment building and nearby: Kuya John is a schoolteacher who lives in a house near the apartment; Atche Auring is an old woman living in the apartment building; Roger is a five-year-old boy who stays occasionally with his grandmother in a nearby house.

Occasionally, she visits with other housegirls living in the neighborhood; one, in particular, is her age and works for a co-worker of Mrs. Ferrer. Another girl her age, a relative of the Ferrers who was her classmate in San Fabian, comes every few months to visit in Dagupan. But when friends of Mrs. Ferrer come to visit, Lisa stays in the background, playing with Nina or helping Mrs. Ferrer's aunts with the cooking.

Her closest ties and greatest interaction are with Mrs. Ferrer: "If I need help, or get sick or need to borrow money, I would go to Mrs. Ferrer. If I had an accident, I would tell Mrs. Ferrer. I would not like to inform my parents. If I had something confidential, secret to tell someone, I would tell Mrs. Ferrer. Or I might tell my friend from across the street. But I don't tell all my secrets to my friends, because Mrs. Ferrer might get angry."[3]

For Lisa's thirteenth birthday, Mrs. Ferrer organized a party; her aunts prepared food, neighborhood children and adults attended, and Mrs. Ferrer gave her a dress as a gift. Lisa received no gifts from her family in San Fabian. A month later, at Christmas, she received a gift of ₱20 from Mrs. Ferrer. At that time Lisa also gave her parents a gift of ₱35.

Lisa did not go home at Christmas, however, but waited until the town fiesta in January, when she spent a night in San Fabian and saw her sisters and friends: "I went to the plaza on Friday night with my friends and saw many of my former classmates there. On Saturday I went to the beach with my cousins and friends." Her trip home for the fiesta was one of the rare occasions when she went to San Fabian, even though it is only a twenty-minute bus ride from Dagupan. Nevertheless, she sees her parents regularly, as they come to Dagupan about once a month, primarily to get money from her.

Family in San Fabian

Lisa's parents, grandparents, and brother and sisters all live in San Fabian. When Lisa visits there, she usually goes to her grandparents' house first. Located on the dirt road that leads to the beach, the house is a dilapidated wood building. Two or three broken steps on the side provide an entrance to the kitchen, a room about four by six feet, with the usual counter for the kerosene stove. A short hallway leads into the sitting room, empty except for two wooden chairs, a table and a built-in cabinet with some dishes. A new clock stands near the entrance to the bedroom, off of the sitting room. Lisa's father's parents live here, and her sisters and brother stay with them most of the time, although occasionally they sleep at their parents' house in the *poblacion*. Lisa's uncle lives next door: his fifteen-year-old daughter works in Manila, but his other five children visit back and forth between their house and their grandparents.

When she wants to see her mother, Lisa can find her at the Ferrers' home in the *poblacion*, where she spends her days doing the washing and ironing in a back room of the house. The room where she works is concrete-block and dimly lit. She does the wash in a large tub there, and irons with an iron filled with hot coals. She and her husband live in a small house behind the Ferrers', on land belonging to the Ferrers' nephew. They pay no rent for the land, and the house, which is part of Lisa's grandparents' former home, belongs to them.

Lisa's father's father came to San Fabian from San Fernando, La Union as a young man. (See fig. 12 for birthplaces and occupations of Lisa's relatives.) He opened a watch repair shop in the market, and now, some fifty years later, continues to repair watches there. He met his wife—Lisa's grandmother—in San Fabian; her father was a fisherman and her

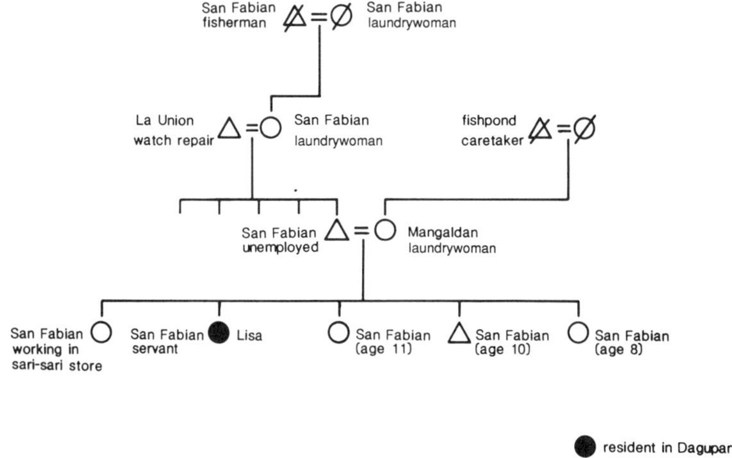

Fig. 12. Lisa; birthplace and occupation of family members

mother worked as a laundrywoman. After her marriage, she too worked for many years as a laundrywoman, primarily for members of the Ferrer family. Lisa's grandparents had eight children, several of whom now live in Manila. Her father was the oldest child; now in his early forties, he has always lived in San Fabian. After completing his second year of high school, he found work as a conductor on buses running between Dagupan and San Fabian. He stopped working five or six years ago and now spends his days visiting in the market and around town; his wife complains that he drinks their money, and Lisa says she is "ashamed" to have outsiders meet her father because he might be drunk.

Lisa's mother was born in Mangaldan, a town near San Fabian. Her father worked as a caretaker of fishponds for a family in San Fabian; she met her husband when she helped out in a small store belonging to her fathers' employer. After her marriage and move to San Fabian, she began to work for the Ferrer family as a laundrywoman, as her mother-in-law had previously done.

Lisa's mother has lived in San Fabian since her marriage except for a few months when she left her husband: "Early this year I got mad at my husband and ran away. I went to Manila and stayed there for four months. He got sick when I was gone, so someone came and called me back." According to Mrs. Ferrer, Lisa's mother left because her husband was beating her and spending money on wine. When she went to Manila, she stayed with the elder Mrs. Ferrer's brother and worked in his household. Later, she worked for a short time for one of the Ferrers' daughters, doing laundry for her. But when she heard her husband was sick, she returned home to care for him.

Lisa has three sisters and one brother; all are in school except her older sister, who works at a *sari-sari* store (small neighborhood shop selling basic provisions) owned by her cousin in the San Fabian market. Like Lisa, her older sister left school after sixth grade. She has worked at the *sari-sari* store for only a year, and is paid ₱1 a day.

Expenses and Remittances of Lisa and Her Family

Lisa's mother earns ₱4 a day working as a *lavendera* for the Ferrers. She works every day, washing and ironing not only for the older couple but also for their daughter and son-in-law. This is the sole regular income from within the household, as her elder daughter's ₱1 a day is for her own expenses. Lisa's mother estimates that she buys about one kilo of rice a day, at ₱2.10; she uses whatever is left for other food, such as vegetables, or occasionally fish. Sometimes the Ferrers give her vegetables and meat.

For nearly all other expenses, Lisa's mother gets money from Lisa. Lisa earns ₱60 a month, and gets food and lodging from Atche Andrea. However, she and Atche Andrea have agreed to tell her parents that she earns only ₱50, because every month her parents come to Dagupan to get half her salary. In this way, she has ₱10 that they don't know about, and which she tries to save in the bank.

When her parents' house needed repair, they borrowed ₱300 from Lisa, given by Atche Andrea as an advance on her salary. When her mother needed medicine, she came to Dagupan to buy it, stopping first to see Lisa and having her accompany her to the drugstore. When her sister hurt her back, Lisa's mother borrowed ₱20. When Lisa and her parents entertained visitors during the fiesta, Lisa gave her mother ₱40 for food.

Lisa's gift giving is limited, but at Christmas she gave her parents ₱35, and at the time of the fiesta, she gave clothes to each of her sisters, and another ₱5 to her father. Any money that is left from her salary she spends on items for herself, such as clothing, and other necessities (see table 42).

Lisa has no plans to return to her family in San Fabian. "I want to live in Dagupan, because I like it here, and Mrs. Ferrer can take good care of me." She says that she would like to return to school, and eventually to "marry a man with a stable job and have one child."

Discussion

In the cases of Lisa and Andrea Ferrer, we see two family groups that have been linked over several generations (see fig. 13). As in patron-client ties based on landlord-tenant relationships, these ties link families occupying very different social class positions. Unlike the more typical landlord-tenant ties, this relationship is not focused on the land. Rather, the Ferrers have employed the women of Lisa's family as servants—*lavenderas* and, in Lisa's case, housegirls. As in other patron-client ties, the bonds have more content to them than a simple employer-employee relationship. The older Ferrers provide a support system for Lisa's mother; her pay is low, but they give her food as well. More importantly, they help out in emergencies. When she decided to leave her husband, it was other members of the Ferrer family who took her in and let her work for them. While the Ferrers have provided jobs and some support for Lisa and her family, they have at the same time obtained for

TABLE 42. Income and Expenses of Lisa and Her Parents

	Lisa	Parents
Income	₱60/month	Mother: ₱4/day × 30 = ₱120/month
	In kind: room and board	In kind: food from employer; children stay with grandparents part of the time
		Remittances: ₱25 from Lisa
		Total: ₱145 plus in kind
Expenses	Clothing: occasional	Rice: ₱2.10/day × 30 = ₱63/month
	Personal items: occasional	Other food, wine: whatever is available from mother's income
	Remittance to parents: ₱25/month	Medicine
	Savings: ₱10/month	House repairs
	Gifts and additional contributions to parents for medicine, repairs, etc.	Special occasions

Note: Based on interviews with Lisa, her mother, and Andrea Ferrer.

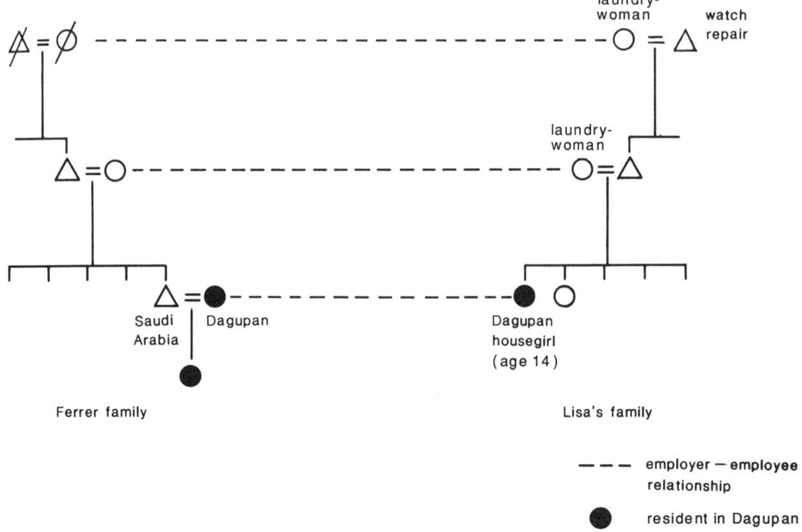

Fig. 13. Ferrer family and Lisa's family; employer-employee
relationships

themselves servants who to some extent see themselves as "part of the
family," who are therefore "loyal" and "do not gossip."

For Lisa's family, work in the service sector of the economy is not
new, nor is it limited to the women of the family. Lisa's father worked as
a bus conductor; one grandfather is a watch repairman, the other was a
caretaker of fishponds. Only three generations back do we find someone
with a primary-sector occupation—her father's mother's father was a
fisherman. The women have had even more restricted employment:
Lisa's mother, grandmother, and great-grandmother were all laundrywomen in San Fabian. Today's generation follows the pattern established by their parents. Lisa's sister works as a shop assistant, as her
mother did before her marriage. When her mother considers what the
younger children in the family might do when they grow up, she suggests that perhaps they, too, can get jobs "in the house," like Lisa.

The family does not fit the typical image of the "rural Filipino"—a
farming (or perhaps fishing) family that only in this generation has
moved off the land by sending some younger members to work in the
city. Migration, like service-sector employment, is not new to this generation. Rather, Lisa's grandfather migrated from his home in the

Ilocano area of La Union to Pangasinan, as did many others at that time. And while her mother's father only went from one small town to a neighboring one to work, he would today be classified as a landless rural worker.

It could be argued, perhaps, that Lisa's move from San Fabian to Dagupan and from the laundry work of her mother to being a housegirl demonstrates a very limited upward mobility. While neither occupation is prestigious or well paid, that of housegirl is somewhat higher in prestige than that of laundrywoman and probably somewhat higher paid, with some important additional in-kind payments such as room and board.[4] Furthermore, living and working in the city, in a middle-class person's home, improves Lisa's material position over that of other members of her family; even though she gives nearly half of her salary to her parents, she still has more money to spend for herself than do others in the family.

Lisa's parents and siblings are dependent on her for monetary support; her remittances provide a considerable portion of the family's income for basic survival needs. The money is used, as we have seen, for food and necessities such as medicine and house repairs. Although the absolute amount remitted is small, it is essential to their survival. Unlike other cases considered, the flow of money and of gifts is unidirectional; Lisa receives nothing material from her parents.

While Lisa's family depends on her, then, she is not dependent on them, and to a large extent, she seems to view her ties to her employer as closer than those to her own parents. Clearly, she is dependent for material goods on her employer: not only for money and room and board, but also for gifts, and for help in emergencies (thus, obtaining advances from her employer to give her parents). In addition, she spends most of her time with Atche Andrea and Nina, and seems in many ways attached to their way of life and even their values, as is suggested by her statements on her future goals and the responses to photos of different types of residences.

Clearly, there is a contradiction between the way of life of her own family and that of her employer, which she herself seems sensitive to in her comments on the photos—noting that "we" are "poor" and that those working as civil servants are "rich." But she lives in the household of her employer, and as a servant, is closely bound to it, yet not completely part of it. More so than for others we have considered, the move to the city represents a major break with those at home, and Lisa, perhaps because she moved while still rather young, seems now to identify considerably more with her employer than with her own family.

In the case of Andrea Ferrer, remittances are again important, but with very different implications. The remittances that she receives from her husband in Saudi Arabia are used for a number of different purposes. There is a considerable amount of what might be seen as conspicuous consumption—new furniture, appliances—things which the average Filipino cannot afford. There is as well purchase of property—the houselot and rice land. And, finally, Andrea and her husband have made a number of investments. For them, his going to work overseas has led to considerable upward mobility, enabling them to purchase items and make investments that could not otherwise have been possible. In noting this, it is important to also note that Andrea and her husband were in a position to be able to take advantage of opportunities for overseas migration, something not open to most Filipinos. Through a combination of his status, skills, and personal contacts, he was able to obtain a job that led to significantly larger earnings than he would have received in the Philippines. Andrea augments these earnings by engaging in a diverse array of sideline activities, in addition to her regular employment.

Like the others whose cases have been discussed, Andrea and her husband maintain extensive ties with members of their natal families. But unlike someone like Lisa, their families are not in any way dependent on them for survival. (Andrea's brother is a possible exception, but he is supported by a number of relatives.) They both do contribute in various ways to family at home, although more through gifts than outright remittances. What is of greater interest is the extent to which they are involved in other activities in their hometowns and continue to retain links there. Even though Tony is away, he and Andrea have bought stock in a company based in his hometown; similarly, when Andrea wanted to purchase rice land, she found some that belonged to a relative. They are also seen by others in their hometowns as people who should be involved in local activities and events, such as making contributions to the town fiesta. When Andrea's cousin died, Andrea was the one who was called to help with arrangements. In other words, the obligations to family and community continue, even after marriage, and even when there is no dependence or absolute need for monetary or material aid. In Andrea's case, she finds that she must represent her husband as well as herself while he is away.

Whereas in a case like Lisa's we find fairly minimal strategizing—the family knows the Ferrer family and knows they will employ her, so she goes to work there—in cases involving overseas migration such as we see in the Ferrer family, quite complex strategies are developed. Such strategies are apparent not only in the decisions made by Tony and Andrea but also in those of other Ferrer family members. Tony and Andrea have clearly decided that they want more than can be earned in the Philippines, and have found a way to pursue that goal. His parents were following still another route, with the goal of enabling their youngest daughter to emigrate to the United States; their strategy requires knowledge of, and ability to use and manipulate, U.S. immigration laws.

In these cases, as in others considered, the extent of family decision making regarding migration is apparent. None of the decisions discussed here—Lisa's, or Tony's, or those of other members of the Ferrer family—were made by an individual acting alone. It is doubtful that Lisa ever actually made a decision regarding working in Dagupan; rather, arrangements were worked out largely between the Ferrers and her parents. As we have seen, most of her activities are in fact circumscribed by her situation, as a domestic servant living and working in a particular household and sending half her salary home. In very different circumstances, Tony made a decision to migrate to obtain better work and pay; but again, family considerations played a major role.

In the two cases discussed in this chapter, then, we see two linked family groups for whom migration has been an important route for access to opportunities and income. But in one family, that of Lisa, it is essentially a survival strategy, a way to try to obtain income for minimum subsistence. In the other, starting out at a much higher social class position, migration—especially overseas migration—has led to social mobility and a variety of new opportunities.

Chapter 9

Conclusion

The case studies in Part 2 provide detailed evidence on the migration process and subsequent rural-urban interaction for a small set of people. What are the implications of such evidence for understanding migrants and migration in general, both in the lowland Philippines and elsewhere? In this conclusion, I will suggest that these case studies, combined with the macrolevel data discussed in Part 1, provide insights into several key aspects of migration. These include (1) the importance of continuing rural-urban links and formation of dispersed family networks; (2) family migration strategies and the role of remittances; (3) the role of women in migration and in maintaining ties following migration; and (4) people's own perceptions of their activities as migrants and the extent to which they themselves focus on rural-urban distinctions.

Rural-Urban Links and Dispersed Family Networks

By following migrants back and forth between the city and their rural homes, we have been able to consider in some detail the formation and maintenance of ties between those resident in Dagupan and those living elsewhere. In particular, ties between family members are maintained and relied on. While migrants have moved away from their family homes, more or less permanently, they continue to be part of the support network of those family members remaining at home. They visit, send those family members remaining at home gifts and remittances and often continue to see the rural place as "home."

Rather similar patterns of rural-urban ties have been described elsewhere, especially in Africa. Gugler and Flanagan state, for example, that studies in West Africa "show, without exception, that immigrants in a variety of urban settings maintain quite strong ties with their areas of origin, with what they consider their 'homes'" (1978:67), while Mayer argues that in South Africa, the extent to which extra-town ties are retained influences migrant behavior and identity and that such ties enable the migrant "to resume his place in a specific tribal community" at a later date (1962:578). Similarly, in East Africa, Ross and Weisner have argued that among migrants to Nairobi, Kenya, "the goal of most migrants is to maintain a high level of contact with their rural families" (1977:360).

However, the situation in the Philippines differs in important respects from that described for African societies. In the latter, the ties are to *place* (i.e., hometown and community), as well as to *people* (relatives or others). For example, Bartle describes the formation of "an extended community," including migrants and nonmigrants in Ghana, that is "dispersed by cyclical migration and bounded by the ethnic identity of migrants with their home towns" (1981:112). Therefore, the ties are maintained between migrants and those *at home*.

While Filipino migrants maintain ties with those at home, they may also have important links with people living elsewhere; the ties are to *people*—especially family—wherever they may be residing, rather than to place. The result is what I would term dispersed family networks, which include interaction and, frequently, support, among people who may be residing in two or more different places. These places may be the rural home and urban residence of the migrant, or they may include people in other cities, and even overseas. In the third case in chapter 6, the family is dispersed between the rural home, Dagupan and Manila; in the case described in chapter 8, ties are maintained among family members in the rural home, Dagupan, and Saudi Arabia. While migrants also retain friendships and other ties in their hometowns, the major interaction and support networks revolve around family ties, regardless of the residence of the family members.

Such dispersed family networks are found among people in a range of socioeconomic situations, including those who are well below the poverty line, as well as those who are relatively well off. In Africa, a major reason for continuing to maintain ties with the home community is to maintain access to land (Gugler and Flanagan 1978; Ross and Weisner 1977); in fact, Ross and Weisner argue that a precondition of the emergence of rural linkages is "the availability of rural resources to the migrant," the most important of which is land (1977:362). That is clearly not a precondition of such links in the Philippines. While some do indeed have an interest in land or other rural resources—with some having in fact purchased land long after migrating, as in the case of the Santoses described in chapter 7—most do not. Even among those who anticipate returning to the rural barrios, or who at least hope to do so, such as the salesgirls in chapter 6, it is unlikely that they plan to engage in farming or to otherwise use the small parcels of land currently farmed by family members.

Of greater importance in these networks is the sharing of resources in both directions, back and forth between those in the city and those elsewhere. In this respect, the interaction patterns are similar to those described by Hugo (1982) for circular migrants in Indonesia as well as to the linkages among "confederations of households" that G. A. Smith (1980) has described in Peru. In both these cases, as in the Philippines, people are engaged in ways of spreading their income-earning possibilities in situations in which there are limited opportunities and in which any single source of support is not likely to be sufficient. Among migrants to Dagupan, such strategies for mutual support are found not only among those whose families are poor, but also among those who are better off. Overall, there seem no clear socioeconomic characteristics that predict the type or extent of ties likely to be maintained (Trager 1984a). What is clear is that, for nearly all involved, migration is a process leading to extensive interaction and support among individuals who may be widely dispersed in space, but for whom such dispersal does not generally lead to a breaking of ties.

How does the existence of such residentially dispersed networks affect the formation and maintenance of households? As we have seen in chapter 5, the most common residential unit in the lowland Philippines is the nuclear family household. If "household" means, as is generally accepted, a residential group sharing a common pot, then how should one interpret the position of a family member who resides elsewhere but who (a) visits home every weekend and thinks of the place as home, (b) contributes a substantial portion of his or her income; and (c) whose contribution affects the possibility of others in the family to eat, go to school, etc. The migrant is not a resident of that household, but is in many ways part of it, and is perceived as part of it by other family members.

In other words, the effects of migration go beyond changes in household composition; migration does not simply lead to the loss of members. Rather, migration adds to the considerable flexibility in domestic arrangements that already exists in the Philippines, leading to situations where family members are residentially absent and yet remain integral to the support of other household members. Families and households engage in a wide variety of activities at different times and in different places as part of the effort to mobilize resources for maintaining themselves; migration is one means of obtaining access to diverse sources of income. In understanding contemporary Filipino family and household organization, it is necessary to examine the total field in which household members operate, the resources available, and how family networks are used to mobilize these.

A similar perspective has been suggested in recent comparative studies of the household. While most discussions continue to define households in terms of residence, some recent definitions stress the examination of sharing of certain key tasks (Wilk and Netting 1984; Carter 1984). Wilk and Netting make an argument similar to that made here. They suggest that, in certain situations "perhaps the most important members are those who are not in residence at all" and term such members *intermittent coresidents* (1984:19). Carter goes still further to argue that "the household dimension of the domestic group . . . is defined by shared tasks of production and/or consumption, regardless of whether its members are linked by kinship or marriage or are coresident" (1984:45). Carter, as well as Wilk and Netting, point to the likelihood that noncoresident households will develop in situations of "economic stringency" (Wilk and Netting 1984:19) in which members must leave, usually temporarily, to seek income elsewhere. While it is certainly true in the Philippines that dispersed family networks involving sharing of resources occur among poor households, such networks are not limited to poor households. In chapter 8, for example, we see dispersed family networks both in the case of the girl working as a domestic servant and helping to support the rest of her family and in the case of the middle-level civil servant whose husband works in Saudi Arabia.

Recent discussions of the household have emphasized the problematic nature of determining not only household membership but also the flows of resources and income among those members (Netting, Wilk, and Arnould 1984; Wilk n.d.). Wilk, in particular, has pointed out the diverse interests of household members and the various possibilities for sharing of resources and decision making. When migration and the situation of absent household members are included in the analysis, the result is even more complex and more problematic. In a discussion based on a sample survey in the Ilocos area, Caces et al. identify what they call *shadow households*, consisting of "all individuals whose principal commitments and obligations are to a particular household but who are not presently residing in that household" (1985:8). However, it is not always possible to determine where "principal commitments and obligations" lie, and there may be sharing of resources and income among sets of people even if that is not the "principal" commitment. In cases such as those of the three young salesgirls and Lisa, it is fairly clear that their principal ties are to their natal households. But the Santos couple and Mrs. Ferrer have diverse sets of obligations, including both urban household members and rural family; Mrs. Ferrer is obligated to, and shares some resources with, her husband's family as well as her own. There can also be overlapping obligations, and nonsharing of resources among those who reside in the same place; in the case of Delia, we find the sharing of some resources between her older sister and her parents, who coreside, as well as restriction on the use of the remittances that her sister receives from her husband to support herself and her children.

Furthermore, the use of a term such as *shadow household* seems to imply some permanence to the existing set of arrangements, whereas key features of the relationships described in this study are their flexibility and changing characteristics over time. Finally, such terminology is even less applicable in situations, such as most of Africa, where the household is a much less central unit than it is in the Philippines, and where even coresiding members do not routinely share or pool resources.

What I am calling dispersed family networks, then, includes households and noncoresident household members, but it may also include others who share some resources and who feel some obligation and commitment to one another. My sense here is similar to what Kearney has recently called the Articulatory Migrant Network (AMN), which has, he suggests a developmental cycle:

[The AMN] is, among other things, an income-seeking organism. Driven out of the sending area by economic necessity, individuals and households move in and out of various spaces that permit often complex economic strategies. In this historic process differentiation of many kinds occurs within the network . . . . Also, individuals and households form various relationships with elements outside the network . . . . The sum total of these changing internal and external relationships constitutes the life cycle of the network. (1986:354)

Family Migration Strategies

The dispersed family networks discussed above form in a socioeconomic situation where migration represents a possible income-generating strategy. As in the case of the Mexican migrants studied by Selby and Murphy, "migration is an income-generating strategy directed at family preservation" (1982:iv). The decision to migrate, then, is not typically an individual one, but is rather taken in a family context. Family strategies are not necessarily focused on migration per se, but are rather concerned with ways of maintaining and/or advancing the household by bringing in income and other resources necessary. Furthermore, family strategies are important not only in influencing a particular individual in the decision to migrate, but also in influencing decisions and activities long after migration.

In the cases discussed in Part 2, we see two broad types of strategy. One represents a strategy for survival, not only of the individual migrant, but also of other family members. The other is an attempt at achieving some upward mobility; this may involve either mobility for the migrant, or longer-term strategies of mobility for the family as a whole.

Cases such as that of Lisa or that of Marie are examples of family survival strategies, in which family members explicitly acknowledge the contribution being made by migrant members of the family. Marie's mother expresses this most clearly when she hopes that her daughter will remain single for a while longer, as the family needs the income she contributes for basic subsistence. Similarly, Lisa's parents rely substantially on the salary she contributes each month. Although the actual amounts are quite small in these cases, contributions from the income earned by migrant members is essential. Furthermore, in such households, there is expectation that younger children who are not yet working will find similar urban employment and make contributions in their turn.

Survival strategies such as these have been observed and analyzed elsewhere; for example, Hugo comments that among circular migrants in Java, "the flow of remittances is absolutely critical to the well-being of many village households" (1982:75). However, there is less discussion of strategies for upward mobility, as found among both poorer farm households and those from essentially middle-class professional households. Such strategies are clear in several of the cases in Part 2. For example,

Delia's family exhibits a pattern in which older siblings have helped pay for the education of younger siblings. In this case, as in that of Flor, there is no absolute necessity for contributions of income from migrant members to the rest of the family, yet such contributions take place and are used in a variety of ways, including in Delia's case, not only contribution to a sibling's education but also aid in obtaining things that will increase farm income, as in the purchase of pigs. These may be seen as activities geared to the attempted upward mobility of the family as a whole, although in the short run, such mobility is likely to be slight or nonexistent. In fact, it is essential to see these activities from the perspective of the family; they may actually be to the disadvantage of the individual migrant. Delia, for example, would prefer to have more of her income available to spend on herself.

In other cases, strategies are directed more toward the goal of achieving mobility for the migrant or migrants themselves. For the Santoses, for example, their purchase of land and other ties with the rural home are focused on increasing their own income and resources, rather than on the income of those in the rural home. Again, in the case of Mrs. Ferrer, the migration of her husband to Saudi Arabia is explicitly directed toward the goal of earning a larger income than would be possible in the Philippines, with the ultimate aim of establishing himself and his wife and child in a higher socioeconomic position.

For families to carry out either survival or mobility strategies, it is not simply a matter of sending out a family member as a migrant. In addition, the family has the expectation that the migrant will fulfill his or her obligations to other family members by sending remittances of goods, money, and so forth. As we have seen, this does in fact take place, even when the individual may prefer to have more of her income for her own use. To understand why this is so, we must examine not only the economic context in which such monetary support is necessary, but also the cultural values that sustain and reinforce the giving of remittances. In other words, "the moral imperatives of kinship and reciprocal obligation that flourish in the household context" (Wilk and Netting 1984:19) must also be considered. In the Philippines, as we have seen in chapter 5, the core value of *utang na loob* expresses the reciprocity and mutual obligation that is expected, especially between parent and child and between siblings. When an individual receives help from other family members, then that individual has an obligation to give assistance in return, when she is in a position to do so. This is a value that is felt, discussed and acted on by members of the society. People frequently comment that something represents *utang*, or, conversely, that someone *walang hiya* (has no shame), meaning that the person has *not* fulfilled expected reciprocal obligations. Among migrants, *utang* is represented symbolically by the small gifts regularly given, such as native cakes, biscuits, and local delicacies, which are referred to as *pasalubong*. Most migrants bring *pasalubong* when they visit relatives (Trager 1984a:323). However, the true extent to which these obligations are enacted is better indicated by the fact that 63 percent of migrants surveyed take or send necessities to family elsewhere, and 50 percent bring or send money on a regular basis (Trager 1984a:324). In other words, the reciprocal obligation indicated by the phrase *utang na loob* is expressed both through symbolic gifts and through the giving of necessities. Family strategies that are based on the expectation that migrant members of the family will aid others are embedded in these values. The expectation that those who migrate, especially young, single family members, will contribute to maintenance of those residing elsewhere is in general, fulfilled in practice.[1]

The Role of Remittances

Although embedded in cultural values of reciprocity and mutual obligation, the ties maintained between migrants and other family members are not simply sentimental and emotional ones. They form part of a set of practical responses to an overall situation in which family maintenance and mobility are difficult. In this context, monetary remittances from the migrant to those elsewhere are especially crucial. While not all migrants give remittances, a large percentage do; and for those who do, the remittances form an essential part of survival and mobility strategies of the family, as we have seen. What is the role of such remittances? Do they in fact contribute to the well being and advancement of the families receiving them? Do they have broader implications, in aiding rural development through the investment of urban income or in reducing income inequality?

It is clear from the cases that remittances do have substantial implications for the families receiving them, that for those on the margins, survival and maintenance would be difficult without them, and that for others, remittances can contribute to the possibility of mobility.

The importance of remittances goes beyond this, however. A central issue in the study of remittances has been whether they contribute to rural development. Rempel and Lobdell have argued that "it seems certain that very little [of remittances] is used directly as investment for rural development" (1978:336). In contrast, Stark suggests the need to look beyond direct investment in production, arguing that there is "sufficient evidence to suggest that rural-to-urban migration and urban-to-rural remittances can and have actually been used to transform agricultural modes of production" (1980:373).

The case data provided here tend to support the argument that remittances from urban migrants can be important for investment in agriculture and hence for rural development. In some cases, direct investment in productive activities is evident: the purchase of piglets by Delia's mother, for example, and on a larger scale, the purchase of rice land and provision of agricultural inputs by both the Santoses and Mrs. Ferrer. The latter case is especially interesting, in that it shows the use of remittances not only from urban migration but also from overseas migration; the money remitted is used not simply for individual and family consumption (new house and furniture) but for rice land and for making agricultural loans to others as well.

In other cases, the relationship between remittances and investment in agriculture is indirect: remittances may help to free other resources for productive activities. In the case of Delia, for example, her contribution to her sister's education has the effect of enabling her parents to spend money they earn in other ways, including on agriculture, as they do not have to contribute to their daughter's education.

On the other hand, there are clearly situations where remittances can have no effect—direct or indirect—on agricultural production; when a family is landless, as in Lisa's case, it is highly improbable that remittances will be used for agricultural investment.

A second issue in the debate on the effects of remittances is whether they help to equalize rural income distribution or to cause greater income inequality. Lipton has argued that remittances are "unlikely to do much to reduce rural poverty" and that those who receive larger remittances are better off to begin with. Hence, he argues that, at the village level, inequality is likely to increase rather than decrease (1980:11–13). Stark, on the other hand, argues that by increasing the income of poor rural households, remittances help reduce overall inequality in rural areas (1978:90). The data and approach taken here cannot directly answer the question of the effect of remittances on rural income inequality. Certainly, remittances to poor households help to improve the overall standard of living of those household members living in the rural area, and as migrants from poor backgrounds working in low-paying jobs seem to be as likely to give remittances as those in higher-paying jobs, it is possible that such remittances help to improve the situation of poor rural households in relation to others in the community. However, rural communities in the Philippines are complex and highly stratified, and seem to be becoming increasingly so as the ways in which people gain access to income-earning opportunities have changed. As the discussion in chapter 2 shows, it is no longer a simple situation of landlords and tenants, but rather one that includes landless, share tenants, leaseholders, those who own some land and are tenants on other land, and so on. The receipt of remittances by a household in any of these groups may change its situation vis-a-vis other households in the community. To analyze the overall impact of remittances in income distribution at the level of the village community, however, requires examination of data for households in all strata within a single community. Although such data do not exist, I think it unlikely that remittances as such are likely to smooth out the large differences that may exist among households in a single community, much less reduce overall income inequality.[2]

Migration of Women

Women play key roles in the family strategies described above and in giving remittances. The large number of women migrants in Philippine cities needs to be viewed in this context, as well as in terms of the economic opportunities that exist for women in those cities. That is, the migration of women needs to be seen both in relation to the macroeconomic structure and in terms of the microcontext of family and household decision making.

As we have seen in chapter 3, there are differential employment opportunities for males and females in rural and urban areas. Relatively few opportunities exist for females in rural areas, whereas in the cities they dominate in three major occupational groups—sales, domestic service, and professions such as teaching. For the most part, these occupations involve low paying, low status work in the informal sector, particularly in secondary cities where, according to Koo and Smith, 94 percent of recent female migrants are in informal sector occupations (1983:224). However, in a provincial and regional center such as Dagupan, migrant women also occupy professional positions, not only in teaching, but also in government agencies (Trager 1984b). Likewise, Bulatao found that, in general, women in small cities in the Philippines are better off occupationally, with more working in professional occupations, than was the case either among women in Manila or in rural areas (1984:350). Hence, in Dagupan, we find female migrants from a considerable range of educational and socioeconomic backgrounds, as exemplified by those described in Part 2.

The family strategies discussed above rely especially on young, single women. Although both men and women are expected to give remittances, and in fact do so, parents seem to feel that daughters are more reliable (Hart 1971). Therefore, a socioeconomic context where employment opportunities exist for women in urban areas has combined with family strategies for seeking out resources and increased income to lead to a situation where the migration of young women is increasingly important. The migration of women is not so much tied to strategies of *poor urban* households, as Koo and Smith (1983) have suggested, as it is to the survival and mobility strategies of *rural*-based households, including both those who are poor and those who are somewhat better off.

An important result of these strategies is that women play key roles in the social networks that result from and aid in migration. They are not simply passive players who get moved as a result of family decision making, but active participants in the creation and maintenance of networks involving the continual movement of people, goods and money. In Delia's family, for example, the daughters have created crucial links that have aided subsequent migration: the eldest daughter married a man from Dagupan, resulting in the establishment of a congenial and free living arrangement for Delia, who, in turn, provided rent for her younger sister in the same household.

In another vein, those who work together or who are in similar situations form social networks useful for communication within the city. The salesworkers at Dagupan Trading can communicate about work and living conditions, while the women whose husbands are in Saudi Arabia, such as Mrs. Ferrer, rely on each other for crucial information as well as for sending and receiving money and goods.

The linkages in social networks created by women have been noted by M. Estellie Smith (1976) in her study of Portuguese immigrants in the United States. She focuses on the ways in which women within an immigrant community provide essential links for the communication of information, for example about jobs. The networks considered here, however, are not limited to a single neighborhood or city, but rather extend between rural and urban areas. They are important not simply in communicating information but also in the sending of necessities that, in effect, maintain the family units of those involved.

It may seem paradoxical that in a society where the family is all-important, families are split and young female members are sent out as migrants in order to sustain and maintain the family. In effect, families encourage the migration of women, with the expectation, based on strong cultural values, that the result of such migration will be continued maintenance of the family unit through support received from the migrant. Given the overall socioeconomic context, however, where few opportunities exist in rural areas and where most households cannot sustain themselves through farming alone, it is hardly surprising.

Are Migrants Migrants?

How do the people engaged in migration view their activities? Do those who move see themselves as "migrants," uprooted from home? Do those living in rural areas see themselves as staying at home? Do they make a sharp distinction between rural and urban places? Much of the migration literature has been concerned with the question of "adaptation" to the urban environment. Is adaptation as problematic as it has seemed, or do people move between places with relative ease and flexibility?

Recent studies of circular migration (e.g., Hugo 1981, 1982) suggest some of the problems with emphasizing distinctions between rural and urban residence. When people circulate between rural and urban locales, leaving husbands or wives in one place while going to work in the other, as in the Javanese villages studied by Hugo, "a rethinking of what constitutes rural or urban 'residence' . . . is needed" (1981:294). In the present study, however, we have considered people who have moved on a relatively permanent basis from rural home to the urban area, at least in the sense that they are working full-time in Dagupan; in several cases, such as the Santos couple, they have lived in the city for many years. Nevertheless, we have found continued maintenance of ties with rural places and people, ties that are in many ways similar to those found among circular migrants elsewhere.

In addition, some of those who are now living in the city talk of the rural family as "home" and see that as the place where they have their strongest social links. This might suggest that they are embedded in a rural social network, involved only in city life to the extent that they must work there but having no further ties there. Yet this is not the case either. Those such as the three salesgirls participate in urban networks to the extent possible; further, their behavior patterns, including language usage, are fully appropriate to the urban context. They do not behave as, or see themselves as, "peasants" in the city. Neither do they behave as, or see themselves as, urban girls no longer able to participate in chores and other rural activities when they return to visit family at home. They, like the others discussed in this book, move back and forth with considerable ease, shifting behavior as appropriate to the context. Similarly, those family members now living in the rural area are also likely to move in and out of the city, at least to visit and in some cases, to stay. They, too, do so with relative ease. As Bartle has pointed out, "an individual need not suffer ambivalence from rural–urban contrasting obligations any more than a person has to suffer ambivalence from the daily contrasts in roles at work and roles at home" (1981:111).

It is, in other words, possible to suggest that those involved in migration carry dual or multiple identities involving combinations of ideas and values from rural and urban settings (cf. McGee 1975) and leading to behavior appropriate to those settings. This suggests, further, that the issue of adaptation to urban settings is less problematic than has often been suggested. In a situation such as the contemporary lowland Philippines, where access to transport is relatively easy and where people travel between places fairly easily and frequently, most adults from rural homes have had some exposure to urban locales, either directly or through contact with others who have lived or worked or visited in cities. In villages close to Manila, people move back and forth for visiting and work (van den Muijzenberg 1973). Those living further away from the capital such as in Pangasinan, have access to smaller cities such as Dagupan, although many also spend time in Manila. Even those living outside the lowlands, such as the relatives of Annie Santos, may well have access to the highland city of Baguio, although they are less likely to come to a lowland city such as Dagupan without prior contacts there.

There is, in other words, considerable mobility, only some of which involves movement to live and work in a new place. Are those who do move more or less permanently migrants? Clearly, from one point of view, they are, in that they can be defined in terms of the type of move they have made. But their own behavior and their own perception of their activities suggests viewing them in a somewhat different way: those who move, as well as those at home, may be seen as participants in a single social and resource system which, over time, may involve movement between a variety of locales, including cities and rural areas. Such a view not only takes into account the perspective of the participants themselves but also emphasizes the fluidity and flexibility of the process being studied. Today's urban migrants may be those in the rural home tomorrow, and vice versa. What is significant for those involved is where, within that social and resource field, they can gain access to resources, in such a way as to be able to participate most fully in the social networks of which they are a part, including, most importantly, the family networks that need to be maintained and sustained.

Migrants and the City

In this study I have taken a perspective that links the consideration of macrostructural conditions and processes with analysis of the microlevel activities of individuals and households. On the one hand, it is necessary to understand the socioeconomic and cultural context in which migration takes place—the structure of constraints and opportunities that affect people in a particular society. On the other hand, individuals and families are not simply passive recipients of imposed conditions. Rather they respond to those conditions, find ways to cope with them, and in the process, make decisions that help to shape the outcomes. At the same time, cultural values and ideas affect the responses and decisions that are made. Hence, there is a continuing, and complex, interaction between socioeconomic situations, cultural values, and the decisions and behavior of people that result in the patterns observed of migration, maintenance of family ties, remittances, and so on.

In utilizing such a perspective, I have focused in particular on intermediate units of analysis—the household, family, and social networks. As I have argued earlier, and as others have suggested as well, such units enable analysis of the decisions and activities of sets of people as they respond to and deal with the situations in which they find themselves. Individuals are important, but their activities are shaped by their immediate social context, which in the Philippines means especially the family context. Family strategies have been examined in some detail. Such "socially-determined strategies" (Leeds 1976:69) result from the responses of families at varying socioeconomic levels to overall conditions and to particular constraints and opportunities affecting them. I have suggested two broad strategies in which migration plays a major part—survival strategies, for those households at the low end of the socioeconomic scale, and mobility strategies, for those who are somewhat better off, or attempting to be so.

The migrants whose activities are analyzed here are all living and working in a regional urban center in an area where the regional economy is dominated by rice farming. While migration statistics indicate net out-migration from the city and the region, we have seen that the city also attracts considerable numbers of migrants, especially from the surrounding region. Regional centers such as Dagupan are likely to do so (cf. Rondinelli 1983:158–61). It may well be that the patterns examined here, of engaging in migration while maintaining close ties with family members in rural homes and elsewhere, are especially possible in medium-size cities, where there are a large number of social and economic links with the surrounding hinterland.

At the same time that the city facilitates family strategies involving migration, migration in turn affects the social and economic dynamics of the city. The large numbers of young women who work at service sector jobs and who live in boarding houses while continuing to see their rural home as "home," for example, shape consumption and demand patterns in the city in ways that have not been fully explored. In general, the effects of migration on medium-size cities have been much less extensively considered than the effects on large and capital cities, where, certainly, the impact of migration is much more evident and dramatic.[3]

The complex patterns of mobility considered here suggest that greater attention be paid to the role of smaller and regional cities in the migration process. In particular, city-hinterland interactions need to be examined. These include not only the rural-urban ties maintained by migrants that are discussed here, but also other economic, political, and administrative links that help to shape the development of different types of locales and the roles that they play in a region.

In sum, rural and urban places are not separate arenas but rather interacting ones. The movement of people, and the continuing ties formed between migrants and their families, involving the exchange of a variety of resources, leads to the formation of rural-urban networks that span a number of locales. Such networks form only one part of the rural-urban arena within which individuals and households make decisions, act, and help to shape the conditions of life in the places in which they live.

Notes

Chapter 1

1. However, Portes and Walton do note as well what they call "micro-structures of migration" in the formation of social networks (1981:59–60).

2. In a recent review of anthropological studies of migration, Kearney (1986) discusses much of the same literature and argues that what he calls the "articulation" perspective provides an approach that bridges the structural historical and individual decision-making approaches and that this perspective reintroduces culture and ideology as well as using the household as a basic unit of analysis. He further proposes the "articulatory migration network" as a unit of study.

3. The survey is described in chapter 4.

4. Philippine censuses and surveys, such as the 1973 National Demographic Survey, have included questions on migration in recent years. In addition, social scientists connected with institutions such as the Institute of Philippine Culture at Ateneo de Manila University, the University of the Philippines, and the University of the Philippines at Los Baños have done extensive research on national and regional social and economic conditions.

Chapter 2

1. Urban areas in the Philippine census are defined in terms of population density, types of establishments and institutions, and occupational characteristics (Philippines [Republic] National Census and Statistics Office 1975b:xii). Each *barangay* (section) of each municipality is classified as urban or rural. In Pangasinan, Dagupan is the only city whose population is classified as fully urban; in other towns and cities in the province the *poblacion* (town center) is usually classified as urban and the other *barangays* as rural. The total urban population of the province is 278,166; Dagupan's population of 90,092 comprises 32.4 percent of the total. *Barangays* are the basic unit used in the census; they are equivalent to what in the past were called *barrios*.

2. Chartered cities are administrative units that have usually been created from heavily populated municipalities, although there are no fixed standards for granting city charters (World Bank 1976:88).

3. Obviously, not all went to Dagupan, but nearly all traveled to or from towns and cities within Pangasinan.

4. Counts of passengers on buses and jeeps entering and leaving the city on each of the three main roads in the early morning hours showed between three thousand and six thousand inbound passengers and between fifteen hundred and two thousand outbound passengers on each of the routes.

5. Published census material does not provide data on employment and occupations in specific cities and municipalities of the province. Rather, it provides a breakdown that aggregates all "urban" areas and all "rural" areas. The occupational data considered here refers to the total urban population of the province. Some skewing no doubt results from this: for example, the number in professional occupations includes many of the schoolteachers who reside in the *poblacions* of the municipalities where they teach. On the other hand, Dagupan probably has fewer in primary sector occupations (farming/fishing) than is the case in the other "urban" areas.

6. The official exchange rate in 1978–79 was 7.5 pesos to the dollar.

7. In 1976, 64.2 percent of Dagupan's household heads were shown to have earned less than ₱3,600 (see tables 3 and 4). Because these data are not corrected for family size and because they include only earnings of household head, they cannot be used to estimate numbers falling below the poverty line in Dagupan.

Chapter 3

1. In this chapter, I focus on Pangasinan Province, as most migrants to Dagupan originate within the province. However, Pangasinan shares many features with the rest of the rice-growing Central Luzon Plain, and much of the available data deals with other parts of Central Luzon. Therefore, the term *region* here refers to an area sharing a set of economic characteristics, in which rice farming is dominant. This area is usually referred to as Central Luzon. This usage does not conform to contemporary administrative regions in the country; since 1973 Pangasinan has been administratively part of Region I, Ilocos. All of the other provinces in that region are mountainous with a narrow coastal plain and therefore quite different from Pangasinan in economic character. Prior to 1973, Pangasinan was part of Region IV, Central Luzon, and many statistically based studies (e.g., Castillo 1977) continue to use that classification. Unfortunately, the change in administrative regions makes it impossible to use comparative regional data for census periods such as 1970 and 1975. See figure 1 for locations of Central Luzon and Ilocos regions, and of Pangasinan Province.

2. A *cavan* is the standard measure used for rice, one cavan equals 44 kilograms of *palay*; one cavan of cleaned rice equals 57.5 kilograms (Lynch 1972:128).

3. Other crops produced in the province include corn (planted on 11.9 percent of farms); tobacco (on 10 percent of farms); sugarcane (on 4 percent of farms); coconut and coffee. Many farmers also raise vegetables, primarily for their own consumption, and keep livestock (such as hogs, *carabao*, cattle) and poultry (Philippines [Republic] National Census and Statistics Office 1975a:xxiv–vii).

4. The data is from the 1971 agricultural census, before the 1972 land reform policies were announced, but there seems to have been little change as a result of those policies; see note 6, below.

5. I use the definition employed by Ledesma (1978) rather than that of Reyes-Makil and Fermia (1978). The latter include tenants as well as those with no access to land for farming at all.

6. Land reform in the Philippines has a complex history. In the 1960s, the focus was placed on shifting tenants to leasehold status; in the 1972 effort, as mandated under Presidential Decree 27, tenants were to become amortizing owners of "family-size" farms of five hectares of unirrigated land or three hectares of irrigated land. Landlords were allowed to retain seven hectares for personal cultivation. Because most farms in Pangasinan were already small, and because the initial efforts of the land reform were directed at large landholdings of twenty-four hectares and above (Harkin 1982:7) there has been relatively little effect in that province. According to the Ministry of Agrarian Reform, in Pangasinan by 1978, 16,452 certificates of land transfer had been distributed to 10,028 tenants, on land owned by 225 landowners (Ministry of Agrarian Reform, Region I 1978: table 4).

7. In Pangasinan in 1971, 46.8 percent of farmers reported using improved rice varieties (Philippines [Republic] National Census and Statistics Office 1975a:xxiv).

8. Not only rural households have this characteristic; a World Bank study of households in the Tondo area of Manila shows the importance of diverse income sources for those households as well (World Bank 1980).

Chapter 4

1. Ilocanos also predominated among the early Filipino emigrants to the United States.

2. The 1948 census shows 41 percent of the population of Manila having "mother tongue" (i.e., first language) other than Tagalog (Philippines [Republic] Bureau of the Census and Statistics 1951:293).

3. Published analyses of migration in the 1970s are based on two sources—the 1970 census, which included information on residence in 1960, 1965, and 1970 for a 5 percent sample (see Fleiger, Koppin, and Lim 1976:4 for description of the data) and the 1973 National Demographic Survey, which included information on residence of the sampled population at birth, 1965, 1970, and 1973 (see Pernia 1975:2). The 1975 census also includes data on change in residence between 1970 and 1975. The discussion below is based on the published analyses as well as on the published 1975 census.

4. No information is provided on interregional moves.

5. That is, they recorded different residences at one, two, or three of the time periods—1965, 1970, 1973; other moves between these intervals are not recorded.

6. Pryor shows that Dagupan has low "migration efficiency" in that there is a large population turnover (1979:233).

7. Women were relatively mobile in earlier periods as well, as Nava notes in his study of intercensal migration between 1938 and 1949 (1959:23).

8. People from Ilocos are called Ilocano and speak the Ilocano language, which

is quite different from the Pangasinan language spoken by those indigenous to the region. As we shall see below, both languages are now widely spoken in Pangasinan province. Despite the linguistic differences, Ilocanos and Pangasinanses share many cultural features that are generally characteristic of lowland Philippine culture.

9. Ilocano-speakers may of course be migrants from Ilocos, but given their relatively small numbers in Dagupan and the existence of Ilocanos there for several generations (see earlier discussion) it is likely that most are either born in the city or migrants from within the province.

10. The percent of Tagalog speakers in the whole province is 1.2 percent; no other municipality has a sizeable proportion of Tagalog speakers. It is possible to say then that most of the counter-stream of Manila-area to Pangasinan migrants identified by Flieger (and see table 7 above) consists of migrants to Dagupan.

11. This survey was taken by Mrs. Christie Dumaran of the University of Pangasinan in 1979. I would like to thank her for kindly allowing me access to her data.

12. The data discussed here are based on information in the Civil Register of Live Births, Dagupan City from January, 1978, to September, 1978. All of those who listed mother's usual residence as Dagupan City were included. Information was available on 2,952 males and 3,002 females. Eighty-seven percent of the males and 95 percent of the females were less than forty years old.

13. The data are based on self-reported occupations in the registry of births; they have been recoded to coincide as closely as possible to census occupational categories. Only occupations of males are given in the registry.

14. This data is based on student enrollment, second semester 1977–78, University of Pangasinan. I would like to thank the Office of the Registrar, University of Pangasinan, for giving me access to these records.

15. I took this survey during a two-week period, using university students as assistants. We used networks and snowball sampling methods to identify potential respondents. Socioeconomic data, migration histories, family data, and information on visiting and remittances were collected.

Part 2

1. These cases were selected from a somewhat larger number because they did involve continuing rural-urban ties. Not all migrants are engaged in such activities. For example, a contrary case is that of a street vendor and her mother. The mother migrated to Dagupan many years ago, while her daughter continued to live in the rural home and later moved back and forth between there and Dagupan. By 1978–79 she lived permanently in Dagupan and did not visit the rural area; there were only distant relatives remaining, and she lacked money for such visits. Out of the 176 migrants surveyed in the sample described in chapter 4, however, only 7 did not visit some relative elsewhere at some point during the year. Further, 50 percent gave monetary remittances of some sort (see Trager 1984a).

2. The data used in the case studies is based on my own interviewing and observation, both in the city and with family members living elsewhere. In addition, several of those studied agreed to keep journals of their activities, incomes, and expenses, and I have drawn on those records. Where quotations are used, these are either comments made to me in English, or, in a few instances, translations of comments made in Pangasinan and translated immediately by my research assistant. I have edited comments slightly, to make them clear, but have tried to leave the original flavor, including grammar that may be acceptable in Philippine English though not in American English. In the cases, I have changed the names of all individuals, but not of places. The time period referred to is the present as of 1978–79; hence, the present tense is used where activities are described that those studied were involved in at that time.

Chapter 6

1. There is an artesian well near her parent's home, and electricity; in Dagupan the town water supply tends to be undependable and there are occasional blackouts and brownouts.

2. One cavan *palay* equals forty-four kilos *palay*.

3. The large difference between reported income and reported expenses requires some explanation. It is possible that it results from overestimation of actual expenses; it is also possible that the family lives constantly in debt. Studies on a large scale in the Philippines show large rates of "dissavings" and there does not seem to be an accepted explanation for this pattern.

4. The case of Delia and her family is considered in less detail in Trager 1981a and Trager 1981b.

5. Research undertaken by Richard Ammann during the same period as my own research shows that language switching is common among migrants to Dagupan (personal conversations).

Chapter 7

1. Both Annie Santos and her husband recorded their life stories for me in English. I have edited and condensed the recorded version in the biographical sections of this chapter.

2. A school run by an order of Belgian nuns.

3. Declaiming is a form of speech making.

4. Baguio is 205 kilometers (128 miles) from Kiangan, and is the major city in the mountain area of Northern Luzon.

5. The barrio from which Mr. Santos comes.

6. It is 432 kilometers (270 miles) from Kiangan to Dagupan. Until the mid–1970s, when a cement road was constructed, travel was over a dirt road.

7. Roberto is the only member of his family still selling cloth in Dagupan. His sister now lives in Mindanao with her husband, two of his brothers are living in the barrio, and the third lives in Cotabato.

8. The market is run by the city government. People own the rights to places in it and pay rents to the government; the rights to stalls can be sold by one individual to another. When a stall is "borrowed" the owner lets the other person use it in return for paying the rent.

9. The term *suki* implies having regular buying and selling relationships; therefore it can refer both to regular customers and regular suppliers.

10. Cursillista was a movement within the Catholic church that was very important in the Philippines in the 1960s and 1970s.

11. The expression *P.R.* (public relations) is used with the same sort of meaning as *pakikisama*, the Tagalog expression that is translated by social scientists as "smooth interpersonal relations."

Chapter 8

1. The interview was in Pangasinan and translated into English.

2. I asked Lisa to record her activities during a two-week period, which she did with the assistance of my research assistant, who was also her neighbor.

3. Responses elicited as part of a set of questions regarding people on whom she depends and people who come to her.

4. On an occupational prestige scale developed by Lauby (1976), *lavendera* (laundrywomen) are rated as 17.1, maids or housegirls as 22.2; the highest rating is for surgeons at 93.4.

Chapter 9

1. This does not mean that all family members share the same goals or that there is no conflict among them (cf. Yanigasako 1984). What it means is that all are operating with the same set of key values that are mutually understood and are, for the most part, acted on. Certainly there are individuals who break ties or who do not reciprocate as expected, but these are relatively few.

2. Ulack (1986) reaches similar conclusions. His data show that there is "no relationship . . . between income or educational level and cash remittances received in rural areas" and therefore, there is no support for the argument that inequalities increase (353). On the other hand, he suggests that while cash remittances do not have a negative impact there is also not much evidence for a "major" effect on rural development (354). Unfortunately, his study does not include data on the uses to which remittances are put.

3. An exception is the recent study by Costello, Leinbach, and Ulack (1987).

Bibliography

Abad, Ricardo G.
  1981   Internal Migration in the Philippines: A Review of Research Findings. *Philippine Studies* 29:129–43.
Abrera, Ma. Alcestis S.
  1976   Philippine Poverty Thresholds. In *Measuring Philippine Development: Report of the Social Indicators Project*, ed. Mahar Mangahas, 223–73. Manila: Development Academy of the Philippines.
Abu-Lughod, Janet
  1975   Comments. The End of the Age of Innocence in Migration Theory. In *Migration and Urbanization,* ed. Brian M. DuToit and Helen I. Safa, 201–6. The Hague: Mouton.
Alvarez, J. Benjamin C., and Patricia M. Alvarez
  1972   The Filipino Family-owned Business: A Matriarchal Model. *Philippine Studies* 20:547–61.
Amin, Samir
  1974   Modern Migrations in Western Africa. In *Modern Migration in Western Africa*, ed. S. Amin, 65–124. Oxford: Oxford University Press.
Anderson, James N.
  1964   Land and Society in a Pangasinan Community. In *Social Foundations of Community Development: Readings on the Philippines*, ed. Socorro C. Espiritu and Chester L. Hunt, 171–92. Manila: R. M. Garcia Publishing House.
  1972   *Social Strategies in Population Change: Village Data from Central Luzon.* Southeast Asia Development Advisory Group Papers on Problems of Development in Southeast Asia. Washington, D. C.: Department of State.
Aronson, Dan
  1980   *The City Is Our Farm: Seven Migrant Ijebu Families.* Cambridge, Mass.: Schenkman.
Bacol, Melinda M.
  1971   Inter-generational Occupational Mobility in the Philippines. *Philippines Sociological Review* 19:193–208.
Balán, Jorge, Harley L. Browning, Elizabeth Jelin, and Lee Litzler
  1969   A Computerized Approach to the Processing and Analysis of Life Histories Obtained in Sample Surveys. *Behavioral Science* 14:105–20.

Bartle, Philip F. W.
  1981   Cyclical Migration and the Extended Community: A West African
         Example. In *Frontiers in Migration Analysis*, ed. R. B. Mandal, 105–
         39. New Delhi: Concept Publishing Co.
Basa, Restituto C.
  1972   *The Story of Dagupan*. Dagupan City: Manaois Press Company.
Bolusan, Carlos
  1973   *America is in the Heart*. Seattle: University of Washington Press.
Bulatao, Rodolfo A.
  1984   Philippine Urbanism and the Status of Women. In *Women in the Cities
         of Asia: Migration and Urban Adaptation*, ed. James T. Fawcett, Siew-
         Ean Khoo, and Peter C. Smith, 317–64. Boulder: Westview.
Bureau of Commerce and Industry
  1922   *Statistical Bulletin No. 4 of the Philippine Islands*. 1921. Manila.
Caces, Fe, Fred Arnold, James T. Fawcett, and Robert W. Gardner
  1985   Shadow Households and Competing Auspices: Migration Behavior
         in the Philippines. *Journal of Development Economics* 17:5–25.
Carrozal, Francisco P.
  1886   *Memoria de Pangasinan, 1885*. Archives of the Dominican Order,
         Tomo 121 (1886): 150–56. Quezon City: Convent of Saint Dominic
         (quoted in McLennan 1973:107).
Carter, Anthony
  1984   Household Histories. In *Households: Comparative and Historical Studies
         of the Domestic Group*, ed. Robert McC. Netting, Richard R. Wilk,
         and Eric J. Arnould, 44–83. Berkeley: University of California Press.
Castillo, Gelia T.
  1975   *All in a Grain of Rice*. College, Laguna, Philippines: Southeast Asian
         Regional Center for Graduate Study and Research in Agriculture.
  1976   *The Filipino Woman as Manpower: The Image and the Empirical Reality*.
         College, Laguna, Philippines: University of the Philippines at Los
         Baños.
  1977   *Beyond Manila: Philippine Rural Problems in Perspective*. 3 vols. Col-
         lege, Laguna, Philippines: University of the Philippines at Los Baños.
Castillo, Gelia T., and Sylvia H. Guerrero
  1969   The Filipino Woman: A Study in Multiple Roles. *Journal of Asian and
         African Studies* 4:18–29.
Chang, Tuck Hoong Paul
  1981   A Review of Micro Migration Research in the Third World Context.
         In *Migration Decision Making*, ed. Gordon F. de Jong and Robert W.
         Gardner, 303–27. New York: Pergamon Press.
Chapman, Murray
  1978   On the Cross-Cultural Study of Circulation. *International Migration
         Review* 12:559–69.
Chapman, Murray, and R. Mansell Prothero
  1983   Themes on Circulation in the Third World. *International Migration
         Review* 17:597–632.

Civil Register Book of Live Births
  1978   January 1978–September 1978. Dagupan City.
Concepcion, Mercedes B., and Peter C. Smith
  1977   *The Demographic Situation in the Philippines: An Assessment in 1977.*
         Papers of the East-West Population Institute, no. 44. Honolulu.
Cortes, Rosario Mendoza
  1974   *Pangasinan 1572–1800.* Quezon City: University of the Philippines
         Press.
Costello, Michael A., Thomas R. Leinbach, and Richard Ulack
  1987   *Mobility and Employment in Urban Southeast Asia: Examples from Indo-
         nesia and the Philippines.* Boulder: Westview Press.
Dagupan City
  n.d.a Dagupan City Framework Plan 1977–2000. City Planning and De-
         velopment Council. Mimeo.
  n.d.b Social Action Development Plan. City Planning and Development
         Staff. Mimeo.
  1976   Socioeconomic Profile of Dagupan City. City Planning and Devel-
         opment Staff. Mimeo.
Dannhaeuser, Norbert
  1980   The Role of the Neighborhood Store in Developing Economies: The
         Case of Dagupan City, Philippines. *Journal of Developing Areas*
         14:157–74.
  1983   *Contemporary Trade Strategies in the Philippines: A Study in Marketing
         Anthropology.* New Brunswick, N.J.: Rutgers University Press.
DaVanzo, Julie
  1981   Microeconomic Approaches to Studying Migration Decisions. In *Mi-
         gration Decision Making,* ed. Gordon F. de Jong and Robert W. Gard-
         ner, 90–129. New York: Pergamon Press.
deGuzman, E. A.
  1975   Occupational Mobility in the Philippines: 1973 Data. Research Note
         no. 38. Quezon City: Population Institute, University of the Philip-
         pines. Mimeo.
Doeppers, Daniel F.
  1971   Ethnicity and Class in the Structure of Philippine Cities. Ph.D. diss.,
         Syracuse University.
  1972   The Development of Philippine Cities before 1900. *Journal of Asian
         Studies* 23:769–92.
Eggan, Fred
  1978   Philippine Social Structure. In *Orientation Readings in Philippine Cul-
         ture,* comp. U.S. Peace Corps/Philippines, 33–67.
Eviota, Elizabeth, and Peter C. Smith
  1981   *The Migration of Women in the Philippines.* Working Paper no. 13.
         Honolulu: East-West Population Institute.
Far Eastern Economic Review
  1987   Philippines Economy: Things are Looking Up. August 6, 1987, 60–
         64.

Fegan, Brian
    1972 Jobs and Farms: The Lessee's Alternatives and Peasantization. In
          View from the Paddy, ed. Frank Lynch, *Philippine Sociological Review*
          20:134–41.
    1979 Folk-Capitalism: Economic Strategies of Peasants in a Philippines
          Wet-Rice Village. Ph.D. diss., Yale University.
Fields, Gary S.
    1980 *Poverty, Inequality and Development.* Cambridge: Cambridge Univer-
          sity Press.
Findley, Sally E.
    1987 *Rural Development and Migration: A Study of Family Choices in the
          Philippines.* Boulder: Westview Press.
Flieger, Wilhelm, Brigida Koppin, and Carmencita Lim
    1976 *Geographical Patterns of Internal Migration in the Philippines: 1960–70*
          Manila: National Census and Statistics Office, UNFPA-NCSO Pop-
          ulation Research Project Monograph no. 5.
Flormata, Gregorio
    1901 *Memoria Sobre la Provincia de Pangasinan.* Manila: La Democracia
          (quoted in McLennan 1973).
Fox, Robert
    1963 Men and Women in the Philippines. In *Women in the New Asia*, ed.
          Barbara E. Ward, 342–64. Paris: UNESCO.
Gibb, Arthur
    1974 Agricultural Modernization, Non-Farm Employment and Low-
          Level Urbanization. Ph.D. diss., University of Michigan.
Goldstein, Sidney
    1978 Circulation in the Context of Total Mobility in Southeast Asia. Paper
          presented at International Seminar on the Cross-Cultural Study of
          Circulation, East-West Center, Honolulu.
Grace, Brewster
    1977 *The Politics of Income Distribution in the Philippines.* Southeast Asia
          Series 25(8). Hanover, N.H.: American Universities Field Staff.
Gugler, Josef, and William G. Flanagan
    1978 Urban-Rural Ties in West Africa: Extent, Interpretation and Implica-
          tions. *African Perspectives* 1:67–78
Guyer, Jane
    1979 *Household Budgets and Women's Incomes.* Working Paper no. 28. Bos-
          ton: African Studies Center, Boston University.
    1981 Household and Community in African Studies. Paper presented at
          the African Studies Associaton meetings.
Harbison, Sarah F.
    1981 Family Structure and Family Strategy in Migration Decision-
          Making. In *Migration Decision Making*, ed. Gordon F. de Jong and
          Robert W. Gardner, 226–51. New York: Pergamon Press.

Harkin, Duncan
  1982   Land Reform in the Philippines, 1972 to 1982. Paper presented at University of the Philippines at Los Baños, March 19, 1982.
Hart, Donn V.
  1955   *The Philippine Plaza Complex: A Focal Point in Culture Change.* Yale University Southeast Asia Studies, Cultural Report Series no. 3. New Haven: Yale University.
  1971   Philippine Rural-Urban Migration: A View from Caticugan, a Bisayan Village. *Behavior Science Notes* 6:103–37
  1977   *Compadrinazgo: Ritual Kinship in the Philippines.* DeKalb: Northern Illinois University Press.
Hayami, Y., M. Kikuchi, P. F. Moya, L. M. Bambo, and E. B. Marciano
  1978   *Anatomy of a Peasant Economy: A Rice Village in the Philippines.* Los Baños, Laguna, Philippines: International Rice Research Institute.
Hollnsteiner, Mary R.
  1964   Reciprocity in the Lowland Philippines. *Four Readings on Philippine Values*, 2d rev. ed., comp. Frank Lynch, 22–49. Quezon City: Ateneo de Manila University Press.
Hugo, Graeme
  1975   Population Mobility in West Java, Indonesia. Ph.D. diss., Australian National University.
  1981   *Population Mobility in West Java.* Yogyakarta, Indonesia: Gadjah Mada University Press.
  1982   Circular Migration in Indonesia. *Population and Development Review* 8:59–83.
Illo, Jeanne F. I.
  1977   *Involvement by Choice: The Role of Women in Development.* Quezon City: Institute of Philippine Culture, Ateneo de Manila University.
International Labor Organization (ILO)
  1974   *Sharing in Development: A Programme of Employment, Equity and Growth for the Philippines.* Geneva: International Labour Office.
Jacobson, Helga E.
  1974   Women in Philippine Society: More Equal than Many. In *Many Sisters: Women in Cross-Cultural Perspective*, ed. Carolyn J. Mathiasson, 349–77. New York: The Free Press.
Kaut, Charles
  1961   Utang na Loob: A System of Contractual Obligation among Tagalogs. *Southwestern Journal of Anthropology* 17:256–72.
  1965   The Principle of Contingency in Tagalog Society. *Asian Studies* 3(1): 1–15.
Kearney, Michael
  1986   From the Invisible Hand to Visible Feet: Anthropological Studies of Migration and Development. *Annual Review of Anthropology* 15:331–61.

Kerkvliet, Benedict J.
  1980   Classes, Consciousness, and Change in a Philippine Village. Paper
         presented at Association of Asian Studies Meetings.
Koo, Hagen, and Peter C. Smith
  1983   Migration, the Urban Informal Sector, and Earnings in the Philip-
         pines. *The Sociological Quarterly* 24:219–32.
Langness, L. L., and Gelya Frank
  1981   *Lives: An Anthropological Approach to Biography*. Navato, Ca: Chand-
         ler and Sharp.
Lauby, Jennifer
  1976   Indicators of Social Mobility. In *Measuring Philippine Development:
         Report of the Social Indicators Project*, ed. Mahar Mangahas, 405–64.
         Manila: Development Academy of the Philippines.
Laya, Juan Cabreros
  1941   *His Native Soil*. Manila: University Publishing Company, Inc.
Ledesma, Antonio J.
  1978   Rice Farmers and Landless Rural Workers: Perspectives from the
         Household Level. Los Baños, International Rice Research Institute
         Saturday Seminar, Agricultural Economics Department. Mimeo.
Lee, Sun-Hee
  1985   *Why People Intend to Move: Individual and Community-Level Factors of
         Out-Migration in the Philippines*. Boulder: Westview Press.
Leeds, Anthony
  1976   "Women in the Migratory Process": A Reductionist Outlook. *An-
         thropological Quarterly* 49:69–76.
Lewis, Henry T.
  1971   *Ilocano Rice Farmers: A Comparative Study of Two Philippine Barrios*.
         Honolulu: University Press of Hawaii.
Lewis, Oscar
  1959   *Five Families: Mexican Case Studies in the Culture of Poverty*. New
         York: Basic Books.
  1961   *The Children of Sanchez: Autobiography of a Mexican Family*. New
         York: Random House.
  1964   *Pedro Martinez: A Mexican Peasant and His Family*. New York: Ran-
         dom House.
  1965   *La Vida: A Puerto Rican Family in the Culture of Poverty: San Juan and
         New York*. New York: Vintage Books.
Lewis, Oscar, Ruth M. Lewis, and Susan M. Rigdon
  1977   *Four Men*. Urbana: University of Illinois Press.
Lipton, Michael
  1980   Migration from Rural Areas of Poor Countries: The Impact on Rural
         Productivity and Income Distribution. *World Development* 8:1–24.
Lomnitz, Larissa
  1976   Migration and Network in Latin America. In *Current Perspectives in*

Latin American Urban Research, ed. Alejandro Portes and H. L. Browning, 133–50. Austin: Institute of Latin American Studies.

Lynch, Frank, ed.
  1972 View from the Paddy, *Philippine Sociological Review* 20.

McCoy, Alfred W.
  1982 Introduction: The Social History of an Archipelago. In *Philippine Social History: Global Trade and Local Transformations*, ed. Alfred W. McCoy and Ed. C. de Jesus, 1–18. Honolulu: University Press of Hawaii.

McCoy, Alfred W., and Ed. C. deJesus, eds.
  1982 *Philippine Social History: Global Trade and Local Transformations.* Honolulu: University Press of Hawaii.

McGee, T. G.
  1973 Peasants in the Cities: A Paradox, A Paradox, A Most Ingenious Paradox. *Human Organization* 32:135–42.
  1975 Malay Migration to Kuala Lumpur City: Individual Adaptation to the City. In *Migration and Urbanization*, ed. Brian M. Dutoit and Helen I. Safa, 143–78. The Hague: Mouton.
  1978 Rural-Urban Mobility in South and Southeast Asia: Different Formulations, Different Answers. In *Human Migration: Patterns and Policies*, ed. William H. McNeill and Ruth S. Adams, 199–224. Bloomington: Indiana University Press.

McLennan, Marshall
  1973 Peasant and Hacendero in Nueva Ecija: The Socio-Economic Origins of a Philippine Commercial Rice-Growing Region. Ph.D. diss., University of California, Berkeley.
  1982 Changing Human Ecology of the Central Luzon Plain: Nueva Ecija, 1705–1939. In *Philippine Social History: Global Trade and Local Transformations*, ed. Alfred W. McCoy and Ed. C. de Jesus, 57–90. Honolulu: University Press of Hawaii.

Mangin, William, ed.
  1970 *Peasants in Cities: Readings in the Anthropology of Urbanization.* Boston: Houghton Mifflin.

Mayer, Philip
  1962 Migrancy and the Study of Africans in Towns. *American Anthropologist* 64:576–92.
  1963 *Townsmen or Tribesmen: Conservatism and the Process of Urbanization in a South African City.* Cape Town: Oxford University Press.

Meillassoux, Claude
  1981 *Maidens, Meal and Money: Capitalism and the Domestic Community.* Cambridge: Cambridge University Press.

Ministry of Agrarian Reform, Region I
  1978 *Annual Report 1978.* San Fernando, La Union, Philippines: Ministry of Agrarian Reform.

Mintz, Sidney W.
  1974 *Worker in the Cane: A Puerto Rican Life History*. New York: W. W. Norton.
Murray, Francis J., Jr.
  1973 Lowland Social Organization I: Local Kin Groups in a Central Luzon Barrio. *Philippine Sociological Review* 21:29–36.
National Cottage Industry Development Authority (NACIDA)
  1977 *Profile of Cottage Industries in the Ilocos*. Northern Luzon Research Institute. Pamphlet.
Nava, E. L.
  1959 *Internal Migration in the Philippines, 1939–1948*. Bombay: Demographic Training and Research Centre.
Neher, Clark D.
  1982 Sex Roles in the Philippines: The Ambiguous Cebuana. In *Women of Southeast Asia*, ed. Penny Van Esterik, 154–75. Occasional Paper no. 9. DeKalb: Center for Southeast Asian Studies, Northern Illinois University.
Netting, Robert McC., Richard R. Wilk, and Eric J. Arnould, eds.
  1984 *Households: Comparative and Historical Studies of the Domestic Group*. Berkeley: University of California Press.
New York Times
  1987 October 18, 1987.
Nicholas, J.
  1977 *Level and Pattern of Income Distribution among Farm Households in 5 Selected Cropping Systems. Pilot Barrios of Manaoag, Pangasinan: An Analysis of Benchmark Information, CY 1974–75*. Los Baños, Laguna, Philippines: International Rice Research Institute.
Pangasinan Development Staff
  1976 Cottage Industries Registered with NACIDA: Pangasinan. Mimeo.
Pantranco Conductor Trip Records
  1978–79 November 1978, December 1978, January 1979.
Pascual, Elvira M.
  1966 Internal Migration in the Philippines. In *Proceedings of the First Conference on Population, 1965*, 315–53. Quezon City: University of the Philippines Press.
Perez, Aurora E.
  1976 The Migrants of Metro Manila. Research Note no. 139. Quezon City, Population Institute, University of the Philippines. Mimeo.
Pernia, Ernesto M.
  1975 Patterns of Philippine Internal Migration. Research Note no. 36. Quezon City: Population Institute, University of the Philippines. Mimeo.
  1977 *Urbanization, Population Growth, and Economic Development in the Philippines*. Westport, Conn: Greenwood Press.
  n.d. Migration Decision Model: Philippines 1965–1973. Mimeo.

Philippines (Commonwealth)
    1940 *Labor Bulletin*, January–February.
    1941 *Labor Bulletin*, March–April.
    1941 *Labor Bulletin*, May–June.
Philippines (Commonwealth) Commission of the Census
    1939 *Census of the Philippines. Summary and General Report for the Census of Population and Agriculture*. Manila: Commission of the Census.
Philippines (Republic) Bureau of the Census and Statistics
    1951 *Census of the Philippines, 1948*. Manila: Bureau of Printing.
    1952 *Summary Report on the 1948 Census of Agriculture*. Manila: Bureau of Printing.
    1962–63 *Census of the Philippines, 1960: Population and Housing: Pangasinan—Population*. Manila: Bureau of Printing.
Philippines (Republic) National Census and Statistics Office
    1974 *1970 Census of Population and Housing*. Vol. 2. *National Summary*. Manila: National Economic and Development Authority, National Census and Statistics Office.
    1975a *1971 Census of Agriculture, Pangasinan Province*. Manila: National Economic and Development Authority, National Census and Statistics Office.
    1975b *1975 Integrated Census of the Population and its Economic Activities: Population—Pangasinan*. Manila: National Economic and Development Authority, National Census and Statistics Office.
Planeras, Oscar F.
    1977 *Social, Economic and Demographic Factors Relating to Interregional Migration Streams in the Philippines: 1960–1970*. UNFPA-NCSO Population Research Project Monograph no. 11. Manila: National Census and Statistics Office.
Polido, Baldonero
    1971 The History of Dagupan City. Unpublished.
Portes, Alejandro and John Walton
    1981 *Labor, Class and the International System*. New York: Academic Press.
Prothero, R. Mansell, and Murray Chapman, eds.
    1985 *Circulation in Third World Countries*. London: Routledge and Kegan Paul.
Pryor, Robin J.
    1979 The Philippines: Patterns of Population Movement to 1970. In *Migration and Development in Southeast Asia: A Demographic Perspective*, ed. R. Pryor, 225–43. Kuala Lumpur: Oxford University Press.
Rempel, Henry, and Richard A. Lobdell
    1978 The Role of Urban-to-Rural Remittances in Rural Development. *Journal of Development Studies* 14:324–41.
Reyes-Makil, Lorna Pena, and Patria N. Fermia
    1978 *Landless Rural Workers in the Philippines: A Documentary Survey*. Que-

zon City: Institute of Philippine Culture, Ateneo de Manila University.

Rondinelli, Dennis A.
1983   *Secondary Cities in Developing Countries: Policies for Diffusing Urbanization.* Beverly Hills: Sage Publications.

Ross, Marc Howard, and Thomas S. Weisner
1977   The Rural-Urban Migrant Network in Kenya: Some General Implications. *American Ethnologist* 4:359–75.

Santos, Bienvenido
1965   *Villa Magdelena.* Manila: Erehwon.

Schlegel, Stuart
1964   Personal Alliances in Lowland Philippine Social Structure. *Anthropology Tomorrow* 10:50–65.

Selby, Henry A., and Arthur D. Murphy
1982   *The Mexican Urban Household and the Decision to Migrate to the United States.* ISHI Occasional Papers in Social Change no. 4. Philadelphia: Institute for the Study of Human Issues.

Simkins, Paul D., and Frederick L. Wernstedt
1971   *Philippine Migration: The Settlement of the Digos-Padada Valley, Davao Province.* Yale University Southeast Asia Studies Monograph Series no. 16. New Haven: Yale University.

Smith, G. A.
1980   Huasicanchino Livelihoods: A Study of Extended Domestic Enterprises in Rural and Urban Peru. *Canadian Review of Sociology and Anthropology* 17:357–66.

Smith, M. Estellie
1976   Networks and Migration Resettlement: Cherchez la Femme. *Anthropological Quarterly* 49:20–27.

Smith, Peter C.
1977   *The Evolving Pattern of Interregional Migration in the Philippines.* East-West Population Institute reprint no. 104. Honolulu: East-West Center.

Stark, Oded
1978   *Economic-Demographic Interaction in Agricultural Development: The Case of Rural-to-Urban Migration.* Rome: Food and Agricultural Organization of the United Nations.
1980   On the Role of Urban-to-Rural Remittances in Rural Development. *Journal of Development Studies* 16:369–74.

Stretton, A. W.
1981   The Building Industry and Urbanization in Third World Countries: A Philippine Case Study. *Economic Development and Cultural Change* 29:325–39.

Szanton, M. Cristina Blanc
1982   Women and Men in Iloilo, Philippines, 1903–1970. In *Women of Southeast Asia,* ed. Penny Van Esterik, 124–53. Occasional Paper no.

9. DeKalb: Center for Southeast Asian Studies, Northern Illinois University.

Tan, Edita A., and Virginia Holazo
1982 Measuring Poverty in a Segmented Market: The Philippine Case. In *Village-Level Modernization in Southeast Asia: The Political Economy of Rice and Water*, ed. Geoffrey B. Hainsworth, 109–40. Vancouver: University of British Columbia Press.

Tiempo, Edilberto
1972 *To Be Free.* Quezon City: New Day Publishers.

Trager, Lillian
1981a Urban Migrants and Their Links with Home: A Case Study from Dagupan City. *Philippine Studies* 29:217–29.
1981b Rural-Urban Linkages and Migration: A Philippines Case Study. In *Southeast Asia: Women, Changing Social Structure and Culture Continuity*, ed. Geoffrey B. Hainsworth, 84–94. Ottawa: University of Ottawa Press.
1982 Family Networks and Rural-Urban Mobility in the Philippines. Paper presented at American Anthropological Association meetings, December 1982.
1984a Migration and Remittances: Urban Income and Rural Households in the Philippines. *Journal of Developing Areas* 18:317–40.
1984b Family Strategies and the Migration of Women: Migrants to Dagupan City, Philippines. *International Migration Review* 18:1264–77.

Ulack, Richard
1975 The Impact of Industrialization upon the Population Characteristics of a Medium-Sized City in the Developing World. *Journal of Developing Areas* 9:203–20.
1986 Ties to Origin, Remittances and Mobility: Evidence from Rural and Urban Areas in the Philippines. *Journal of Developing Areas* 20(3): 339–55.

United Nations
1978 *Statistics of Internal Migration: A Technical Report.* Department of International Economic and Social Affairs. New York: United Nations.

University of Pangasinan
1978 Office of the Registrar, Student Enrollment, Second Semester, 1977–78. Dagupan City.

van den Muijzenberg, Otto D.
1973 *Horizontal Mobility in Central Luzon.* Pub. no. 19. Amsterdam: Anthropoligisch-Sociologisch Centrum, Universteit van Amsterdam.
1975 Involution or Evolution in Central Luzon. In *Current Anthropology in the Netherlands*, ed. Peter Kloos and Henri J. M. Claessen, 141–55. Rotterdam: Anthropological Branch of the Netherlands, Sociological and Anthropological Society.

Villegas, Bernardo M.
    1987   The Philippines in 1986: Democratic Reconstruction in the Post-
            Marcos Era. *Asian Survey* 27(2): 194–205.
Vreeland, Nena, Geoffrey B. Hurwitz, Peter Just, Philip W. Moeller, and R. S.
Shinn
    1976   *Area Handbook for the Philippines*. 2d ed. Washington, D.C.: Govern-
            ment Printing Office.
Wilk, Richard R.
    n.d.   Household Ecology: Patterns and Processes. Paper presented at
            American Anthropological Association meetings, November 1987.
Wilk, Richard R., and Robert McC. Netting
    1984   Households: Changing Forms and Functions. In *Households: Com-
            parative and Historical Studies of the Domestic Group*, ed. Robert McC.
            Netting, Richard R. Wilk, and Eric J. Arnould, 1–28. Berkeley:
            University of California Press.
Wood, Charles H.
    1981   Structural Changes and Household Strategies: A Conceptual Frame-
            work for the Study of Rural Migration. *Human Organization* 40:338–
            44.
    1982   Equilibrium and Historical-Structural Perspectives on Migration. *In-
            ternational Migration Review* 16:298–319.
World Bank
    1976   *The Philippines: Priorities and Prospects for Development*. Washington,
            D.C.: The World Bank.
    1980   *The Philippines: A Study of Income and Expenditure Patterns of House-
            holds in the Tondo Foreshore Area (Summary Findings)*. Report Series of
            the Monitoring and Evaluation of Urban Development Projects, Ur-
            ban and Regional Report no. ME-6. Washington, D.C.
Yanigasako, Sylvia Junko
    1984   Explicating Households: A Cultural Analysis of Changing House-
            holds among Japanese-Americans. In *Households: Comparative and
            Historical Studies of the Domestic Group*, ed. Robert McC. Netting,
            Richard R. Wilk, Eric J. Arnould, 330–52. Berkeley: University of
            California Press.
Yu, Elena, and William T. Liu
    1980   *Fertility and Kinship in the Philippines*. Notre Dame: University of
            Notre Dame Press.

Index